'A WINNER'

'James Herriot, the best-selling vet, often
says that his huge international success began
only when his second book was enthusiastically
reviewed in the Sunday Express. That was
five years ago, when I forecast a massive
success for the unknown Yorkshire vet
even though his first book had only sold a few
hundred copies. I have a similar hunch about
the first book in another new autobiographical
series, this time by an ex-priest, who has
written a delightfully entertaining and
hilarious fictionalised account of life as a man
of God.'

GRAHAM LORD *in the* SUNDAY EXPRESS

Bless Me, Father

Neil Boyd

CORGI BOOKS

A DIVISION OF TRANSWORLD PUBLISHERS LTD

BLESS ME FATHER

A CORGI BOOK 0 552 10669 0

Originally published in Great Britain by
Robert Hale Ltd,

PRINTING HISTORY
Robert Hale edition published 1977
Corgi edition published 1978

This book is set in Plantin 10/10½ pt.

Corgi Books are published by Transworld Publishers, Ltd.,
Century House, 61–63 Uxbridge Road, Ealing,
London, W5 5SA

Made and Printed in Great Britain by
Richard Clay (The Chaucer Press), Ltd., Bungay, Suffolk.

Contents

I *My First Confession*

Freedom at last! Six years of seminary studies and spartan discipline were behind me. On my plate at breakfast after ordination at the Cathedral in the early 'fifties was an envelope. In it was a card with details of my first appointment and a Latin document granting me 'faculties' to hear confessions in the diocese.

My curacy was to be in the parish of St Jude in Fairwater, part of the Borough of Kenworthy in West London. I was told it was not fashionable like Chelsea nor unfashionable like Poplar in the dockland district of the East End. A mixed area but mostly working class.

After a two-week vacation with my parents in Brighton, I alighted, one bright Saturday morning in early summer, from the red double-decker bus in the High Street. In each hand I carried a suitcase crammed with essential belongings. My bicycle and a hundred or so books which I imagined would be of help to me in saving souls were to follow by courtesy of British Railways.

I soon left the busy High Street near the Town Hall for the quieter Chindell Road where stood the grey-brick, fifty-year-old parish church of St Jude.

Before knocking on the adjoining presbytery, I entered the church to pray before the Blessed Sacrament. There, the first thing to catch my eye, was a confessional at the rear bearing my name: FR NEIL BOYD.

I knelt down before I fell down. Worse, this, than seeing my picture in the newspaper without prior warning. I prayed fervently in the half light of the church that I would make a good curate and particularly a kind and compassionate confessor. For eighteen years, since I was six, I had been a penitent myself. I had had my share of scruples and known the embarrassment of having to accuse myself of secret sins. In the seminary, I had confessed like the other students, at the knees of the Spiritual Director every Saturday night. At least the ordinary Catholic was spared that nobbly ordeal.

When I had recovered my composure, I looked about me at the statues, the baroque High Altar and the second confessional over which was printed in yellowed lettering FR CHARLES DUDDLESWELL. Then I genuflected and left the church.

The presbytery door was flung open before I could ring the bell by a large, lumpy, white-haired lady in a green dress and flowery apron on which she wiped both her hands before trying to snatch my suitcases.

'Mrs Pring,' she informed me, 'housekeeper.'

'Neil Boyd,' I said, not yet used to calling myself 'Father', and resisted her efforts to help.

She insisted on grabbing the cases while calling over her right shoulder, 'Father Neil's arrived.'

From a room on the right came the scratchy sound of

> None shall part us from each other
>   One in life and death are we,
> All in all to one another,
>   I to thee and thou to me.

And the plump parish priest appeared in a dishevelled cassock. The top button was in the second hole and the mistake was repeated twenty times down the line. It looked as if all his ribs were dislocated.

'Hello, Father Neil. A hundred thousand welcomes. You have just saved me life, d'you know that?' I smiled modestly at having done prestigious service so soon. 'I have been dying for someone with a ha'porth of wit and intelligence to talk to.'

Fr Duddleswell pumped my hand and peered cheerfully with his big blue eyes—their roundness accentuated by round steel-rimmed spectacles—into mine.

Already Mrs Pring was struggling up the stairs with my suitcases.

'Come into me study, Father Neil,' said Fr Duddleswell. When he had ushered me in and stopped the gramophone he called aloud, 'Mrs Pring, a nice hot cup of tay for Father Neil,

8

if you please.'

This pronunciation of tea was, I soon discovered, one of his ways of touching his forelock to his Irish ancestry.

'That woman,' he said, indicating Mrs Pring's broad back, 'came to me twenty years past. The best instance I know of the worst coming to the worst.' He offered me a chair. 'Bishop O'Reilly informs me he has but recently made a priest of you.'

'Three weeks ago, Father.'

'Well, now, since you are a holy innocent, a seminary seedling, so to speak, the Bishop has asked me, the white-whiskered one, to teach you the tricks of the trade.'

He lifted his glasses on to his forehead and pushed up his sleeves a little as if he was about to do a bit of conjuring.

'First trick, Father Neil, always keep something up your sleeve.'

'What sort of things, Father.'

'That,' he said, pursing his lips, 'I cannot tell you.'

'No?'

He shook his head. 'If I did that, would I not have to change what's up me sleeve?'

I said I supposed so.

'Second, Father Neil.' He extended both hands in front of him, back to back, as if at any moment he was going to scoop water aside and swim out of the room. 'What's this, now?' he challenged.

'Siamese twins, Father?'

He made as if to spit but checked himself bravely. ' 'Tis your right hand not knowing what your left hand is doing. Keep 'em total strangers to each other and you will come to no harm.' I nodded, acknowledging the undoubted wisdom of the man. 'Third,' he went on, 'listen like a woman to parish gossip—'tis your duty to know what is not going on around you—but hold your tongue.' As I nodded again, he put his tongue out, broad and pink as a pig. 'Bite it, if need be, till your teeth bleed.' He gave me a painful demonstration of what he meant. 'Finally, when speaking to the good people, make sure you do not *tell* them anything. Pull down the shutters of your mind.'

With the middle finger of each hand, he closed his eyelids, gave two angry snores and opened his eyes with a start. 'You are still there, Father Neil?' he enquired. 'I must have dozed

9

off. Where was I?'

'You were saying a priest has to be discreet.'

'Indeed. Cards to the chest, tight lips, stony-eyed—in a word, like our Blessed Lord Himself. Now, what else must a holy priest be like?' He warmed to the subject. 'Kind at all times, of course, patient, full of considerateness and love for everyone ...'

Mrs Pring checked his flow by putting her head round the door. 'Sugar and milk, Father Neil?'

'Herself,' groaned Fr Duddleswell, 'would bloody-well interrupt Jesus in the middle of a miracle.'

'Both, please,' I said, and Mrs Pring, smiling the smile of the just, closed the door behind her.

'Now, Father Neil, Catholic priests do not marry. And why not?'

Mrs Pring's head reappeared to provide the answer. 'Because there's not enough crazy women around.' Then she put her head back on and left us to chat about parish matters. Before the tea arrived we were off on an inspection of the house.

'On the ground floor here, next to me study, is the dining room. *There* is the big committee room—we call it the parlour—and down that corridor is the kitchen.'

Mrs Pring, who had just descended the stairs, said, '*My* kitchen.'

Fr Duddleswell pouted amusedly. 'Women,' he sighed, 'almost as difficult to comprehend as nuns. That one beats eggs just by talking to 'em.'

He lifted the skirt of his cassock—without noticing that the buttons were awry—and proceeded to climb the stairs.

'My bedroom,' he said, nodding to his left.

He led me into the middle room which was to be my study, bare of ornament but for a few potted plants, then to my bedroom, overlooking the street, in which Mrs Pring had deposited the suitcases. The bedroom was small and dark with a wash basin, brown utility wardrobe and chest of drawers. At the head of the iron bedstead was a faded copy of Velasquez's Crucifixion.

'Run the hot water for a minute or two,' he said. 'It comes eventually if you pray hard enough to St Anthony. I only hope that bed is going to be long enough for you. Why was I not forewarned, then, you were two yards tall? It does look a big bit on the little side.'

I muttered something about being used to sleeping knees up in beds considerably smaller than myself.

'Good,' he said, 'that will save me executing your legs off as I did with me last curate.'

He showed me the bathroom and ended by pointing up the next flight of stairs. 'Up there, a few feet below God's own blue heaven, is Mrs Pring's domain.' He waved his index finger warningly. 'Trespassers *will* be, I can assure you of that, now. Herself does not own much, which is why she is so fiendishly possessive.'

By this time, the maligned Mrs Pring had brought a cup of tea, black as syrup, into my study. I noticed her sturdy forearms, rough elbows and her smooth red cheeks.

'Now, Mrs Pring, leave the lad alone,' said Fr Duddleswell. 'Do not smother him with your maternal ministrations.'

Mrs Pring began, 'I was only going to say ...' but he stopped her with a lordly gesture.

'Indeed, Mrs Pring, but we do not have an hour to spare, you follow?'

When Fr Duddleswell had shooed Mrs Pring out I was left to settle in. Having drunk my tea, I tried the bed for size, tidied away my clothes and tested the efficacy of prayers to St Anthony.

I had a premonition I was going to like it at St Jude's.

A few minutes later and my few books were on the shelf and my framed papal indulgence was hanging on the wall. There was a gentle knock on the door. Mrs Pring had come to water the fuchsias.

'Don't be put off by him,' she said comfortingly. 'He's really a very nice man until you get to know him. If you have any difficulties with that one, just give Churchill a ring. Winnie's been longing for a good dog-fight since he finished Jerry off five years ago.'

'Oh, yes,' I stammered.

'Him and me are what you might call a hellish combination. I do the weeping and he does the gnashing of teeth.'

Her comforting was not having the effect she was intending. 'What time do you serve meals, Mrs Pring?'

'He's terribly suspicious, you know. His dad was in antiques. If you ask me, he thinks everything's a fake but himself.'

'Lunch is at one, I suppose.'

'It's as if,' said Mrs Pring, 'he's seeing things in a mirror. He don't notice because *everything* is back to front.'

A sharp rap on the door startled her. She grabbed her watering can saying, 'The Day of Judgement, flee the wrath to come.'

Father Neil, I was . . .' Fr Duddleswell's smile vanished like a T.V. picture when the set is switched off. One moment it was as wide as his face, the next it had contracted to a dot before popping out altogether. 'Woman,' he growled, 'I do not want you walking up me curate's sleeve. Did I not tell you to go West to your kitchen for a while? I *will* be obeyed here.' He stamped his foot. 'I will not have you wearing the cassock in this house.'

'I should think not,' the housekeeper said without flinching. 'That skirt went out of fashion in Queen Victoria's time.'

'Ah, Father Neil,' said Fr Duddleswell, the gleam in his eye showing he conceded a temporary defeat, 'she is more at me throat than is me collar itself.'

'What time is lunch, Father?' I asked.

Mrs Pring drove home her advantage with, 'Never trust the son of a cow.'

'One o'clock, Mrs Pring?' I put in with a trifle more urgency.

'Father Neil,' said Fr Duddleswell, 'are you one of those curates who is always thinking of his belly?'

'I'm not hungry, Father,' I hastened to say.

'Then why in the name of Beelzebub d'you keep asking when lunch is?'

Mrs Pring touched my shoulder. 'Poor Father Neil.'

'I will not have the pair of you ganging up against me,' Fr Duddleswell said. 'Go, Mrs Pring, before I take me tongue to you.'

Mrs Pring carried on with her condolences. 'I'll put lunch forward if you're peckish, Father Neil.'

I attempted to bring peace by insisting that I didn't mind if she served lunch at three.

Fr Duddleswell was not pleased by my magnanimity. 'He is not above one hour at St Jude's and already he is changing the times of meals.' Then he dropped his shoulders and relaxed. 'I repent me of me loutish behaviour,' he grinned.

'I'm sorry, too,' added Mrs Pring. 'I don't know what came over him.'

In spite of the colourful exchanges, I sensed at once that the parish priest and his housekeeper were only indulging in banter which, while heated, was neither harsh nor bruising.

''Tis the problem of living year by year in one another's shoulders,' explained Fr Duddleswell. 'I only came to tell you I am intending to give you a whistle-stop tour of the parish before lunch.'

I thanked him for that.

'Do you not wish to know what time lunch is?' he asked.

'Not particularly, Father.'

He gave me an incredulous smile. 'What a strange lad y'are surely. You keep on asking questions and have not the slightest decent interest in the answers.'

First stop, the maternity-wing of the hospital. From behind a glass-partition we gazed admiringly on half a dozen newly-born.

''Tis an extraordinary thing, Father Neil, yet there is but one father of all these.'

'A sex maniac in the parish?' Humour is not my forté but I was doing my best.

'I was speaking in a spiritual sense, if you're still with me.'

'You mean God, then.'

'No, Father Neil. I mean me. This is why we priests do not marry, so we can be 'father' to the whole tribe.' I followed the dab of his finger. 'Look at that little boy ... or girl. 'Tis hard to puzzle which when he or she is back to front and upside down.' Too true, I thought. 'By the way, how would *you* tell the difference between a boy and a girl?'

I hummed for a few seconds without coming to any articulate conclusion.

'How old are you, Father Neil?' he laughed. He beckoned my ear downwards. 'Boys have blue eyes and girls have pink eyes. Did your mother never tell you that?' I removed my ear from the vicinity of his lips. 'And if they are asleep, what then?'

'I don't know,' I said stubbornly.

'A priest must use his initiative, like. While nobody is

looking, you prise their little eyes open.' When he laughed this time I joined in. 'Ever hear the story, Father Neil, of two families holidaying together? First morning on the beach, the little Catholic boy of four summers is playing on the sands with the little Protestant girl, both of them skin-wrapped as they came into the world. Know what the Catholic boy says to his mummy?'

'Yes, Father.'

He was taken aback. 'You do?'

'Yes.'

'What?'

Somewhat shyly I said, 'Mummy, I didn't know there was that much difference between Catholics and Protestants.'

Fr Duddleswell's eyes came over glazed. 'What difference are you speaking of, Father Neil?'

'Um. *The* difference, Father.'

'Which is?'

'The difference, um, everyone knows about.'

'Excepting me, it seems.' A leggy nurse chanced to walk by. 'I will just ask this lovely young nurse if she knows what difference 'tis you are referring to.'

'Please, *don't*,' I begged.

He shrugged in acquiescence. 'A further thing is perplexing me. How would seeing a little girl in the state of nature make the little lad so sure she was a Protestant?'

'It wouldn't, Father.' Lamely, I added, 'And that's the joke.'

'The joke, you say. Would you be so kind as to explain the *joke* to me?'

'I can't, Father.'

He heaved a deep sigh. 'So, then, Father Neil, you have learned your first important lesson at St Jude's.'

'Lesson?'

'That if you steal me best punch-lines, you must expect to suffer.' Without a change of pace, he pointed to a six or seven pounder, 'Anyway, what would you baptize him with?'

'It's a *her*,' I said beaming defiantly.

'And you pretended not to know the difference,' he said. 'Well, what would you baptize her with?'

'Water, Father.'

'I knew you would not use pea soup but what would you

14

pour the water from, a fire-bucket?'

'A cup, Father?' I asked, improvising.

'Even that might drown the girleen or give her the pneumonia. A cupful is, to one that size, the same as a swimming pool to a Jehovah's Witness.'

'A thimble, Father.'

'A thimble,' he echoed. 'Now, where would you get one of those in a maternity unit?'

I used my initiative. 'I could borrow one from Mrs Pring.'

Well in the driving seat by now, Fr Duddleswell said to himself, 'The lad is wanting to use Mrs Pring's thimble for a font.'

'I can't think of anything smaller, Father.'

Fr Duddleswell picked up a syringe from a surgical trolley. 'You would use one of these. But make sure first it has water in it and not, say, hydrochloric acid.'

'Baptism isn't legal with hydrochloric acid,' I said, in case he didn't know.

'Not legal,' he said, 'but lethal, like. So you test it out on your skin, like this.' He squirted some of the syringe's contents on to the back of his hand. 'If it brings up a blister, do not use it on the baby's head.' He paused to rub his hand where the liquid lay and blew on it anxiously. 'Oh my God,' he cried. The leggy nurse had returned. 'Nurse, nurse, what the divil is in this syringe?'

'Water, Father.'

Fr Duddleswell licked his hand before lifting his head in relief. 'Thank God for that, 'tis only tapoline. Next, an important question, Father Neil. If a child is born premature, what would you do?'

'Call a nurse quick, Father.'

'Brilliant,' he almost sang. 'What if after the baby is born premature a nurse calls *you* to the incubator?'

'I'd baptize it—him or her, according to the difference—in case the baby died.' Fr Duddleswell nodded encouragingly. 'With a syringe.' Another friendly nod. 'Not hydrochloric acid.' He slowly shook his head.

'What else would you *not* do?'

As if to give the lie to my words I said wildly, 'I wouldn't panic, Father.'

'You would not ... light ... any ... candles.'

'No, Father?'

'No. Because with all that oxygen around, if you struck a match the poor little mite would go unbaptized—poof!—to Limbo.'

It took me a second or two to recover from the explosion. 'Father,' I said.

He was looking down paternally on all the infants in their cribs. 'Yes?'

'Is it nearly time for lunch?'

It wasn't. We stood side by side in the tree-lined cemetery gazing dreamily over the grassy and concrete beds with tombstones for headboards.

'Our last resting-place, Father Neil,' he whispered. 'Before we go off to lunch, I am meaning.'

Glad of a few moments' rest, I murmured, 'It's very peaceful here.'

'You would hardly expect it to be a riot,' he said. 'Not with all those corpses stretched out and decomposing six feet below.'

I asked him if this was a special plot for deceased Catholics. He nodded gravely and gave it as his opinion that Holy Mother Church was wise not to allow mixed funerals. 'At the Last Day,' he proclaimed cheerfully, 'St Michael will blow loud the Trumpet Blast, and winds wild as angels on horseback will blow from the four corners of heaven, and the Almighty God will start His resurrecting, like, in this sacred little plot of Catholic earth.'

I was in no mood for questioning the Lord's geographical preferences on Doomsday.

'Stand up, Seamus Flynn, the Lord will cry.' Fr Duddleswell's evocation made me jump to attention. 'Stand up, Mary Ryan. Stand up, Micky O'Brien, if you are yet sober.'

Joining in the festive mood, I chanted, 'Thigh bone connected to the hip bone.'

He rounded on me. 'And what will God say to Paddy Reilly who had no legs to stand on in life due to a motor accident?'

'Sit down, Paddy?' I suggested.

'Where is your faith, Father Neil? At the resurrection, God will put on Mrs Pring's thimble and the legless Paddy Reilly will have new ones sewn on. A marvellous sight to behold. One thing, though.'

'Yes, Father?'

As he moved on, he called over his shoulder, 'I only hope I am not around to see it.'

A bit further on we came to the grave of 'FR FREDERICK CONNORS, PARISH PRIEST OF ST JUDE'S, 1890–1938.'

'Your predecessor, Father?'

He nodded. 'I remember well that day twelve years since when we buried Freddie Connors.'

'Only forty-eight years old,' I said, after a quick calculation.

'Surprising he lasted so long, Father Neil. Always had trouble with his internals.'

'Weak heart?'

'No, his housekeeper was a really shocking cook.' He became solemn again. 'The whole parish of St Jude's was here, living *and* dead. Oh, 'twas a gorgeous day for a funeral. A cold, gusty, end-of-the-year, end-of-a-life sort of day. The corpses were the warmest bodies here. Trees bare. The short grass faded, almost white. And not one bird sang.'

'Did *you* officiate, Father?'

He shook his head. 'Fr McNally did the honours. Tall and lean. A beanpole of a man, draped in black, McNally. With a booming voice and a huge red beak on him like an eagle with 'flu.' He stopped to pull up a weed and threw it casually behind him. 'Same old clichés—no less true for that, mind. "Our beloved Brother, Frederick, departed this mortal life ... ashes to ashes, sod to sod ... vanity of vanities ... what I am, he was, what he is, I will be." '

His head dropped on his left shoulder as if it was too heavy for his neck alone to support. 'The pall-bearers slowly lowered the coffin and frozen earth dropped like thunder on the polished wood. I stood on the edge of the gaping hole there and looked down, dizzy-like, to pay me last respects to a dear old buddy. Wailings, loud as Jews', all around me, but through me tears I just managed to whisper, "Thank God, you are dead, Freddie boy." ' A heave of his chest and a loud sniffle. ' "You would never have lived through your funeral." '

Out of the corner of my eye I saw him looking at me out of the corner of his eye.

'And now, Father Neil,' he announced breezily, 'I am sure

17

you *must* be ready for a bite to eat.'

At lunch on the dot of one, Fr Duddleswell said grace and presided under a gaudy print of Blessed Pius X.

I shook out my table napkin in expectation of replenishment at last. 'Is the food good, Father?'

''Tis foul as can be, but one consolation—there is plenty of it. In spite of rationing, herself still manages to provide us with three square meals a meal.'

Mrs Pring arrived puffing and blowing, laden down with a tray. She asked if she had heard us discussing her cooking.

'Indeed,' confessed Fr Duddleswell, 'I was on the eve of telling Father Neil there is nothing wrong with your cooking, provided we do not have to eat it.' Mrs Pring started to serve a pot roast. 'And why are we lunching late again?' It was two minutes past the hour.

'I've had trouble with ...'

'Always an excuse readier than an apron, Mrs Pring.'

'The cooker,' she finished.

He touched my wrist as the plate was put in front of me. 'Father Neil, you have made your will? Well, now, this evening your confessions are from 5 to 6.'

I did my best to look unconcerned. 'Fine, Father.'

Mrs Pring interjected, 'If he's not been in the box before, he's probably scared out of his wits is poor Father Neil.'

'Rightly so,' retorted the parish priest, unscrewing the top of the sauce bottle. 'He is probably thinking you will come yourself and unload on him your own heinous sins.' Turning to me: ''Tis better to have a fixed time for confessions because in that way you gradually build up your own clientèle, you follow? The good people get to know when and where to find you.'

'And how to avoid the priests they can't abide,' said Mrs Pring.

'Good day to you, Mrs Pring,' the parish priest said, and, showing her the hairy instrument, 'the back of me hand to you. I have now to discuss confessional secrets with me new curate.'

'If you want something,' said Mrs Pring before closing the door on herself, 'just call and I'll come bouncing back like an egg off the wall.'

In a loud whisper, Fr Duddleswell confided to me, 'Her husband chose the better part. He left her in the First World War, so he did.'

I was shocked. 'Divorced, Father?'

'No, no, I mean he laid down his life nice and easy, like, on the field of battle.' The essentially kind-hearted priest added, 'God rest him,' and made a sign of the cross so swift no angel would have recognized it.

Not knowing quite what to do or say, I blurted out, 'Amen'.

'Now, he said, coughing and adopting a brisker tone once more, 'about this holy sacrament which turns the sinner's wages from death to life. First, a word of advice. Never let on you know who 'tis that is confessing to you. You must *not* say, for instance, 'You really have improved since last month, have you not, Mrs O'Kelly?' or 'Leave the door ajar after you, Mr Tracey.' Above all, you must not be querulous ever and say, 'But Mr Jones, your wife just admitted to using contraceptives *seven* times, not *five*.'

'I promise not to be querulous, Father,' I said, suspecting that one of my long legs was getting rapidly longer. 'But does that sort of thing happen often?'

'Using contraceptives?'

'No, Father, lying about it.'

Showing mild surprise, he asked, 'Did I mention the word "lying"? 'Tis rather like on the golf course, Father Neil. The men are such marvellous proud creatures they tend to underestimate how many strokes they take to the hole. There is no malice to it.'

'Just bad addition, you mean.'

'And sometimes subtraction,' he responded knowingly. 'At the start,' he said confidentially, bowing towards me a domed head over which was slanted his thinning brown hair and skewering me with his eye, 'at the start, I am sorry to have to tell you this, you are likely to get the more ...' He reached for a word, missed and reached again, 'hardened sinners.'

'Hardened' was accentuated but softly.

My spine grew icicles but I tried to brave it out by joking, 'Not you and Mrs Pring?'

He pointed to my plate. 'Take a mound of mustard with that and you might be lucky enough not to taste the food at all.' I obeyed. 'Some'll think—quite mistakenly, to be sure—

you are a greenhorn who's not yet heard that sin has been invented. Others'll take advantage of the fact that you cannot fix a voice to a face. But in two shakes of a black sheep's tail you will only have your fair share of *hardened* sinners.'

The thought of being initially saturated with more than my fair share of trouble was to be a lemon in my mouth for the rest of the afternoon.

'Any questions, Father Neil?—apart from the time of supper.'

'Tea-time, Father?' I ventured. Since it brought no reaction, I tried again. 'Is it interesting?'

'Are you referring to the time-table of meals in this house or the holy sacrament? No, Father Neil, 'tis not at all interesting sitting there by the hour with harmless women and children spitting sins into your unprotected ear. 'Tis bloody tedious, if you want to know, especially'—he tapped his thigh —'if you suffer from the occupational hazard. Mind you, if you have a nice juicy murder this very evening, that is another matter surely. Your first penitent perhaps.'

I knew he was teasing me but I still gulped and said, 'That's not likely, Father.' When he did not reply: 'Is it?'

'Oh, at a guess and on the basis of me own experience, at least four to one against. Sex, now, is another kettle of fish.'

'Sex comes up more frequently?'

'Well,' he tutted, 'since you brought the indelicate subject up, I tell you. If an Irish girl confesses to company-keeping, be sure to investigate that thoroughly.'

'By questioning?'

He looked at me as if to say, How else? 'To a colleen, Father Neil, company-keeping can mean anything from holding hands in the park to multiple adulteries. And watch out for the way English people—not Americans who are decent and straightforward folk—slip their mortal sins into the middle of a pack of peccadilloes. Now, as to birth control.'

To prove the adequacy of my seminary training I told him that scientists were reported to be working on a contraceptive pill.

'And no doubt,' he replied scornfully, 'the same Lucifer-like fellows think that one day they will fly to the moon. To practicalities. Contraception is a grievous sin because there is interference with nature to make sure that one and one do not

20

make three.' I smiled, hoping it was expected of me. 'The Lord said to our first parents, 'Multiply' not 'Stultify'. And, by the by, what would have happened, like, if Adam and Eve had used contraceptives?'

'Nothing, Father.'

'Indeed. For a start, you and I would not be here conversing and the whole world would be one gigantic zoo without any keepers to look after the animals. Could anything demonstrate better the evils of contraception?'

I shook my head to show his argument had convinced me.

'Father Neil, what *natural* methods of birth control are permitted by the Church?'

'Complete abstinence, Father.'

'From what?' he asked. 'From the drink? From flesh meat? Fish and chips? Be specific, if you would.'

'From sex.'

He pursed his lips approvingly. 'Complete sexual abstinence is pure. And effective, certainly. Especially if husband and wife take the precaution of sleeping in separate towns.'

'The other method,' I said, 'is using the safe-period.'

'But once the intercourse of man and woman has begun,' he said, lowering his fork, 'what may lawfully interrupt it?'

That was the moment Mrs Pring chose to poke her head round the door to say, 'Plum pudding and custard?'

Fr Duddleswell told her with measured impoliteness that when he was ready for his plum pudding and custard he would let her know. He repeated his question about any exceptions to the general rule of not interrupting intercourse—'apart from Mrs Pring's dessert.'

I played for time. 'You do mean married couples?'

'If they are unmarried, boy, they should interrupt it before they start.'

I had never asked myself such an intimate question before and so I enquired distractedly if an earthquake would do.

'Surely, Father Neil, but do you mean that as cause or effect?' When he saw I had finished guessing he put it to me, 'Suppose the children come unannounced into their parents' bedroom.'

'During ...'

'Yes.'

'For a drink of water, Father?'

'For any reason whatsoever, whether to drink water or to pass it.'

'Ah,' I exclaimed, as my memory came into focus, 'it's all right to stop sex—in the middle—if the bed breaks, Father.'

'Correct!' He slapped his knee in applause. 'Provided of course their intention is not to prevent conception but only to restore a semblance of order to the room.'

When lunch was over, Fr Duddleswell led me into the church. After a prayer, he showed me my confessional at close quarters.

'You will notice,' he said, 'I have seen to it there is a black-out curtain over the grille. The good people like to think you cannot tell them from Adam and Eve.'

'And *can* you, Father?'

'The priest in the confessional, Father Neil, is like a blind man: all ears. Consequently, his hearing becomes very acute, if you're still with me. In a while you will recognize every voice in the parish. More,' he spoke with a certain professional pride, 'before they even open their mouths, you will know who is there from their footsteps, from how they open the confessional door, from the squeaks they make when they kneel down on the prie-dieu—even from the way they breathe.'

My breath caught in my throat on hearing of Fr Duddleswell's remarkable talent for detection.

'Often, Father Neil, you will know their sins before they confess them.'

'Even the mortal, Father?'

'*Especially* the mortal.'

I guessed he was finding me an audience very much to his liking.

'Sometimes you will smell it on them like booze or garlic. But most horrible of all . . .'—I waited, my mind boggling at the prospect of what was to come—'you know which of them should visit their dentist. The sins themselves are odious enough but bad breath! Phew. Now, finally,' he seemed relieved he had got that off his chest, 'deaf-mutes.'

Disconsolate, I could only repeat the latest source of my troubles.

'There are two problems with them,' he said briskly. 'They cannot hear you and . . .'

22

'You cannot hear them.' He was pleased I was so quick on the uptake. 'How do you hear their confessions, then?'

'Unless you can work a miracle, you cannot. See here.' He entered the confessional and showed me a drawer under the grille which he pulled out. 'It opens two ways. The deaf-mute writes his sins on a piece of paper and sends it to you. You then write his penance underneath, return it to him and give him absolution. If it says on the paper, "A pound of sausages and two lamb chops," you know the butcher has just received a very interesting order.'

'What,' I objected, 'if the deaf-mute can't read or write?'

He looked at me a little wearily. 'Father Neil, must you be ever manufacturing difficulties for yourself? Whoever heard of a deaf-mute going to confession if he cannot read nor write.'

'But suppose one does.'

'Oh,' he concluded, as if no solution could be more obvious, 'you pull down the curtain, lad, and use sign-language.'

Mrs Pring served tea at four and it lasted a quarter of an hour. I did not take in much of what was said to me. Immediately afterwards, I went to my room to prepare myself for the impending ordeal. I was quivering as, I imagined, a surgeon is before his first operation—except I know the harm I could do was far worse since it was harm to *souls*.

I put on my cassock, recently purchased from Van Haigh's, the clerical tailors, for my ordination. My parents, though not well-off, insisted I have it. There were no soupstains down the front. It had all its buttons. My hand trembled so, I had difficulty in fastening them up.

Fr Duddleswell came to my study to lead me, as he said, 'through the milling crowds' to my confessional.

I expressed gratitude for his support.

'I only hope, Father Neil, that your dear knees are not knocking their heads together.'

We descended the stairs and passed through the door connecting house and sacristy. Thence, apprehensively, into the church.

It was empty.

I had expected to find benchfuls of sinners waiting to make their confession. For some reason, the emptiness had a more damaging effect upon my constitution than if the place had been crowded out. It made me feel more isolated than Moses on the mountain top.

'Good heavens, Father Neil. There is not an individual here. I should have placed an Ad. in the paper.'

Genuflecting with a wobble, I walked with him down the side aisle to my confessional, our footfalls echoing as in a museum. There he shook my hand with emotion and left.

I opened up my side of the box and put on the purple stole that was draped across the chair, closed the door and sat down. At least I was privately alone there and not publicly alone as in the church.

The door of the box had a top section of smoky glass. Through it, I saw amorphous shadows dancing in the flickering light of candles. The irreverent thought came to me that this was like sitting on an ancient lavatory.

I had almost succeeded in pulling myself together when I became aware that I was not alone after all. There were *noises*.

I imagined someone had either tip-toed into the penitent's side of the box or been hiding there all along. I listened. I said, 'Yes?' in case there was a penitent waiting to begin. No speech, only noises.

I felt some *thing* brush against the bottom of my cassock.

With a yell, I pushed open the confessional door and jumped out of my seat with an almighty crash. It was a mouse—rodents always give me the creeps—a mother mouse followed crazily by two smaller mice. They must have been nesting there since spring behind the radiator. They scuttled away into the gloom.

I could not follow their course because I saw another spectre. An elderly lady in a flowerpot hat had entered the church at the very moment I burst out of the box. Unaccustomed to such a wild display from an unknown clergyman, she screamed and ran from the church.

There goes my first penitent, I reflected. I hoped she would not report me to the police.

I returned warily to the box and saw that in my haste to escape I had kicked the chair from under me and smashed one of its legs. It hung on by a sliver of wood.

I would have fixed it on the spot if I had been a practical man. But it so happens I'm what my father calls 'maladroit'.

Even my right foot is left-handed, so to speak. Guiltily, I crossed to Fr Duddleswell's box carrying my chair and exchanged it for his.

Back in my own box, I switched on the naked bulb above my head. Having assured myself there was no daddy mouse lurking in a corner waiting to pounce, I opened my breviary. This was a grotesque piece of self-deception. Prayer was impossible and I had already recited my office for that day in any case. But the black leather-bound book gave me a much needed feeling of warmth and security.

In the seminary, our professor of moral theology, Canon Flynn, had advised us to copy out the Latin formula for confession in case we should forget it in a moment of crisis. I had written it out in capitals on a sheet of paper. When the penitent came in, the custom was to extinguish the light which meant the letters had to be large if I was to read them.

I was grateful for Canon Flynn's advice. By then I would have found it hard to recite even the Lord's prayer without a prompter.

Ages seemed to pass. My watch, which never panicked, told me it was eight minutes past the hour. Then came the sound of feet brushing hard on the rough mat at the entrance to the church. Someone knelt noisily and with a sigh near my confessional box but beyond my range of vision. I wondered if the lady with the flowerpot hat had summoned up enough courage to return, and, if so, what would I say to her? And what would she say to me?

'Bless me, Father, for I am a sin.'

In my relief, I could have given my invisible young penitent a big hug for making such a shambles of the opening formula.

'*Dominus sit in corde* ... May the Lord be in thy heart and on thy lips that thou mayest truly and humbly confess thy sins, in the name of the Father and of the Son and of the Holy Ghost.' I made the sign of the cross.

The child's voice went on, 'Father ...'

'Yes?'

'This is my *second* confession.'

My first, I thought. I said, 'And when was your first confession?'

There was a pause before the voice answered. 'Just before

my first Communion.'

'When was that?'

'Two weeks ago. Everybody knows that.'

'Well,' I explained, 'I'm new to the parish, you see.'

'Oh,' the voice said, not very convinced.

Another silence broken by the voice asking, 'Are you still there, Father?'

'Yes,' I said, grateful for some sign that my penitent hadn't abandoned me. 'What are your sins, dear?'

I was pleased with that. 'Dear' was a good indefinite English word with which to address a child whose age and sex were undetermined. Of course, Fr Duddleswell would have had the edge ...

'I called the grocer a pig.'

So it wasn't only the Yanks who were frank about their faults. 'Yes,' I murmured non-committally. I didn't want to appear either to condone the offence or be shocked by it.

'Two times, Father.'

'Why did you call him that?'

' 'Cos he deserved it. He *was* a pig.'

'I see,' I said, unable to test for myself whether there was a sufficient justification for the epithet. 'What made you *suspect* he was a pig?'

'He wouldn't give me a chocolate marshmallow when I asked him to.'

Another pause, so I said, 'Was there something else?'

After a silence broken only by the rocking of the prie-dieu, the voice whispered, 'I committed adultery three times.'

I blinked in the darkness. Was I dealing with an older person after all—say, a dwarf with a high-pitched voice? I managed to get out a question Canon Flynn had advised us never to put: 'What exactly did you do?'

'I took three pennies out of mummy's purse.' Then the voice corrected the mistake: 'No, that's the next commandment, isn't it, the funny one? I know what it was, I stoled three times.'

'Mummy trusts you, dear,' I said, gently rather than reproachfully, 'and you shouldn't let her down, should you?'

'She don't,' returned the voice.

'Doesn't what?'

'She don't trust me, she's a wise 'un.'

'Anything else?' I asked, ready for a change of subject.

'She owed it me for washing up.'

'Anything else?' I repeated.

'She did, too.'

No comment.

'I committed an immortal sin.'

'A mortal sin? How?' I bit my tongue. Another prohibited question.

'I didn't go to Mass last Sunday.'

'Why was that? Were you ill or something?'

'No,' replied the voice, sighing and blowing on the bottom of the confessional veil so it billowed and touched my ear. 'Marge wouldn't come with me.'

'Is Marge your sister?'

'No, Marge is my mum. Everybody knows that.'

'I'm new ...,' I began but gave up. 'Doesn't your father go to church?'

'My dad, you mean?'

'Yes, your dad.'

'He came to my first Communion.'

'Not otherwise?'

'He says next time he comes it'll be in a bleedin' box, Father.'

I quieted my soul with the reflection that the child was only quoting. 'Is he a Catholic?'

'No, Father.'

'Is he a believer, then?'

'No, he's a bus-driver.'

'Well,' I said, having sat in judgement long enough already on my first penitent, 'for your penance I want you to go to Our Lady's altar and say one Our Father and one Hail Mary for your mummy and daddy. Now make a good act of contrition while I give you absolution.'

I spread out my sheet of paper on my knee and started to quietly read the absolution. I tried to be conscious of the solemnity of the occasion. For the first time in my priestly life I was forgiving sins in Christ's name.

'Misereatur tui, omnipotens Deus ...'

I had gone some way and still no sound of the act of contrition from the penitent. I halted and said encouragingly, 'O my God, because Thou art so good ...'

The voice repeated, 'O my God,' and, satisfied it would continue under its own steam, I finished off the absolution.

At the end, I said, 'Go in peace, dear, and pray for me.'

There was a creak and a shuffle before the voice said, 'I forgot my penance, Father.'

'One Our Father and one Hail Mary.'

The other side of the box banged open. I saw a pint-sized shadow flitter by and heard the clip-clip of a child's feet going down the church.

Someone else had entered the box with a heavy sigh and a creaking of the prie-dieu. I suspected I wasn't going to be let off so lightly this time. I gave the blessing. I listened. No sound.

'How long is it?' I asked. Since there was still no sound I repeated my question, only louder.

The clip-clip in advance of a shadow was already on the way back past the confessional. There was a light tap on my window and my first penitent said, 'Bye-bye, Father.'

'Goodbye, dear,' I said, as tiny footsteps were swallowed up in the open air and the voice went home to Marge. Now I could concentrate on my second penitent. 'How long is it since your last confession?' I could hear heavy breathing continuing so I banged nervously on the box to get some reaction.

Then the situation became painfully clear. A deaf-mute? Must be a deaf-mute.

I opened up the drawer. Nothing there. Frantically I wrote on the back of my sheet of paper: 'WHAT ARE YOUR SINS?' and put it in the drawer. I waited for a few seconds until the sound of scribbling on the other side of the grille had ceased, then pulled the drawer out again. Underneath my question, written in the clearest hand, was the answer: 'MIND YOUR OWN BUSINESS.'

Angrily I pulled aside the curtain to see Fr Duddleswell's cherubic face beaming at me through the grille like a fish in a net. 'Do not forget to replace me chair when you have finished with it.'

'No, Father.'

'And, Father Neil.'

'Yes, Father?'

'May your stay at St Jude's continue as happily as it has begun.'

28

II *An Unusual Pregnancy*

My earliest impression of my parish priest was that, notwithstanding his bland exterior, he was a wily old bird. This impression was soon to be confirmed.

We were standing side by side outside the church one Sunday morning. He was still wearing his vestments because it was his custom, immediately he had celebrated the late Mass, to leave the sanctuary while the choir was still busy chanting the prayer for the King and race down the aisle like a rabbit to greet the parishioners as they filed out.

'We priests have got to be as sociable as sun and rain,' he'd said to me, as the "good people" emerged blinking into the daylight, he shook their hands, spoke to each of them and wished them 'God's blessing on you and yours.'

Fr Duddleswell introduced me to any number of the congregation, mentioning their names and addresses. It was like expecting me to memorize the telephone directory. But towards the end of the line, he introduced me to a couple whose name had a familiar ring.

'Father Neil, I'd have you meet Mr and Mrs Macaulay, stalwarts of the parish.'

They beamed at the compliment and shook my hand with Irish *bonhomie*.

'And this,' added Fr Duddleswell, 'is their married daughter, Mary Frost.'

I exchanged greetings with Mary Frost, a little alarmed as celibates tend to be, at the fact that she was so advanced in pregnancy.

'Father Neil,' said the obviously dominant Mrs Macaulay, 'our Tim has often spoken of you.'

Then I was certain I was being introduced to the family of Tim Macaulay who'd been my best pal in the seminary.

'Our Tim's turn next, Father,' Mr Macaulay softly said to me.

'And a grand priest he'll make, too,' said Fr Duddleswell.

'It so happens,' said Mrs Macaulay, telling me what she must have realized I knew as well as she, 'our Tim is a sub-deacon, but this time next year he'll be celebrating his first holy Mass in St Jude's.'

'God willing,' added the quiet Mr Macaulay.

'And how is Mary?' asked Fr Duddeswell, turning to the round and lovely daughter who reminded me very much, feature-wise, of her brother.

Mary said blushingly, 'As well as could be expected, considering, Father.'

'Delighted to hear it,' responded Fr Duddleswell.

'Father married Mary and Patrick in St Jude's a little over nine months ago,' Mrs Macaulay announced to me in a volume more appropriate to a loudspeaker.

'A great occasion,' said the parish priest. 'Will I ever forget it? I never will.'

'And the power of Fr Duddleswell's blessing will soon be made manifest to all the world,' said the eloquent Mrs Macaulay.

I thought the world had a grandstand view already.

Next to me, Mr Macaulay shuffled his feet and whispered, 'We're very much looking forward to the happy event, Father.'

'In a couple of weeks,' said his wife, 'Mary is going to present us with our very first grandson. Isn't that so, now, Mary?'

Mary blushed a deeper hue. 'God willing,' she murmured.

Sharing Mary's discomfort, I attempted to put her at her ease. 'And how is your husband, Mrs Frost?'

'Very well, Father, thanking you. He's in Birmingham. I'm just down for the weekend.'

'Mary,' said Fr Duddleswell, 'I think you are a very brave girl coming all this way from the Midlands on your own at this time.'

'I'll be all right, Father, and Pat's going to pick me up at Birmingham New Street tonight.'

Mrs Macaulay put in: 'So it'll mean another baptism for you not too long hence.'

'I look forward to every christening,' said the parish priest. 'Now run along with you and do not keep poor Mary on her feet one second longer than she needs.'

As the happy family group departed, Fr Duddleswell was repeating mostly to himself: 'A lovely girl, a lovely girl that Mary, lovely girl.'

At lunch, I remarked on the striking likeness between Mary and her brother, Tim.

'Provided she does not take after her mother, she can count herself blessed among women.'

'Her mother is a strong character, I could tell.'

'Strong as Gorgonzola cheese and proud as a paycock.'

I thought his tone uncharacteristically acid. 'She seemed a pious sort of person,' I ventured.

As he flicked over the pages of the *News Of The World*, he said: 'Oh, she is pious all right. A Pharisee of Pharisees, if you ask me.'

'She's looking forward to a little grandson, Father.'

'Not this time round.'

I was silent for a moment, wondering whether he were a prophet or gynaecologists were at last able to determine a child's sex before birth.

'Are you sure, Father?' I said.

'Quite sure.'

Fr Duddleswell suddenly closed his newspaper with a swish, raised his spectacles on to his forehead and said: 'Promise me you will not let on.'

I promised, not knowing what this was all about.

'*Sub sigillo*, I mean it,' he continued. 'Treat this as a confessional secret. The truth of the matter is: Mary Frost is not pregnant at all. At least, I hope to God she isn't.'

It was on the tip of my tongue to ask him if he might be mistaken. Each time he opened his mouth I was becoming more confused.

'Father,' I managed to say, 'she *looks* pregnant.'

'She is supposed to look *very* pregnant. But, in fact, Mary Frost had her baby a couple of months ago.' He must have seen my look of disbelief, for he added, 'And 'twas a girl, not a boy. Mrs Macaulay has a grand-daughter and that is more than she deserves.'

'And why, Father, does Mary look pregnant when she isn't?'

'An old trick. Cushions, Father Neil, cushions.'

Grudgingly he explained. 'Mary Macaulay was made pregnant by Paddy Frost two months before they married. Mary's no whore, let me assure you of that. The first and only time she went company-keeping, Paddy got her in the family way. Their proficiency was entirely due to inexperience, you follow?'

'A popgun wedding?' I asked.

'A *shot*gun wedding is the more common phrase,' he said, smiling faintly, 'but I reckon, Father Neil, that your description is the more apt.'

'I meant they had to get married.'

'In a manner of speaking, but they loved each other, mind. Paddy is your typical Irishman, not disposed towards marriage unless there is sufficient reason for it. His unexpected talent for paternity supplied the precipating reason and they got wed without argument. Nothing like a child, as they say, to bring a couple together.'

Fr Duddleswell went on to say he'd had to resort to subterfuge on account of Mrs Macaulay's excessive pride.

'Mary knew well enough the kind of mother she had inherited. If she had owned up to her condition, Mrs Macaulay would have shown her the door and used her timid little man for a doorstopper.'

'Would she *really*?'

'Not a doubt about it, Father Neil. Remember the woman comes from the heart of bogland. Did not she name her daughter after the Blessed Virgin herself? 'Tis a marvel to me she let her darlin' Mary enter the lustful condition of matrimony at all. Anyway, the real light of her life is Tim, who is destined to be a priest and thus guarantee a place in heaven for all the family. Mrs Macaulay could not bear the thought of it being whispered abroad that her holy son has a harlot for a sister.'

'I know the kind of thing you mean, Father. There was an Irishman entered the seminary with me who gave up after six months and ...'

'And he could not return to his native Dublin on account of him being 'a spoiled praste' and a disgrace to his bloody family.'

'It was Galway, actually.'

'What *can* you do with people of that mentality, Father

Neil? Two months after the ceremony, before anything showed, I parcelled the newly-weds off to Birmingham. Paddy is only a bricklayer and he can lay one brick on t'other as well in Birmingham as anywhere else. They rented a room on the edge of town. They are finding it tough financially, you know how 'tis, starting with two mouths and two salaries and now three mouths and one salary. But they manage. They are contented just being away from Mother Macaulay.'

I worked my way through most of my first course before daring to say, 'One small question, Father. How do you manage to ... ?' I hesitated.

'To square it with me conscience?'

'What I meant was ...' I couldn't delicately express what I meant but he seemed to understand.

''Tis like this, Father Neil: Mary is not saying she is pregnant. Neither am I.'

'Everybody else is, Father.'

''Tis true. But that is their look-out, is it not?'

'And you don't feel in any way responsible for their misunderstanding?'

'Father Neil, Mary is making a justifiable mental reservation. You know what a mental reservation is?'

I thought, 'Putting a cushion up your jumper and letting folk believe you're pregnant when you're not.' But I only dared say, 'It's the art of letting people deceive themselves without actually telling them lies.'

'A definition worthy of St Thomas Aquinas,' he exclaimed appreciatively. 'There are times, believe you me, when to lie would be a sin and to tell the truth would be a disaster.'

'And silence?'

'Silence ... Silence can be very ... pregnant, if you will forgive the expression. Silence can arouse the very suspicions you are aiming to eliminate.'

'I suppose so, Father.'

'Father Neil, a priest has to become a good poker player. He has so many secrets, confessional and otherwise, he cannot reveal that he has to be a skilled practitioner of the mental reservation.'

To change the subject, I asked, 'When have you decided the baby's going to be ... born?'

'In a day or so, Mary's hubby, Paddy, is due to send a

33

telegram to Grannie Macaulay. Here, I'll show you.'

He took two pieces of notepaper out of his wallet.

'This first is the telegram. It reads: 'Mother and baby doing well. It's a girl. Love Pat.' I'm not sure Paddy can write, so I have to put words on the lips of his pen, like. And this here,' he said, waving the second sheet, 'is a letter from Mary to be sent a couple of days later. In it, Mary explains that the baby having been born premature ...'

I looked up. 'Premature, Father?'

'Two months premature, in fact. Due to this, shall we say, early delivery, a priest in Birmingham baptized the baby, naming her Kathleen after her grandmother.' He gritted his teeth at the reference to a lady whose excessive pride, he considered, was causing him much inconvenience.

'*Is* the baby baptized, Father?'

'Of course. You do not think I would ask Mary to tell a lie on my behalf, do you? I baptized little Kathleen three days after birth in Paddy's flat.'

'*You're* the Birmingham Priest?'

'The priest *in Birmingham*,' he corrected me.

'But, Father'—I spoke as politely as I could—'I was taught you can only baptize a baby in private when there's danger of death.'

'Quite right, Father Neil. And was there not an imminent danger of death when Kathleen came into the world?'

'You mean she really *was* premature?'

'Not at all. She was born nine months to the second after she was conceived. I mean there was danger of spiritual death, you follow? Now don't you try telling me that is not what canon law intends. 'Tis what the Almighty intends that matters.'

'Spiritual death?' I echoed, hoping for some sort of explanation.

'Would there not be slaughter of souls all round, Father Neil, were the truth to be broadcast? Mrs Macaulay would disown her daughter and die like the Pharisee she is, Mary and baby Kathleen would be deprived respectively of mother and grandmother—no great loss from an outsider's point of view but distressing perhaps from theirs.'

At this juncture, Mrs Pring came in to remove the remains of the first course and supply us with strawberries and custard.

Pointing to the bowl of strawberries, Fr Duddleswell said, 'Sacred Hearts again, Mrs Pring?'

'Yes, your irreverence. There's a glut of 'em in the market, so the price has fallen faster'n Lucifer himself. If they go down much more I can see you having 'em for breakfast besides.'

'And *custard*?'

'I know you likes it, so why shouldn't I pamper you?'

As Mrs Pring prepared to depart in a clatter of cutlery and dirty dishes, Fr Duddleswell said for her benefit, 'We had an American priest supplying here last summer, Father Neil, and he suggested that in England the taps should be marked Hot, Cold and Custard.'

Mrs Pring snorted like a cow on a cold morning and lifted her nose in disdain.

'Oh, and by the way, Mrs Pring,' Fr Duddleswell said, before she could screen herself with the door.

'I know. Midwifery again tonight.'

'Mary will come to the side at 8 o'clock as usual and I'll run the both of you to Euston Station.'

'This'll be the third time I've delivered that bairn.'

'And the last, Mrs Pring.'

'I'm pleased for Mary's sake you've finally agreed to let Kathleen come into the world. Must be the longest pregnancy on record.'

When she had gone, Fr Duddleswell's comment was: 'She has her uses, does Mrs Pring. *Très formidable*. Arms like Moses. Should have been a windowcleaner.'

He went on to explain that Mary was currently carrying Mrs Pring's kitchen cushion. He and Mrs Pring were meeting Mary at Euston on Fridays, where the foetus was implanted in the Ladies and the miscarriage took place on the Sunday evenings following.

'There is only the christening to think of now,' said Fr Duddleswell. 'Kathleen has been baptized; all that remains is to supply the rest of the ceremonies in St Jude's.'

'When will that be?'

'No hurry. We will wait awhile so 'tis not so easy to judge how old the child is. Everyone will say that Kathleen is very advanced for her age, and that will make her old granny prouder and fitter for the Fire than ever.'

To stir things up a little, I put forward a hypothesis of my own: 'What if Mary really is pregnant again and another child turns up too soon after the first? Won't you have to go through all this trouble again?'

'Not on your life, I won't. I won't. No. I won't. I would not care now if the next babe were born two days after its conception. That would be a miracle, no doubt, but no aspersions would be cast on its legitimacy. So!'

'Aren't you afraid, I asked finally, 'that Mary and Patrick will give you away?'

'Not a chance, Father Neil. They are terrified of that old harpy, can you not see that? And,' he added less convincingly, 'they are terrified of me, too. I have warned 'em that if they let the cat out of the bag, I'll whip 'em to a pulp with me rosary.'

'It seems safe enough, then.'

'Of course,' he added, 'I put the fear of God into them for good measure. Told 'em I considered the whole matter is under the seal of confession. They will not breathe a word of it now, even to their guardian angel.'

A few weeks later, I went to the reception at the Macaulay's after Kathleen's christening. There I made the acquaintance of Paddy, an incoherent lad with freckles who had originated the whole train of events, and I said 'Hello again' to Mary, now a trim, relaxed young woman.

Across the room, I could see Fr Duddleswell listening with growing agitation to something Mrs Macaulay was whispering in his ear. He was becoming redder and redder, and he kept raising his spectacles and lowering them on his nose, a gesture I interpreted to mean he was furious about something.

After a couple of minutes, he suddenly broke away from the conversation, proclaiming with masterly self-control. 'Charming little grand-daughter, you have, Mrs Macaulay, to be sure, charming.' But as he grazed past me to get to the door, he was muttering so only I heard: 'The bitch. The bloody bitch. Deceiving me all this time.'

He left in an almighty hurry.

Mrs Macaulay, for her part, followed Fr Duddleswell with

a beatific smile. Then she came across to me and led me to where Kathleen was lying asleep in her cradle.

'Fr Duddleswell ...' she began.

'Yes?'

'He's a real saint is that darlin' man and innocent as a new-born babe. As the saying is in the Emerald Isle, may he be in heaven half an hour before the devil knows he's dead.'

'I'm glad you think so highly of him,' I said, saddened that her kindly sentiments towards my parish priest were not reciprocal.

'Yes,' said Mrs Macaulay. 'I can tell *you*, Father, because you're a praste. It was Fr Duddleswell himself saw to it that our Kathleen was born legitimate, like.'

III *The Bell*

'Hope I am not interrupting you.'

I was seated comfortably in my study reading my breviary one morning when Fr Duddleswell appeared.

'Not at all, Father.'

'I was not talking to *you*, Father Neil.' He pointed aloft, smiling. 'The Guvnor.'

'Ah, yes,' I said, and invited him to take a seat.

'Just time for a wee chat about this and that, and that and this.' He settled down and lifted his glasses on to his forehead. 'You have been here how long?'

'A month, Father.'

'Tut-tut. How time drags. Seems more like nine to me. How long does it seem to yourself?'

'*About* a month,' I replied honestly. 'Give or take a day.'

He lowered his glasses again as if to examine more closely a specimen of manhood with such a peculiar sense of time. 'Uh huh. I was just after wondering what you do with your afternoons.'

'I can do anything you like, Father. What would you like me to do with them?'

His reply was firm. 'Nothing.'

'Nothing?'

'Y'see, Father Neil, since you have been stationed with me nine months—or thereabouts—I thought you might have discerned how *I* spend me afternoons.'

'Sleeping, Father.'

'*Trying* to sleep, Father Neil.' He spoke as if he was used to engaging in some heroic post-prandial enterprise. 'Do *you* sleep well, Father Neil?'

Aware that he wasn't directly interested in my sleep-pattern, I said, 'Very well, thank you.'

'God bless you for that. Perhaps one of the reasons for it is that when you close your eyes at night I do not switch on the radio, like, or whistle the all-clear at you like Mrs Pring's kettle, or stamp around in ten league boots.'

I said I was sorry.

'What for, Father Neil?' He put on his bewildered look. 'Have I said anything to blacken your character? Have I openly criticized you for something at all?'

'No, Father,' I lied.

'And I am sure I never will have to.' He turned his attention elsewhere to show how highly he thought of me. 'Mrs Pring, now, our frolicsome widow, that is another topic entirely. For twenty years—or centuries—I have had to put up with her moaning from crow o'cock to the song o' the red breast. Mind you,' he broke off, 'she has been a good housekeeper ever-and-all to me. I have to say that. Because I am a good Christian, you follow?'

I held up my breviary. 'I can pray, if you like, in the afternoons.'

'Aloud?'

'To myself.'

'You cannot pray to yourself, lad,' he said, his eyes fluttering.

'I mean quietly, Father. At the bottom of my voice.'

'That is fine, fine.' He looked up again. 'If that is all right with Yourself.' Finding that joke now a little worn, he went on to tell me he had already to contend each afternoon with Billy Buzzle's pigeons.

He paused to prove his point. The gentle cooing of pigeons came through the window, refreshing as sunlight.

'What a bronchial racket is that for Billy Buzzle to answer for!'

The gentleman in question lived beside the church and had his back yard next to ours. I had often seen him whiling away the afternoon hours among the flowers. He always looked the same: mottled face, square jaw, bushy eyebrows, a wisp of hair curled by tongs jutting over his right eyebrow. Invariably he wore a smart pin-striped suit, from the sleeves of which emerged large stiff white cuffs, with diamond links which made it seem as if both his arms were in splints from the elbows down.

'Father Neil, when Jesus said, 'Love your neighbour as yourself,' d'you think he also meant the people next door?'

I pointed out to Fr Duddleswell that I was 'next door' to *him*.

'So y'are. Then a word of loving advice to me next door neighbour.'

I waited without encouraging him.

'If you want to be happy as a priest,' he began didactically, 'let the chaff go with the wind and the wood with the stream. You follow?'

'I'm not sure, Father,' I said, understating the case.

'Uh huh. Try again. Aim not, if you are wise, to make water run uphill nor try pulling milk from the udders of a billy-goat.' He leaned back, pleased with the exercise of his poetic powers. 'Any clearer?'

I shook my head.

'What I mean is, while you are at St Jude's do not contradict nature.'

'How would I do that, Father?'

'By not doing what I damn well tell you.' He grinned and waters of joy filmed his eyes. 'Not so solemn Father Neil. Remember legs are not only sticks for walking on.'

He went on to tell me that he was about to perform one of his chores of office. The board of school governors was meeting in the parlour and he was Chairman.

'I am chosen every year by a show of hands,' he said. 'This time, though, I am going to insist on a free and secret election so they can all choose me democratically.'

Mrs Pring came in to announce that the governors were arriving.

Fr Duddleswell told her that she was not to waste time nattering while he was 'choring'. ' 'Tis not the nodding of the head that rows the boat.'

As he led me down to introduce me to the governors he declared, with exaggeration, 'There is suffocating dust everywhere in this bit of a house. D'you know, Father Neil, once I bought herself a bunch of artificial flowers and in three days they died.'

We stood together at the front door greeting the governors as they arrived in twos and threes. Last to float in view, chauffeur-driven in his Daimler, was Major Timmins, a retired army officer. His first words to Fr Duddleswell were:

'How'd you like a bell, Padre?'

'What sort of a bell, Major?'

'Cast-iron ... bell-shaped ... you know what a bell's like.'

Fr Duddleswell had previously told me the Major was a rich kindly gentleman of few words and he certainly lived up to this non-description.

'Weighs a couple of hundred pounds,' the Major said. 'Bought it in my village in Wiltshire.'

Apparently, it really was the Major's village. His family had owned most of the farmland in the area for generations.

'Is it very old, Major?'

'Victorian. Tip-top condition. Taken from the Anglican church at the end of the war. Meant to boost the war-effort —cannons, shells, that sort of thing. And after,' snorted the Major, who obviously hated inefficiency, 'they couldn't put it back. Nitwits rebuilt the tower and the damn bell wouldn't fit.'

'That is very generous of you, Major.'

'Not at all,' said the Major, blustering at the compliment. 'Only cost me £50. Thought of you immediately, Padre.'

As Fr Duddleswell led the Major into the meeting, the old soldier was muttering, 'Glad to see, by the way, you've got yourself a new recruit.'

Mrs Pring enticed me into her kitchen for a cup of tea. 'Full of wiles, that one,' she said as she stood over the stove. 'Father D could give you ninety yards start in a hundred and still beat you by fifteen.'

It was dawning on me that Mrs Pring and Fr Duddleswell liked to shadow-box like a couple of butterflies.

'He's that belligerent,' she said, 'every time he picks up a knife and fork they start to fight.'

'Very interesting,' I said, slightly embarrassed at the revelation.

'In spite of it all,' said Mrs Pring, filling the pot, 'he has a heart as big as a barn. He loves big—and he hates big. Or tries to. Mostly he hates out of a sense of duty and it's just comical. My advice to you ...'

'You have advice for me, Mrs Pring.'

'Bite the bulldog's tail. The only way to make a bulldog take his teeth out of you is to bite his whatsit.'

I thanked her for her counsel.

'Poor Father Neil,' she said, 'I can tell he's been at you already with his blackthorn stick.'

I assured her our main subject of conversation was Mr Buzzle. Mrs Pring, unlike Fr Duddleswell, had a high regard for him.

'It's not just the pigeons,' she explained. 'Billy runs a Night Club, "The Blue Star," Father D don't approve of that. Thinks it's shady. And then Billy's a Bookie.'

Billy, it seemed, employed several 'runners' who took bets on his behalf at street corners, in pubs, factories, cafés and on building sites where many Irish navvies worked. These runners were occasionally picked up by the police and fined. Billy paid the fines with the money he saved on income tax.

'But,' concluded Mrs Pring, 'the real reason Father D keeps fighting Billy is because they're too much alike. But I think he's lovely. Billy, I mean.'

'Hello there, young 'un.'

I was busy in the garden when Billy Buzzle addressed me in this friendly way across the fence.

'Good morning, sir.'

'Billy Buzzle. Call me Billy. Mrs Pring tells me you're Fr Boyd.' As we shook hands he said, 'May I introduce you to Pontius.' A superb black labrador. 'When I bought him he was only a puppy. His first owner called him Pilot. I christened him Pontius in honour of your boss-man.'

I said I was sure Fr Duddleswell appreciated the compliment.

'My Pontius, too,' he said, 'is very good at washing his paws. Shall I tell him to have a good lick?'

Fr Duddleswell entered the garden fresh from the Governors' meeting. 'Father Neil,' he called, 'what're you doing fraternizing with the enemy?'

Billy's behaviour took an immediate turn for the worse. 'I can see the Third World War starting over this fence.'

'Mr Buzzle,' Fr Duddleswell said, as he approached, how many times must I reprimand you for the unseemly behaviour of your blankety-blank birds you have billeted without leave in my tower?'

Billy banged the fence with his fist. 'Right *there* the war'll start. Right over this bloody fence.'

'Am I to put up forever,' began Fr Duddleswell, only to conclude in chorus with Billy, 'with the noise of 'em and the mess of 'em and the stench of 'em?' Solo again, Fr Duddleswell demanded to know, 'Well, *am* I?'

Billy drew back from the brink. 'But aren't they *holy* birds, now, Fr O'Duddleswell?'

'Holy birds would not do the things *they* do in my tower.'

'And isn't your God Himself a pigeon fancier?' went on Billy unperturbed.

'Rhubarb, rhubarb,' was Fr Duddleswell's response to that.

'Well, He used one to tell the world the Flood was over didn't He?'

' 'Twas not Jesus but Jehovah that soaked the world with a Flood, you heathen, and never was a scraggy pigeon used in the Bible-period anyway.'

'What about that pigeon that perched on Jesus' head when He got Himself baptized?'

'That,' snarled Fr Duddleswell, was *not* a blankety-blank pigeon.'

'What was it, then?'

' 'Twas a dove, I tell you, a beautiful snow-white dove.'

'What's the difference, Fr O'Duddleswell?' Billy challenged.

'People do not *shoot* doves.'

'You lay one fat finger on my pigeons,' said Billy with menace, 'and I'll get Pontius to eat you alive. Even if it does make him ill.'

Fr Duddleswell turned to me. 'Lunch time, Father Neil.' He sniffed the air. 'I think 'tis, yes, 'tis definitely pigeon-pie.'

At table I asked how the Governors' meeting had gone.

'Not entirely to me satisfaction.' I sympathized with him. 'I must tell you plainly I am no longer Chairman of the board.'

I expressed surprise that he hadn't got all the votes.

'I did not get *one*. In advance, I did not consider it necessary to vote for meself, like.' He tapped the table irritably. 'That is what always happens, Father Neil. Give the laity their freedom and they promptly abuse it.'

When I suggested they simply wanted a change he confessed himself at a loss to know why they should want a change for the worse. He would have to counter-attack, of course, by not signing cheques for any of their bills. The laity would want to elect the Pope next if they could.

Mrs Pring came in with the food-tray, humming pleasantly to herself.

'Good,' said Fr Duddleswell. 'After choring and jawing all the morning I am as hungry as an Irish jury.'

Then he saw what was in store for us. 'Well, woman,' he demanded, 'are you not going to introduce us? What is it?'

'Risotto.'

'It looks more like a poorhouse porridge bleeding to death,' he said.

'Whining while dining as usual, Father D,' she said. '*You* try and do any better with the rations we get.'

Fr Duddleswell handed me a plate. 'Better eat it, Father Neil, before it eats you.'

'One thing, Father Neil,' Mrs Pring said as she ladled the stuff out, 'that one'll never go to hell.' I smiled too soon. 'The devil would never let him in.'

'Ah,' said Fr Duddleswell, 'the troubles across the water are as nothing compared with the troubles under this roof.'

I had the impression that their relationship was like a knotted piece of string. The more they pulled apart by arguing the tighter they came together.

When Mrs Pring asked me how I liked Billy Buzzle, Fr Duddleswell intervened to swear that at last he was going to eject Billy's pigeons from his tower. The bell would do it. In answer to my question, he said our own bell had been taken away ten years before, with the railings round the church, and no reprieve for them.

'This bell,' said Mrs Pring. 'How much?'

'To us, nothing,' Fr Duddleswell replied gleefully. 'Just think, Father Neil, from now on we will be able to toll the bell at funerals and weddings and christenings—just like in the old days before the war.'

'And the Angelus, Father.'

'Indeed, yes. Oh, yes, indeed. The Angelus ringing out morning noon and night. 'Twill sound all the sweeter, believe you me, for having been rescued from a Protestant temple. 'Twill remind the whole Borough of Kenworthy of the time when the Angel Gabriel announced to the Blessed Virgin she was to be the Mother of God, won't it just?'

'Billy Buzzle won't like that,' said Mrs Pring.

'Say that again, sweet lady,' he said, ''tis music to me ears.'

I asked him why he kept saying 'blankety-blank' to Billy. He replied:

''Tis because I have no wish to demean meself by swearing in his presence. No bloody fear,' he giggled. 'And by the way, Father Neil.'

'Father?'

'What are you intending doing this afternoon?'

'Praying, Father. So quietly God Himself won't be able to hear.'

'Great luck to you, lad.'

'One thing, Father.'

'What is that?'

'What is the real difference between pigeons and doves?'

'Whose side are you on?' he came back at me.

'I'm not on anybody's side,' I said. 'Not in the matter of pigeons and doves.'

'I see.' He pondered. 'The difference between pigeons and doves.'

'The Old Pretender!' said Mrs Pring.

He touched my arm. 'Son of me heart, me darlin' priestling, the real difference?'

'Yes,' I said.

He crammed his mouth with risotto. I just made out the words. 'I have not the faintest bloody idea.'

A couple of days later I was in Fr Duddleswell's study as we pored over a map of the parish.

'Your half of the parish is circled in red, Father Neil, and mine is circled in blue.'

'Isn't the red half ... ?'

'Ah, so you have noticed. Yes, the red half is considerably *bigger* than the blue half. But then my legs are shorter than yours.'

'But I thought you visited the parishioners by car.'

He looked mystified. 'What has me car got to do with the shortness of me legs?'

I had to admit there was no logical connection.

He changed the subject by telling me that the architect

45

confirmed that our tower could easily accommodate the new bell. He was delighted with the news.

'We will get it installed as soon as I can fix things with Major Timmins. Ah,' he reflected nostalgically, ''twill take me back to me student days in the Venerable English College in Rome. The Holy City was as full of bells as a Suffolk garden is full of roses in the month of June. And on Sundays and festas, they'd be a-ringing and a-singing, dong, dong, dong.'

Mrs Pring came to say an electrician had asked for admittance to the sacristy. She had let him in. Was that all right?

Fr Duddleswell confessed that he was having to hire a contractor to put in an electrical time-switch and automated ringing device.

'Is Major Timmins installing that for free?' asked Mrs Pring.

'Now, Father Neil,' what were we talking about?'

'About your legs, Father.'

Mrs Pring said, 'He knows he hasn't got one to stand on.'

The phone rang. 'Fr Duddleswell ... Three men *and* a driver ... *How* much?' He glanced guiltily towards us. 'I know how far Wiltshire is from here but you are supposed to be shifting a bell not Cleopatra's Needle ... All right, you have me authorization.' And he slammed down the phone.

Mrs Pring got in before me. 'How much is your free bell costing now?'

'So far, £400.'

'Would you repeat that?' gasped Mrs Pring.

'I do not cook me cabbage twice,' he said. He turned to me for understanding. 'Where is the sense in letting our money deteriorate in the bank? At best it grows there as fast as the legs on an old man. But'—he found a bright side—'we will economize in other ways.'

'Like on tea and sugar?' asked Mrs Pring.

'Perhaps.'

'We *could* pass the basin round the parish, I suppose,' she said, keeping up the challenge. 'Need to, to make up that tidy little sum.'

'Go, woman,' he warned, 'before me wrath becomes incontinent.'

'Hold your row, Father D. It's only a walking funeral, *you'll* have.'

'Mrs ...' But she was gone before she could be named. 'Father Neil, I cannot help meself. Sometimes the cold blast of her mouth goosepimples me all over faster than a February frost.'

I asked him if he was sleeping any better in the afternoons.

'Surely, Father Neil. As a result of your silent prayers, no doubt, I am sleeping as sound as a bell. Which reminds me ...'

It arrived on a lorry one Tuesday morning. The impressive shiny black object caused Fr Duddleswell to tap his chest with both hands and exclaim good-naturedly. ''Tis indeed exceedingly bell-like and no mistake, *exceedingly* bell-like.'

A wooden frame, five feet high, had been built and placed in readiness in the centre of the sanctuary.

'What's it doing here?' enquired Mrs Pring casting her eyes over it. 'I thought bells were supposed to be hung high up.'

'The Bishop,' explained Fr Duddleswell, 'finds it easier blessing it here than fifty feet up the tower.'

'Ah,' said Mrs Pring with sharp intuition, 'I forgot *he's* got little legs as well.'

In an excess of high spirits, Fr Duddleswell pulled back the tongue of the bell and released it with a bong that made the air vibrate with ear-tingling sound for nearly thirty seconds. 'Ask not for whom the bell tolls,' he sang. 'It tolls for ... Billy Buzzle's blasted pigeons.'

The ladies of the parish clucked away, busily decorating the frame with roses, lilies and brightly coloured ribbons. And the next day, outshining even the decorations in his purple robes, the Bishop appeared. I had not seen Bishop O'Reilly since my ordination. It is hard to convey the feelings a young priest has for the Bishop who has shared with him the inestimable gift of the priesthood, given him *ex gratia* the power to celebrate Holy Mass and the sacraments.

The Bishop was a small, distinguished-looking, simple-minded man and very Catholic. I mean he understood, as few did, the Catholic mystique: the emphasis on pageantry and hierarchy and obedience. I felt doubly indebted to him for first accepting me as a junior seminarist, since his general policy was to turn down any candidate who wasn't first or second generation Irish. He used to say privately—or so it was rumoured—that the Irish and Italians are the nations dearest to God's own heart. Looking at the calendar of the saints, bursting with Celts and Latins, I thought this an opinion beyond dispute.

Bishop O'Reilly had given us deacons—there were six of us—a short homily in his private chapel at Bishop's House the night before he ordained us. In my naivete I was expecting a fiery sermon on the high office and onerous but rewarding duties of the priesthood. Instead he contented himself with warning us off the twin dangers of 'Punch and Judy', the clergy's term for 'drink and dames'. I assumed he had his reasons, based on twenty years of episcopal experience, for concentrating on these earthly topics.

In the sacristy before the service of consecration, I heard the bishop say to his private secretary, Monsignor O'Connell, 'Now, remember, Pat me boy, lead me mighty slowly around the church so the congregation get a generous view of me. They love it, so they do. It's not every day of the year, they get a chance to cast eyes on their beloved Bishop.'

As the Monsignor dressed the Bishop like a doll, he kept promising him a suitably slow gyration. He made him put on three chasubles and two pairs of gloves—only *then* the ring —and large shuffly buckskin slippers. Next, he pressed the tall golden mitre down on his head, keeping the second, the Precious Mitre, in reserve for solemn moments in the ceremony. Finally, he handed him a silver crozier almost as big as the Bishop himself.

I admired the way Bishop O'Reilly sat there meekly and passively as he was clothed by a breathless, sweating Monsignor. It was one example of the burdens a Bishop has to bear.

In the opening, tortoise-like procession, I walked alongside Fr Duddleswell and only two yards in front of the Bishop. I imagined I could feel upon my back the unswerving episcopal smile and the ringed hand raised in countless benedictions. I did not like it when a six year old, standing at the end of a bench said in a loud voice, 'Mummy, why is she wearing that funny hat?'

I suppose Bishop O'Reilly was used to being thought a fool for Christ's sake. Fr Duddleswell's comment to me as we genuflected together seemed discourteous. 'Out of the mouths of babes and sucklings,' he whispered.

The choir struck up *Ecce Sacerdos Magnus*, Behold Our Great High Priest, and the hour-long service began. My memory of it is fuzzed by the innumerable anointings and blessings of the bell which the Bishop made with exemplary patience. There were also lots of prayers and stirring hymns, after which all ten invited clergy present on the sanctuary were permitted like schoolboys to ring the bell after the Bishop. I admit I enjoyed that bit of the ceremony best.

The 'incident' occurred as we were sitting while the choir sang a Latin motet. Because of the crowd and the intense heat, the west door had been left open to let fresh air blow through the building.

It wasn't until he was half-way down the central aisle that I saw Pontius. He came in sniffling to right and left, surprised that for all his friendly sniffles and energetic wagging of his hind-quarters, no one in that huge crowd paid him any attention. He had a hurt look on his dignified face as if he could not understand the waning of his popularity. Those of the congregation who saw Pontius didn't want to know.

On he marched until it became clear he was heading for the sanctuary. Maybe the clergy were drugged by the heat or lost in the music, but, whatever the reason, not one of them stirred.

'Father Neil.' Fr Duddleswell whispered out of the corner of his mouth so the Bishop on the other side of him could not hear.

'Yes, Father.'

'Do you see what I see?'

Fear made me sit as blind and still as a pepper pot. 'No, Father.'

' 'Tis bloody Pontius. What d'you intend doing about it, Father Neil?'

Still with my eyes closed, I said, 'Pardon?'

'Canon law distinctly says no animals or ladies are allowed on the sanctuary. What're you doing?'

'Praying, Father. Hard.'

'Save it for me siesta,' he said, in a tone that accused me of hypocrisy.

The Bishop lowered his head towards his secretary. 'Pat, Pat."

'My Lord.'

'Can you not see the black monster yonder?'

'It's a dog, my Lord.'

'I know, I have seen one before. Are you a man, Pat, that's the thing. Get rid of it.'

Fr Duddleswell had at last to admit to the foreign presence on the sanctuary. Slowly, and with as much dignity as circumstances allowed, he rose, bowed to the Bishop and his fellow-clergy, and went across to try and grasp Pontius' collar. Pontius swerved, eluded Fr Duddleswell's outstretched hands and made towards the Bishop as being the most interesting figure there.

The Bishop, faced with this menace to his dignity, sat as far back as he could on his pontifical throne, cowering. The benign Pontius, drooling and undeterred, approached him and with a jump laid his forelegs on the Bishop's lap.

Bishop O'Reilly tried pushing the panting dog away with his crozier but only succeeded in dislodging his mitre so it fell over his eyes, temporarily blinding him.

All this time, the choir, who had a grandstand view of events from the choir-loft, were gradually slowing down like Fr Duddleswell's old gramophone badly in need of a rewind. Then they gave up the ghost and ceased altogether.

In the uncanny silence, Bishop O'Reilly's voice was now a screech. 'Pat, why aren't you *doing* something?'

Perhaps the Monsignor had a phobia about dogs because in in this episcopal emergency he was of no use at all.

By now, Fr Duddleswell had made his way tip-toe to the Bishop's throne. Uttering friendly clucking noises, he succeeded in grabbing Pontius' collar. But when Pontius went sharply into reverse, he went too. He was dragged, off balance, by the great labrador half-way across the sanctuary on his back.

Losing his sense of direction in the fray, Pontius bumped into the scaffolding and the considerable weight of man and dog made the bell give out one enormous bong followed by several lesser bongs.

Pontius was so shaken by the noise, he tore himself free, barked stupendously and fled unopposed from the church like the Wind of Pentecost.

I rushed to help Fr Duddleswell to his feet and removed a lily that had become wedged in the frame of his spectacles. He was muttering something about Billy Buzzle which, I am sure, he afterwards repented and confessed.

The Monsignor rearranged the Bishop, the choir resumed their motet, and the rest of the ceremony passed off without incident.

At the end, still seated on the sanctuary, the Bishop cleansed the oil from his fingers in the medieval way with segments of lemon and breadcrumbs. Then we all processed slowly round the church again so that the congregation could have a final filial look at their father in God.

In Fr Duddleswell's study afterwards the Bishop sat, tired-looking and sipping a glass of milk.

'I must have walked a mile of road around the church giving my blessing.'

Monsignor O'Connell, Dr Daley, the portly friend of Fr Duddleswell, and myself murmured sympathetically and Fr Duddleswell said. 'The good people appreciated it and all, me Lord.'

'I always tell Monsignor Pat here,' the Bishop said, 'the people love it, do I not, Pat?'

'You do, my Lord.'

The Bishop turned to Dr Daley. 'So you, Doctor, are personal physician to our two good fathers here.'

Dr Daley, a bit shaky on his feet, said, 'Yes, my Lord, and I make sure they drink plenty of the juice of the cow.'

'And you, Father Neil,"—it was my turn—'you remember what I preached you about the night before I made a priest of you.'

'Yes, my Lord.'

'Especially beware, when you are young, the Judies with their V-necks wider than a duck's wake and their see-through stockings. I always say to Monsignor Pat here, "All the theological difficulties of my young priests come in silk stockings," do I not, Pat?'

'You do, my Lord.'

'A good crowd tonight, my Lord,' said Fr Duddleswell, trying to cheer the old chap up.

'Whenever I see a crowd of our good people like tonight I

want to sing not "Faith of our fathers" but "Faith of our mothers", d'you see? That is where the faith resides. As I always say to Monsignor Pat here, the faith is in the hearts of our dear mothers. Do I not, Pat?'

'You do, my Lord.'

'If the faith is not learned at the mother's knee,' the Bishop went on, 'it will hardly be learned at the father's elbow.'

Unthinking, the secretary said, 'You do, my Lord.'

Mrs Pring came to say that the Bishop's car had arrived. It was time for adieus.

Dr Daley knelt and kissed the Bishop's ring. 'May the luck stick to your Lordship like a beggar from the bog.'

The Bishop was moved to say in return, 'May God and Mary and St Patrick bless you a hundred thousand times.'

My turn to kiss the ring and then Fr Duddleswell. To him the Bishop said coldly as he handed him his empty glass, 'I would be grateful if, when I visit you in the future, Father, you see to it no wild animals are issued with tickets.'

Fr Duddleswell gave him the assurance he sought, handed the glass to me and went to see the Bishop off the premises.

'Ah,' said Dr Daley to me, relaxing, 'how many days Indulgence do I get for kissing his ring?'

'A hundred days, I think, Doctor.'

'Surely there must be easier ways of gaining a good seat in the Hereafter.' He scratched his bald head. 'But did you notice anything odd about the Bishop, Father Neil?'

'No.'

'Didn't you see how he kept swaying from side to side.' He showed me how.

'No, Doctor.'

'Are you drunk, too?'

I told him I didn't drink.

'Then have you a bilious attack or swallowed a pendulum or what?

'Well, Donal,' said Fr Duddleswell cheerfully enough on his return, 'at least I was "beheaded handsomely".'

'He was like a shirt left out of a frosty night to you, Charles.'

'The Bishop,' Fr Duddleswell agreed, 'has a sharp, blunt tongue on him and no mistake.'

'Charles,' the Doctor said, 'the sight of that white stuff in his Lordship's glass has ...' For conclusion, he pointed sickly to the region of his stomach. 'I don't suppose you have a drop of Punch here.'

'Not here, Donal, and not any other where in this bit of a house. You have a glass eye on you already and an attack of the staggers.'

'Are you drunk, Charles, or did you crack your head on the sanctuary floor?'

'I did that surely. And oh, Donal, how me black heart is straining wild within me for its revenge on Mr Billy Buzzle.'

'Did you sleep well last night, Father Neil?'

It was breakfast time and I assured Fr Duddleswell he need have no worries on my account. In fact, he was sorry that both Mrs Pring and I had failed to hear the first ringing of the Angelus at six that morning.

'Nothing ever wakes Mrs Pring,' he said. 'Not during the daytime, any way.'

A ring on the front door was followed by the raised voice of Billy Buzzle demanding entry. The dining room burst open and there he was.

'*You* ...' he hurled at Fr Duddleswell. 'I'm going to take *you* to court.'

Fr Duddleswell professed ignorance of the cause of such a cruel intention.

'That noise,' fumed Billy, 'that, that infernal racket early this morning.'

'Take a seat, Mr Buzzle,' Fr Duddleswell said soothingly, 'and let us discuss this quietly like a couple of gentlemen lunatics.'

Billy sat down. 'That bloody bell ...'

'Please, Mr Buzzle. I will not tolerate swearing in this holy house.' Fr Duddleswell turned to Mrs Pring. 'Fetch him a coffee cup so we can calm the troubled waters of him.'

'That bell nearly bloody well ...'

'Tut-tut.'

'Blasted me out of bed,' continued Billy. 'You know my bedroom's on the back and that bell let rip like Big Ben only a few feet from my head.'

'I *am* sorry,' Fr Duddleswell said without a spark of repentance.

'What I want to know ...'

As Mrs Pring had just delivered a cup and saucer, Fr Duddleswell interrupted him again with, 'Coffee?'

'What I want to know ...'

'With milk?' Billy nodded and prepared to speak again. 'And sugar?' The same. 'Two?' Billy nodded.

'Why so early?' Billy managed to get out.

'Six o'clock. Is that early would you say?'

'Yes, I bloody well would, especially as I only get back from "The Blue Star" at 3. And once I wake up, no more sleep for me.'

Fr Duddleswell seemed amazed at Billy's experiences. 'Did *you* hear the bell, Father Neil?'

'No, Father.'

'Mrs Pring.'

She shook her head.

'Then all I can say,' Billy cried, 'is they've got bloody coconuts for heads.' He sipped his coffee angrily.

Fr Duddleswell waited a few moments before asking, 'And how is Pontius these days, Mr Buzzle?'

Billy shrugged. 'Fine.'

'You did hear of his trespassing? You did. Now, while the Lord bade us forgive them that trespass against us, he did not, I am thinking include black labradors.'

'He's house-trained,' said Billy proudly.

'He is not House of God-trained,' said Fr Duddleswell.

'What d'you expect him to do, genuflect and kiss the Bishop's ring?'

'I expect him, Mr Buzzle, to leave our Bishop alone. He is not licensed to eat Bishops.'

'A regular St Francis, you are,' said Billy.

Fr Duddleswell held out his hand. 'So we are evens.'

'Suppose so.'

'I repeat I am sorry you got woken up.'

Billy, quite softened by now, said, ''S all right. Just this once. But make sure it don't happen no more.'

Fr Duddleswell withdrew his hand as if it had been stung. 'I cannot promise you that, Mr Buzzle. In fact, 'tis me religious duty to assure you of the exact opposite. The Angelus will ring out every day at six, midday and six in the evening as Holy Mother Church has always decreed.'

'Fr Duddleswell,' pleaded Billy, 'if I become an insomniac

that's one thing, but think of my poor pigeons.'

'They did not pay one penny's rent in me tower.'

Billy explained that he wasn't worried about them losing their lodgings. When the bell rang that morning three of them had flown away never to return, which he interpreted as a form of pigeon suicide.

In the end, Billy wanted to toss for it but Fr Duddleswell's attitude was why should he wager when he could win without.

'I thought,' shouted Billy, 'you were bloody well supposed to love your neighbour as yourself.'

'Oh,' said Fr Duddleswell punching his own arm and recoiling from the imagined pain, 'but I care for you far more than that.'

'Religious people!' said Billy in a scornful voice.

'Mr Buzzle, I love you as a Christian but that is as far as I am prepared to go.'

'God must have made you with His left hand behind His back,' growled Billy. Then his final threat, brought on by what he saw as manifest injustice. 'Okay. If it's war you want, it's bloody war you'll get. If *I* don't sleep, I'll see to it *you* don't sleep, neither. Mark my words.'

'What is Billy up to, d'you reckon, Father Neil?'

Peeping through the curtains of my study which overlooked the gardens, I said, 'No idea.'

He touched my arm accusingly. 'Are you sure you should be spying on our next door neighbour?'

I let go of the curtain at once with an expression of regret.

Two days before, six rolls of wire-netting had been delivered to Billy's back garden. An hour later, a couple of men appeared and erected wire enclosures over the whole area. The following day, huge crates turned up with birds in them. At first, we though Billy was increasing his stock of pigeons but the crates contained about a hundred chickens.

'Pigeons and hens,' mused Fr Duddleswell, mystified, 'the gentlest of God's creatures.'

Losing my self-control, I again peered surreptitiously through the curtains. 'Wait a second, Father,' I said.

'Father Neil, keep your eyes to yourself, will you not? Remember where curiosity landed the first parents of the human race.'

'There are some men with more crates,' I told him.

'What is in them, then?'

I said I didn't know.

'Well, Father Neil, why are we having a heel-cooling here? Let's go fast and bloody well find out.'

Billy was on the patio of his garden. Wearing protective leather gloves, he was gingerly removing the lids from the crates with an iron bar. And there, one by one, were revealed the ten wickedest cockerels in England.

'Sleeping well?' Fr Duddleswell asked Billy slyly.

'Not a wink for some days, Fr O'Duddleswell. And want to take a bet? No? From this moment on, you won't sleep neither.'

'But I have a clear conscience, Mr Buzzle, and why should I not?' Receiving no reply, he said, 'What're you doing, raising chickens?'

'No, Fr O'Duddleswell, raising hell. See those cockerels. No love-making for them. They're going to be sacred bachelors'—he indicated us—'like you and him. Thwarted lovers, you might say. Sex-starved cocks, the lot of them.'

Each cockerel was placed in a roofed-in wire pen on its own, adjacent to the large enclosure where the hens were left free-ranging.

Already the noise of frustrated poultry was wretched enough but soon the midday Angelus rang out. The blend of pealing bell, barking dog, madly fluttering pigeons, clucking hens and trumpeting cocks was indescribable.

Fr Duddleswell knelt to say the Angelus and, I suspect, a few extra prayers not to be found in any manual. When he arose, Billy said:

'Now Fr O'Duddleswell, let's see if, even with your lime-white conscience, you can sleep through *this*.'

'The Third World War,' barked Fr Duddleswell, banging on the fence. 'Right here the war will start. Right over this bloody fence.'

When he retired to his bedroom to take his siesta, I knew he wasn't likely to find much repose. I heard him restlessly pacing up and down his room, and, from time to time, opening and closing his window with a bang. Once I heard him open his window and yell, 'Do you not know that cock-fighting is against the law, you gambler, you?' Then he slammed

56

his window shut with a clonk that broke the cord and smashed one of the panes. Before evening, the whole window frame was double glazed, but it didn't seem to help.

Fortunately for me, my bedroom, like Mrs Pring's above, was on the front of the house. During the hours of sleep, I didn't catch the full blast of the bell or the ravenous excitement of the cocks. Poor Fr Duddleswell was in the cocks' direct line of fire twice a day.

Within a week, he was but a shadow of his former self. He had lost weight and there were large bags under his red-rimmed, blood-shot eyes. He, like Billy Buzzle, was becoming an insomniac.

At Mrs Pring's suggestion, I persuaded Fr Duddleswell to phone Dr Daley. I was in his study when the doctor arrived two hours afterwards.

'Sorry to only answer your call at this late hour, Charles,' he said breathlessly, 'but I'm afraid the polis summoned me for drunken driving.'

'I am distressed to hear it, Donal. But did I not tell you you would be nabbed one fine day?'

Dr Daley was amused at that. 'I wasn't the party accused, Charles. I am just after examining a suspect for the polis.'

'And *was* he drunk, d'you reckon?'

'One of us was, that's for sure,' Dr Daley said, with mischief in his voice. 'But I gave him the benefit and presumed it was myself.' He turned to the patient before him. 'Now what's this I hear that you are not sleeping too well, Charles?'

'Not sleeping at all,' said Fr Duddleswell spiritlessly. 'Not for ten days.'

'Not even during your sermons?' said Dr Daley, as if recalling painful memories. 'If you had told me earlier I would have lighted a candle for you before the Virgin's statue.'

'I have lighted so many for meself, Donal, there is a danger of a shortage in the diocese.'

Dr Daley didn't like the implications of that. 'If God and Mother Mary have given up watching the candles that's a terrible waste of beeswax surely.'

'Ah, Donal,' Fr Duddleswell said pathetically, 'I have a famous appetite on me for a large loaf of sleep.'

'Have you tried counting the lost sheep, Charles?' The question was not well received. 'Cocoa? Ovaltine? Cyanide?

57

And nothing works.'

Fr Duddleswell, with an effort, shook his head, once each way.

'It's a strange thing, Charles.' Only Fr Duddleswell's look said, What is that? 'Four days ago, I was called in by a neighbour of yours.'

Fr Duddleswell froze and into his eye came the familiar glint. 'Billy Buzzle?'

'The same. He was suffering from the exact same disability as yourself. Except his was caused by a strange ... ringing in his ears.'

'Did you help him sleep, Donal, that is the thing?'

'That very night,' Dr Daley said with a touch of pride. 'Next day he phoned to say he had slept fourteen hours and was completely cured.'

Fr Duddleswell's face was a muddle of bitterness, envy and hope. 'Tell me, then, Donal, what must I do?'

'D'you happen to have a drop of ...'

'I do not.'

'It is not for me, Charles.'

'I beg your pardon, I am sure.'

'Not for me *only*, any way. But no matter.' He began to extract from his black bag a bottle of whiskey and two glasses. 'I have your healing right here in my hands.' He poured two stiff ones. 'Now, Charles, take four of these pills with your refresher. If *they* don't knock you out, the Heavyweight Champion of the world will do no better." He took a sip of whiskey and rolled his tongue round the bars of his teeth. 'Mind you, Charles, there is but one infallible cure for insomnia.'

'Which is?'

Dr Daley looked surprised he didn't know. 'Sleep, Charles. Sleep.'

Fr Duddleswell obediently downed his tablets and they sat sipping quietly together and conversing as if I had not been there.

'Is this the way you cured Mr Buzzle, Donal?'

'Not at all,' replied Dr Daley. 'He didn't need the tablets.'

'The whiskey only?'

'Not even that.'

'Tell me, then,' said Fr Duddleswell, peering contemplatively into his glass, 'how *did* you cure him?'

'Simple,' Dr Daley said. He took a sip, then another. 'I told him to go sleep at "The Blue Star".'

Next morning at breakfast, Fr Duddleswell looked worse than worse. In answer to my polite query, he said:

'If I slept well, would I look now like a sorry mashed potato?'

'The tablets, no good?'

'I saw every inch of the night through, Father Neil,' He filled his lungs and exhaled slowly. 'I am that bored with keeping me own company through all the days and nights! Worst of all,' he snarled, 'is that bloody Angelus bell driving into me head like a hammer at six in the morning.' He made a sign of the cross in contrition. 'And Billy Buzzle is missing all the fun.'

'At "The Blue Star"?'

'Yes, Father Neil, and that is where I am sending you.'

'But I'm sleeping fine,' I said.

'Do not play puppies with an old dog,' he said wearily. 'Go to "The Blue Star" around midday and tell Billy, *ask* him—no, *plead* with him to come visit me here.'

'You're not going to silence the bell, Father?' He almost hooked his lips together. 'But you said the sound of the bell is the voice of God Himself to the good people.'

He let out his breath jerkily like an engine that refuses to start. 'Me downy chick of a curate,' he whispered, 'if you desire to live in peace with me, do not say as I say, just *do* as I say.'

In his office—decorated with pictures of dogs, horses and ladies just as scantily clad—Billy was reading his paper and nibbling away merrily at his breakfast. He agreed to my request without a murmur and within fifteen minutes we were at the presbytery.

Fr Duddleswell was in his study spread out in an armchair with his feet on a stool. On the coffee table by his side was a folded tartan blanket as well as a whiskey bottle with two glasses.

He did not rise when we entered. 'Good of you to come, Mr Buzzle,' he said wanly. After inviting Billy to sit, he asked, 'And how is yourself?'

'Never felt better,' Billy said, and I could see powerful reasons why that was so.

'And me dear old friend Pontius?'

'In splendid nick.'

'Fine. That is fine.' He selected from his repertoire a more regretful tone. 'I realize, Mr Buzzle, I have not been acting in a very priestly way towards you.'

Billy smiled as if to say he hadn't noticed any difference but he contented himself with 'No?'

'No. I never intended, God help me, to drive you out of house and home.'

'No?'

'No. An Englishman's home is ... Those cocks.'

'Oh, yes?' said Billy, with the magnanimity of a conqueror.

'They have stirred me conscience as they did the conscience of St Peter, Prince of the Apostles.'

'Your messenger boy indicated you have some kind of proposition to put to me.'

Fr Duddleswell was pouring into the glasses. 'Yes. Care for a drink?'

'Please.'

'Would you ever consider removing those birds, the walking ones, from your garden?'

Billy took his drink. 'Will *you* promise not to ring your bell before ten in the morning?'

'Me solemn word. Not even if Martians invade the parish.'

'Nor if my Pontius swallows your little Bishop?'

'Especially not then.'

'A bargain.'

'Drink to it?'

'Yes.'

They tipped their glasses and both said 'Your health'. It was a moving moment.

Billy said, 'I was wondering if I could interest you in a little wager. A horse at Sandown Park tomorrow. Well fancied. In the 2.30.' He glanced across at the forlorn figure in the chair. 'Father. Fr O'Duddleswell?'

His adversary's eyes were closed and, in spite of heavy breathing, he was clasping his glass in both hands with unnatural steadiness.

Billy looked at me, drained his glass and tip-toed over to

the armchair. He gently took Fr Duddleswell's glass from his grasp, put in on the desk and helped me to pull the blanket over his defeated frame.

The Angelus pealed out then. The sleeper stirred, spluttered and began to snore. Billy, his face shining with the innocence of a child's, raised Fr Duddleswell's glass to him as to a gallant foe, gulped it down and was gone from the room before the final stroke of the bell.

IV *The Parish Bazaar*

I had nearly finished breakfast when Fr Duddleswell came in and ostentatiously placed an envelope on his side plate.

I folded my newspaper and said, '*Good* morning, Father.'

'Hadn't noticed,' he said in an offhand way. He went through the motions of a brisk grace and, as he sat, put his huge serviette under his chin with a flourish. He removed his glasses, pointed to his straggly hair and said, 'Short back and sides, please. But be sure not to take off more than I've got.' He smiled. 'And how are you this morning, Father Neil?'

I told him I was very well so far.

He leaned over and tapped my cup. 'Is that a strong cup of coffee you have there?' I nodded. 'Uh huh. Fine, that is fine. Because'—he came over confidential—'I want to talk to you about . . . the facts of life.'

I wondered if I had heard correctly since it was only breakfast time. I had. His theme was, What makes men and women really happy; what makes things tick.

I sipped my coffee like wine and gave it as my considered opinion that it *could* be stronger.

'What every curate ought to know, Father Neil.' He paused to fill his own cup. His method was to raise and lower the pot like a yoyo as he poured. 'Money,' he said.

'Money?'

'What does the Holy Bible say about money?'

'That it's the root of all evil.'

'True, true,' he conceded, 'but what did our Blessed Lord himself say?'

'You cannot serve God and money.'

He received this information with a grateful shiver. He was expecting, he said, another 'more striking' of Jesus' sayings.

I reflected before proposing, 'It's harder for a rich man to get into heaven than for ...'

'Mrs Pring to get through the eye of a needle. I know it, Father Neil, but surely the Lord had more *cheerful* things to say about money.'

'Happy are the poor?'

'Not in my experience,' he retorted. 'Oh, I see, you are quoting our Blessed Lord again.' I said yes. 'Then 'tis absolutely true, Father Neil, and never you doubt it. In some unfathomable sense the poor are definitely very ... happy. Not so you would notice, of course, but, yes, happy. But what I had in mind was the dictum, "The Lord loves a cheerful giver".'

I broke it to him that it was St Paul who said that and even he was quoting.

Mrs Pring bustled in with a tray on which rested a couple of boiled eggs for the landlord.

He thanked me for correcting his slip of the tongue. 'Now, money,' he began, 'is like an English summer ...'

'It comes in slow,' said Mrs Pring, 'and is gone before you've noticed it.' She had heard it before, annually at least.

'Study each of her remarks very carefully, Father Neil. It could turn out to be the silliest thing you have ever heard.'

'Only when I'm quoting you,' said Mrs Pring.

Fr Duddleswell grabbed his spoon and banged the top of an egg as a substitute for a more satisfactory target. " 'Tis not only the love of God that surpasses understanding,' he sighed. 'To continue: Money.'

'Jesus didn't keep on appealing for money like you, did He?' asked Mrs Pring. 'When He gave the Sermon on the Mount, He didn't keep passing the basin round, did He?'

Fr Duddleswell said, 'That is true,' as he started to remove tiny fragments of shrapnel embedded in the white of his egg. 'But Jesus did not have the double misfortune of running a cheap car and an expensive house-keeper, either.'

'No,' Mrs Pring said, turning to me, 'He walked everywhere *and* He cooked for Himself.'

'Mrs Pring,' Fr Duddleswell said, enjoying the rally, 'would you go before I beseech the Blessed Virgin to box your bloody ears?' Then to me: 'Herself has such a sense of her own importance, she behaves as if she were the seventh son of a seventh son.'

'And *he's* got great stage talents,' came back Mrs Pring.

'Would've made a wonderful actress.' She stood at the door brandishing the coffee pot. 'I'll just get you some more coffee, Father Neil.'

Fr Duddleswell mumbled a few dire imprecations until he was sure she was out of hearing, then he rounded on me. 'I know what you are thinking, Father Neil.'

'I'm not, Father,' I hastened to say.

'What are you *not* thinking?'

'I'm not thinking what you think I'm thinking. In fact, nothing is further from my mind.' For emphasis: 'I'm completely thoughtless.'

'You are thinking,' he affirmed steadily, 'that I treat herself abominably.' He would not accept my denial. 'Because, you see, 'tis true. And the only thing to be said in me defence is that she entirely deserves it and more.' His plate was now a mosaic of eggshell. 'Ah, but what would I do without her and all?' I realized he was not inviting suggestions from me. 'How would I ever learn discipline, patience and self-sacrifice?' He shrugged as if to say even he had no answer to that. 'Now, money.'

I dipped into my pocket. It was lost on him. He removed a sheet of paper from the envelope on his plate. 'Know what this is?'

'A bank-statement, Father.'

'More like an ultimatum. See all those evil-looking figures typed in tomato juice? Debts. Each year we have to find a thousand pounds for the school alone. Then there are rates, gas, electricity, a house-keeper of sorts—and now an expensive addition.'

I thrice beat my breast in sorrow.

'Yes, *you*,' he said. 'Listen, O little soul of mighty deeds, me sweet potato-bud, soon cometh our annual Bazaar.'

Mrs Pring must have caught the last word as she returned with the coffee and she made a lot of Father D's talent for making money.

'That woman gives me six headaches at once,' he said, and she assured me his head was more than big enough.

He feigned annoyance, stood up and declared, 'If *you* stay, Mrs Pring, I'm going to stretch me legs.'

'Even half an inch would help.'

For some reason that reply put him in a distinctly darker

mood. 'Gas, gas, gas,' he groaned. 'That woman could commit suicide just by putting her head in her mouth.'

Mrs Pring was obviously sincere in praising his ability to raise money. It made her wonder why he didn't try harder. Last year's Bazaar, she instanced, had raised £250.

Fr Duddleswell considered that an achievement. With genuine emotion, he said, 'The generosity of the good people brought a big lump to me throat.'

'Did you swallow your tongue, then?' asked Mrs Pring. At that moment, he had difficulty swallowing something. She took advantage of his temporary incapacity to say he ought to try this year for £500.

'Five hundred,' he choked. 'Ridiculous.' He took a swig of coffee and that cleared his tubes. 'I *could* do it, if I wanted, of course.'

Mrs Pring laughed aloud at that. He lacked faith, that's what. And for proof, she cited his hiring a marquee for five years running at £50 a time.

'Talking to you, woman,' he said, 'is a breathless walk up a steep hill.'

According to Mrs Pring not an eyeful of rain had ever fallen on the Bazaar. 'No faith. None.'

He was really riled by now and banged his second egg so hard it collapsed and splayed out in a yellow mess. 'I will show you whether I have faith or no,' he bawled. 'This year I will do without the marquee and raise *six* hundred pounds.'

I felt sure he would regret such an unpremeditated boast. Mrs Pring said, 'You and how many legions of angels?'

'As sure as God Almighty is sitting on His throne, I will fight like a brick to get me £600.'

'And if you don't?' Mrs Pring wanted to know.

'I will fall down before you on me knees.'

'Make it your head and it's a deal,' she said.

'If I fail,' he said, contemplating the carnage on his plate, 'I will have an Irish row with the Almighty, besides.'

The Bazaar committee met in Fr Duddleswell's study. Sarah Sneezum was a bespectacled lady with a nervous tic, approaching middle age. George Groper was a giant of a man, young and prematurely bald. The chairman was Tim Fogarty, wiry and worried-looking. Tim was manager of a small catering firm. His other occupation was soon to be revealed.

'Has your wife given birth to another little stranger, Tim?' Fr Duddleswell asked.

'It's not for two or three weeks yet, Father,' Tim said, without a trace of the brogue for all his obvious ancestry.

'Anyway, for what your wife is about to receive may the good Lord deliver her.' For my benefit, Fr Duddleswell said, 'Tim has a power of children already. How many at the last count, Tim?'

'Eight, Father.'

'Bless 'em. And bless you and Margaret, too, for not using a stitch in time. Soon you will have enough little ones to string a rosary.' Fr Duddleswell then asked Tim to take over the meeting.

First, the target for this year's Bazaar had to be decided. Miss Sneezum suggested nervously that the previous year's £250 was an ideal figure. The forthright Mr Groper, having recalled the trials of reaching that amount, wanted to limit it to a couple of hundred.

Fr Duddleswell marvelled aloud at George Groper's lack of faith and insisted we could do better if we tried. Tim Fogarty and the rest of the committee were astonished to hear him name the sum he had in mind. Together they exclaimed:

'*Six* hundred!'

'Good,' said Fr Duddleswell. 'I'm glad we are all agreed on that. You are not dissenting, I take it, Father Neil?'

I would sooner have admitted at that moment to being an atheist.

'Looks unanimous, then,' Tim Fogarty said, eyeing Fr Duddleswell uneasily. 'The marquee, I assume, is a formality.'

Fr Duddleswell said no, more like foolishness, especially as 'not one shower of soft wet arrows' had fallen on the Bazaar in years.

There wasn't much business after that. Tim Fogarty promised the committee would organize the stalls and the amusements while Fr Duddleswell volunteered to use the pulpit for publicity. Handshakes all round and the quiet meeting came to an end.

Tim Fogarty was the last to leave. To him, Fr Duddleswell said:

'You managed the meeting marvellously, Tim. Without your firmness it might have got out of hand. I pray you reach your target of six hundred.'

With a spark of rebelliousness, Tim Fogarty replied, 'I've only got eight so far, Father.'

When we were alone, Fr Duddleswell said, 'Ah, 'tis wonderful to see the faith and enthusiasm of the laity. And,' he squeezed my arm, 'grateful to you for your support.'

I put it to him on my own account that a marquee would at least give cover to the perishable goods.

'Have you no faith in the protection of the Almighty, Father Neil?'

I remarked that I *had* known instances of believers being rained on.

'You cannot mean real believers, *true* believers,' he said, with fluttering eyes that revealed his lack of seriousness.

'Catholics, Father.'

'In name only. I have never known in me long life any project entered into by *true* believers that foundered.'

It seemed a wonderful thing, that Old Testament faith of his.

'Did y'ever hear the story of the drought in Ireland, Father Neil?'

Having been on the receiving end of so many, I took the coward's way out and said I couldn't remember.

'Well, 'twas in County Donegal. There was this drought which lasted ... Come to think of it, now, 'twas County Cork and all. Anyway, it lasted for eight weeks, like, and the potato crop was in peril of ... Correction, Father Neil, I am quite sure at last 'twas County Cavan. Perhaps you remember the tale now?'

I assured him that now I remembered it even less well than before.

'Whenever there was a drought, y'see, the parishioners of the Church of the Annunciation processed with their statue of Our Lady into the tater field and begged her to rend the heavens and favour them with a shower or two. "Rain, O Blessed Virgin, rain," they cried and they chanted and they sang.

'Well, now, on this occasion, after eight weeks of intense, lip-licking drought, you recall, they prayed aloud: "Rain, O Blessed Virgin, rain." And'—he eyed me challengingly—'what d'you think came to pass?'

'It poured?'

He looked at me suspiciously. 'You *have* heard it before.'

'An inspired guess,' I said humbly, 'but please go on with your story, Father.'

'Thank you kindly. Well, there was this cloudburst of apocalyptic proportions, a veritable avalanche of rain, y'might say, and all the faithful people of County Cork or wherever the bloody County was, sang and chanted and cried, "Stop, O Blessed Virgin, *stop*." '

He laughed merrily and I laughed with him.

'You are *sure* you have never heard it before?' he stopped to enquire.

'Um.'

'You *have*.' He was not pleased. 'Why did you not ... ?'

'Not in that precise form.'

'Which form, then?'

'Much less amusing.'

He was still not satisfied. 'How exactly?'

'There was far less *rain* in the version I heard.'

'Oh?'

'And I laughed a lot more this time, Father.'

'Y'did? Rain has that effect on you?'

I decided to change the subject. 'But what's the moral of it, Father?'

'Moral?' he asked, drawing back his head and shoulders in disbelief. 'Does every rib-tickling tale have to have a moral to it? What a funny solemn English feller y'are, to be sure.'

I remember Fr Duddleswell standing in the pulpit in his green vestments the following Sunday morning to fulfil his sad duty of talking again about the sordid subject: money.

'Did not the Lord Jesus Christ'—a lift of the biretta at the mention of the Holy Name—'say, 'You cannot serve God and money' and 'Happy are the poor'? Now I am wanting you all to serve God and become exceeding happy by giving to our Bazaar.'

He outlined the plan of campaign: posters all over town; a raffle ('Overcome your diffidence and natural timidity, Tickets for the raffle should be purchased with avidity'); programmes sold in advance at threepence a time, reduced to tuppence for the under sevens and the over sixty-fives. Most important of all, each Sunday in the porch, there would be wicker-baskets to hold the commodity requested for that week: tinned foods, toys, clothes, knitted goods—and books.

'Books of a helpful and edifying character, you follow? No lurid, titillating paper-covers, if you please. No naked ladies or seducting gentlemen. No *Gone With The Storm* sort of thing on our Catholic bookstall. Not, me dear people, that I am exactly asking you to bring only the Holy Bible or *The Imitation of Christ*, either.'

Having given them this year's target, he concluded:

'May Christ's Holy Spirit inspire you to heroic feats of generosity in the coming weeks. Above all, have faith and pray mightily for perfect weather so our Bazaar is a huge success. Sometimes the Lord is hard of hearing so use a hammer.'

He signed himself to show the first appeal was over. Then:

'Now who is taking this morning's collection? Is Tim Fogarty there?' He peered shortsightedly down the church. 'He is not. I am not going on with this Holy Mass until somebody grabs that plate and ...' He paused to listen to what someone was calling out from the back. 'No plate there? Is this a Catholic church or is it not?' He cupped his hands to his ears before saying agitatedly, 'Somebody has stolen all the collecting plates? Jesus Christ!' He had the presence of mind to remove his biretta and this gave him the idea. 'Use this for the time being. And, Father Neil? Has me curate been stolen, besides?' I was forced to come out of hiding from behind a pillar and bring my own biretta into service. His last words before continuing with the Creed of the Mass were, ' 'Tis enough to make St Jude himself despair.'

A couple of Sundays later when the last congregation of the morning had gone home, Fr Duddleswell and I were examining the haul for that week. As we wandered among the Ali Baba baskets he was saying to himself, 'Such good, generous people.'

I seconded him but pointed out that it was hardly worth £600.

'Where is your faith, Father Neil?' he demanded to know. Besides, there were admission fees, a fun fair and an amusement arcade.

'But no marquee,' I said.

'Father Neil, d'you think the Almighty God is hoarding up rain to pour it over our Bazaar? Has He not better things to do with His eternity than play practical jokes on a good sinful man with a white collar?'

Whether through pride or humility, I realized he did not mean me.

He was peering down into the basket marked BOOKS. A black hole. He tried to touch the bottom and couldn't. I reached into the basket for him and drew out the only contribution: one of our own hymn books.

'And look at this,' he demanded, holding up a brassiere which was lying on top of the clothes basket. 'Who on earth donated this?'

'A lady, Father?'

'But why couldn't the generous donor'—he stretched the thing out to show its full dimensions—'and the donor is excessively generous, why could she not wrap it up decent, like, in grease-proof paper?'

' 'Morning, Fr O'Duddleswell.' Billy Buzzle was standing in the porch. He looked about him. 'Starting a delicatessen?'

'I am just after saying Mass,' said my parish priest, 'so I cannot swear at you this moment.'

'I've come with a proposal,' said Billy.

'I have no wish to marry you.'

'No, seriously,' said Billy. 'I could run a good book at your Bazaar. 'Good book,' he repeated, laughing, seeing his unintended joke, 'Whatever profit I make on bets, you get ten per cent. What could be fairer than that?'

'A stick of liquorice,' said Fr Duddleswell. 'I intend raising £600 by the generous offerings of the faithful, not by tempting them with the hope of sordid gain.'

'One point of view,' Billy said, 'but if you change your mind, come and see me.' And he left.

'I agree with your stand, Father,' I said.

'What are you trying to do, Father Neil, make me think I did the wrong thing?' His eyes alighted on a lawn-mower. 'Look you here, Father Neil. In mint condition.' He pushed it back and forth. 'Perfect. I have been needing one of these for the last couple of years.'

'You're not intending to ...'

'Pinch it? What are you, a jury or something?'

'Take it away,' I said.

'Without paying for it?' I was silent. 'Of course I intended paying for it.'

'I assumed that, Father. I meant take it away *now*.'

He looked it up and down. 'How much would you say 'tis worth?' I shrugged to indicate I had no idea. ''Tis badly in need of a lick of paint, like.' No comment from me. 'And the blades look terrible rusty. And that handle-grip is a bit perished.'

'It does look under the weather for a mower in mint condition,' I said.

He moved his head from side to side to show he was making a reasonable bargain with himself. 'What would you say to five?'

'Thanks a lot,' I said. Seeing that was not appreciated, I said, 'Um, yes. Five pounds seems a very fair price to me.'

'I meant five *bob*. What d'you think?'

'Do you really want my honest opinion, Father?'

'Like a stomach ulcer.' He slapped me on the bottom. 'Let's go eat, you wicked feller.'

On Tuesday, five days before the Bazaar, I said to Fr Duddleswell:

'There are signs that the fine weather's breaking up. The Met. Office says that perhaps by the weekend ...'

'Prophets of doom have beguiled thy faint heart, Father Neil. I repeat to you, I have run ten Bazaars since I came to St Jude's and many prior to that. And have I had one of them fail me yet? Indeed, I have not.'

I had already admitted defeat and needed no reminding of Christ's words, 'Ask and you shall receive,' and 'If you have faith, you can move mountains.'

'Come along with me to the school, Father Neil.'

It was the third lesson of the morning. Fr Duddleswell's custom was to knock abruptly on each classroom door, steam in and take charge of a class for a few minutes at a time.

The children stood up at his behest to pray for the success of the Bazaar and sat down to hear his homily about gloommongers who prophesied we would never make £600 on

71

account of the bad weather. The boys and girls, sweating in the humid heat of that blazing summer thought this a sick joke.

'Father Neil,' I was asked afterwards, 'tell me truly, are you not ashamed when you see the faith these youngsters have? If only we could become as little children.'

The children got littler and littler because, after we left school, Fr Duddleswell drove me to the orphanage. Any child old enough to walk and kneel on his own was rounded up to pray for the success of the Bazaar.

'Father Neil, d'you think that the Lord who loves little children can refuse the petitions of his darlin' little ones?'

Mentally, I buried my head in my hands. What reply can you make to Biblical blackmail?

Cloudless days followed throughout the week. Nonetheless, the temperature was falling slightly and faint winds stirred the topmost branches of the apple trees in the garden. On Friday night, I couldn't see the stars.

Saturday morning dawned, dull and grey. In my room, I expressed my anxieties to Mrs Pring who also thought him foolish not to hire a marquee. 'The trouble is,' she said, Father D believes in God more than God does.'

At Mrs Pring's suggestion, I telephoned the Met. Office. I had just got through when Fr Duddleswell barged in.

'Father Neil.' '

'Sorry,' I said in a panic, waving my free hand, 'won't be a minute, Father.' Then into the mouthpiece: 'Mr Fogarty, is that you?' The lady on the line said, not surprisingly, it was not.

'Father Neil, what're you doing?'

I took no heed of him. 'You are expecting your wife's baby any hour now, Tim,' I said. 'I do hope everything comes out all right.'

'If that is Fogarty, chairman of our Bazaar committee,' said Fr Duddleswell sharply, 'perhaps I could ...'

'Hello, hello,' I said, as the lady at the Met. Office accused me of obscenity and slammed down the phone. I made a resolution not to play that trick ever again. 'I *am* sorry, Father, the phone's cut me dead.'

'Saved me the trouble,' he growled. 'A very remarkable man is Tim Fogarty.'

I agreed with him but asked him to elaborate.

'Well, here are you talking to Tim on the phone about his wife expecting any hour.'

'Yes. How is that so remarkable?'

'And Margaret gave birth to her ninth only yesterday.'

'That *is* remarkable ... bad luck, Father.'

'And Tim himself is downstairs this minute in me study waiting to go with us to the Bazaar.'

In my chair, I folded my arms and legs to stop myself falling apart. 'Then who on earth was I talking to a moment ago?'

Fr Duddleswell closed his eyes. ' 'Twas a very wicked man, I am thinking.'

As we got out of the car under a mackerel sky, I imagined I could already smell rain in the air.

Though it was only nine o'clock, the Argos playing fields were a hive of activity. Stalls were being erected on the perimeter of the cricket pitch. Two huge trucks arrived packed to the roof with tinned foodstuffs and toys. Vans chugged up in convoys to the entrance of the car-park, bedecked with bunting and Union Jacks. There were two station-wagons bearing household pets: rabbits, hamsters and lots of white mice still odious to me in spite of their pink eyes. Then came a large truck out of which trotted half a dozen shaggy donkeys; and two men with pitchforks heaved out big bales of straw to supply their needs for the afternoon.

A loudspeaker system was being set up all over the field—it was on loan free of charge from Pimms and Sons, the electrical shop in the High Street. Coconut shies and an amusement arcade were soon erected. And over and above all this, there was a constant stream of Fr Duddleswell's 'good ladies of the parish' bearing the most delicious-looking products of their ovens: cakes, buns, doughnuts, pies, biscuits.

Fr Duddleswell himself was here, there and everywhere at once, greeting, thanking, cajolling, chastising, encouraging and, no doubt, praying.

He and I had the misfortune to stop at the cake stall run by Miss Sneezum. 'Were all these buns baked in your oven?' he asked. Receiving an affirmative reply, he said, 'You must have a marvellous capacity.'

She offered him the pick of the stall. He made his selection but had difficulty in making an impression on it with his teeth.

'A rock cake, Miss Sneezum?'

'That one is a fairy cake, Father.'

'Uh huh,' he said, and to me in a whisper, 'Just flour and heavy water.'

'How about you, Fr Boyd?'

'Thank you, Miss Sneezum, but ...'

Fr Duddleswell insisted we stick together. 'Jam tart, Father Neil,' and handed me a large one.

We touched our hats to Miss Sneezum and retreated for safety to the pet stall.

'You will not need any fillings in your teeth for some years after you have eaten that, lad,' he told me.

I carried that tart in the palm of my hand but made no effort to eat it.

At the pet stall, Fr Duddleswell offered his fairy cake to a black rabbit which refused it. A white mouse was equally wise and I warmed to it a little.

We passed on to the coconut shy manned by George Groper. Fr Duddleswell handed George his cake. 'In case you run out of balls, George. For the coconuts.' He then relieved me of my jam tart. He stick it firmly under a coconut and handed it to Mr Groper. 'Put that on a stand, George, and they can throw ten ton bombs at it all afternoon and still not win a coconut.'

We stopped to admire the donkeys. 'Such gentle, humble creatures, Father Neil. Small wonder our Blessed Lord had one of these to carry Himself into Jerusalem.' When I went to stroke them, however, he held me back. 'One kick from them would break your bloody leg,' he warned.

Finally, Fr Duddleswell ascended a platform to make sure the loudspeaker system was working.

'Testing, testing,' he yelled. And then quickly, 'Our Father who art in heaven. Hail Mary, full of grace, the Lord is with thee.' He bowed his head. 'Glory be to the Father and to the Son and to the Holy Ghost.'

'As it was in the beginning,' I took up, 'is now and ever shall be.'

'World without end.'

'Amen,' I said, as I gazed apprehensively at the sky.

'Father Neil. Tut-tut. Father Neil.'

No further remonstrances were needed. I too prayed that despite the auguries, all would be well. God love little children, I begged.

He borrowed a sixpence from me to buy a ticket in the raffle for a bottle of whiskey and we drove home for a bite to eat. His confidence in his mountain-moving God was undiminished. In fact, it seemed to be growing.

Mrs Pring told him at lunch he would regret not hiring that marquee. 'You can't by a prayer turn a little potato into a big potato,' she said.

'But you can by that method, woman, turn a little faith into a big faith.'

'The weather forecast is terrible,' she told him.

'And who made it, the Angel Gabriel?'

'Oh,' she snorted, 'he's well educated so there's no drumming any sense into him. Take your galoshes with you, Father Neil.'

'If he does,' swore Fr Duddleswell, 'he is no disciple of mine. I repeat, with faith we will make our £600.'

Mrs Pring was adamant we wouldn't so he asked me whose side *I* was on.

I pretended ignorance of the issue that was dividing them.

'The case is reducible to this,' he said. 'Are you taking galoshes or not?'

'No, Father.' I was sorry to ruin his pleasure. 'I don't have any galoshes.'

'But if you did have a pair?'

'I wouldn't take them,' I said. Catching Mrs Pring's eye, I added, 'Not both of them.'

'Father Neil.' She was disappointed in me.

'One at least,' I said.

The other combatant showed *his* feelings. 'Father Neil.'

'One at most,' I said.

'Poor Father Neil,' said Mrs Pring, aiming to annoy the boss, 'I'll buy you a pair of galoshes for Christmas.'

'And I,' sighed Fr Duddleswell, 'will buy him a bloody fence. No wonder the human backside is shaped the way 'tis.'

On our return at 1.30, we saw the gaily decorated entrance

to the playing fields. Over it, a huge banner proclaimed: ST JUDE'S BAZAAR—TODAY 2–6 p.m.

The Bazaar was to be opened by T.V. personality Frosty Jones, a local boy with a dead-pan face who was the straight man in a popular comedy doubles act. He put in an appearance at ten minutes to two and remarked at once on the ominous signs of rain.

'If it pours, where do we take cover?' he asked.

'Under the umbrella of the Almighty,' joked Fr Duddleswell, evoking no response on Frosty's professionally frigid face.

Twelve minutes later, with only half a dozen customers added to the fifty or so helpers, Frosty Jones declared the Bazaar open with a speech 'notable', as Fr Duddleswell was to put it, 'for its audacious economy'.

Frosty kept looking anxiously at the black-jowelled clouds racing overhead, and, having said his piece, shook the parish priest and me by the hand before making a dash for his Jaguar.

The wind had freshened considerably by this time and was threatening to become a gale. We had to hang on to our hats and almost needed a torch to find our way about.

At precisely eight minutes past two, the heavens opened. No Hollywood Bible epic ever caught a downpour such as this on celluloid. Orange lightning dazzled us and the thunder accompanying it deafened us. I have never seen such a sky-quake. I expected Moses to appear in person and thrown down the twin tablets of stone. Instead, there was only this huge, grey scroll of tumbling water.

'Four inches of rain fell in fifteen minutes,' the local press was to claim. An exaggeration, but for those of us who lived through it a pardonable one.

The gallant helpers scattered to their stalls to try to keep them intact against the screeching wind and blinding rain. The few books were immediately soaked. Almost all the tins lost their labels so it was impossible to know whether the contents were rice pudding or baked beans. The donkeys went wild and kicked over everything in sight including the wire-fronted hutches containing the rabbits, hamsters and white mice. I watched two assistants squelching in the mud on hands and feet attempting bravely to domesticate them again. Miss Sneezum was heard to say, 'My cakes have all floated away.'

76

Fr Duddleswell afterwards claimed that as the only first-class miracle of the afternoon.

I felt a tug on my jacket and looked down to find a drenched six-year-old tearfully asking for his tuppence back.

The parish priest was all this time running round with gay frenzy crying again and again, 'Stop, O Blessed Virgin, stop.'

It took too long for his message to reach the Holy Mother. By the time she heard and answered his prayer, the playing fields were a disaster area. When the rain ceased completely at three o'clock, there was nothing for it but to clear up the mess and go home.

Fr Duddleswell knocked into me. 'Me spectacles,' he said apologetically. 'They keep misting up on me. Nothing dry enough to wipe 'em with.'

'Mind you don't catch cold, Father,' I said, without caring very much at that moment what happened to the stubborn old boy.

He must have read my thoughts. 'Good job we did not hire that marquee, Father Neil,' he remarked, peeping over the top of his blurred spectacles.

'Tell me more,' I said with what I took to be ferocious irony.

'Would have blown down in that gale as sure as sure and somebody, a child, for example, might have been killed.'

I pondered this as the local authority dustmen came to shovel all the cakes and books and most of the toys into their cart; I pondered it as the R.S.P.C.A. came in response to a phone call to claim the tinier pets and calm the donkeys before removing them, still braying in protest, in a lorry.

The sun came out. Over in the west, I saw a double rainbow.

'What,' I asked Fr Duddleswell, 'does the Bible promise about there never being another Flood?'

'Father Neil,' he said, 'do you not consider that the Almighty can bring good from evil?'

I showed him the takings for the afternoon: one shilling and nine-pence.

'There's an awful lot of evil here, Father, for him to draw good from.'

That evening at supper, Fr Duddleswell was sober, self-contained. Mrs Pring failed to rile him with her comments on the days proceedings.

'No marquee needed, eh?' His ears were double-glazed. 'What about reaching your target now?' He held his peace.

Later, when I heard him ask Mrs Pring for a hot water bottle, a couple of aspirins and a lemon drink, I regretted my cruelty to him at the Bazaar.

Next morning, Fr Duddleswell rose for the early Mass but said from the pulpit that he couldn't preach because he'd caught a chill. The tinned food and the toys that could be salvaged, he explained, had been sent to the orphanage. He thanked from his heart all who had contributed to the Bazaar and said he did not doubt but that the takings, when they were counted, would show we had, as usual, reached our target.

'God bless you for your prayers and unswerving faith,' he said. 'And now who is taking the collection? Just because we make £600 on our Bazaar, it does not mean we can afford to do without our ...'

Later, I told Mrs Pring what he had said. 'He seemed ever so quiet and humble.'

'Yes, I could see he's not himself, Father Neil, that's why I've ordered him to bed.'

'I hope he hasn't caught his death, Mrs P.'

'He's harder to kill than a flea, that one, but I phoned Dr Daley just in case.'

I showed the Doctor into Fr Duddleswell's bedroom. He was propped up in bed without his glasses on.

Dr Daley stuck a thermometer in his mouth and took hold of his left wrist while he softly sang, 'Oh, my love has got a red, red nose.'

'Enough of the comicals, thank you, Donal,' Fr Duddleswell said.

'You have not been eating your apple a day, Charles.'

'I am come over queer as drunk,' said the patient, 'so I am seeing double with both eyes.'

'There is nothing the matter with you, Charles, that a holy death cannot cure.'

'Is me pulse all right?' I was surprised to see that Dr Daley did not bother to look at his watch while taking his pulse.

'Oh,' the Doctor said, 'I was but holding your hand for old time's sake. But, yes, your pulse is very normal for one in your appalling condition.' He took the thermometer from Fr Duddleswell's mouth. 'Um. Tut,' and a deep sucking in of air. 'It makes the saddest reading since the sinking of the *Titanic*.'

'Have I a temperature, Donal?'

'Let me put it thus, Charles. If you breathed your last this very second and were fortunate enough to squeeze into Purgatory, you wouldn't notice the difference.' He touched the cigarette in his mouth. 'Your thermometer is even hotter than mine. Now, tell me what happened and all?'

'Everything was prospering with us,' Fr Duddleswell said, 'till a cloud burst.'

'Myself,' Dr Daley said, 'I will never look at the rain. Filthy stuff.'

'A deluge. There has not been the like since the days of Noah and his ark.'

'Tut-tut.'

'Without the slightest warning there came over this crow-black cloud and bit the wick off the sun.'

'Tut-tut, tut-tut, tut-tut, tut.'

'How was I to know the Almighty God was emptying out the bathwater of all the saints over our Bazaar? And the wind.'

Dr Daley tutted that in sympathy, too.

'I swear to you, Donal, the only thing left standing for a mile around was a solitary coconut.'

'You must be in the Almighty's black books, Charles.'

'He is certainly in mine for this queerness of me head, Donal. Still,' he muttered mysteriously, '*six hundred pounds*. The good God has not entirely emigrated from the parish.'

'You haven't a sup of whiskey hid away in your hot water bottle, I suppose.'

'I have not. You have had a drop taken already on the way, too. I could smell it on you with a peg on me nose.'

Dr Daley slumped down on a chair beside the bed. 'You are uncommon severe with me, Charles, you know that? Have you forgotten our Lord's own sensible words, "There is but one thing necessary, one thing."'

'He was not talking about the liquor.'

'Oh, no?' Dr Daley said challengingly. 'Did our Blessed Lord choose wine or water for the Holy Mass?'

'Wine.'

'And did He or did He not turn water into wine?'

'That He did.'

'And can you tell me one instance in the Holy Book where He turned wine into water?'

'I am not able.'

'There,' he exclaimed in triumph, 'doesn't that show the way our Blessed Saviour's mind was working? Had He changed wine into water, now, which of us would believe He was the Son of God?'

Without removing his cigarette, the Doctor performed the remarkable feat of blowing a superb smoke ring. It hovered before ascending slowly like a shaky symbol of eternity.

Suspecting their theological argument was likely to last for some time, I excused myself and went down to lunch.

Dr Daley came in to the dining room at the coffee stage.

'How is he?' Mrs Pring asked, trying to mask her concern.

'He got a rough handling from the water,' said Dr Daley, 'and that stuff has no medicinal properties as I've noticed. It's gastric 'flu.'

'Poor Father D,' said Mrs Pring. 'He did look pale. As if he'd just caught sight of himself in the mirror.'

'A face white as Connemara stone,' confirmed Dr Daley. 'When I left him he was bankrupt of argument and not excessively well. Coughing like a cow with a turnip down its throat and he has turned political.'

'Pardon,' I said, not knowing what he meant by the expression.

'He will have a seat in the cabinet for a day or two but then he will be in health. The good Lord Himself has not sharp enough teeth to bite the thread of him altogether.'

Mrs Pring said, 'May he live and feign for ever and ever.'

'He will,' Dr Daley said, 'provided you are diligent with him and keep him in bed in between his diplomatic journeys to and fro. He's got a temperature of 103 and *delirium non tremens*. Keeps muttering something about £600.

On Wednesday morning, Fr Duddleswell rose, celebrated a private Mass and afterwards joined me in the dining room wearing one of his most sheepish smiles. On his side plate was an enormous pile of letters.

'There's another two bundles in your study,' Mrs Pring told him.

Fr Duddleswell, in between mouthfuls of toast, was slitting open the envelopes with a butter knife and giving me a running commentary on 'this unexampled generosity of our good people.'

'Here is a note from an old-age pensioner, Mrs Wright, and her postal order for two pounds ten shillings. What d'you think of that, Father Neil?' he asked as his spectacles steamed up from emotion. 'And here is a letter from Colonel Sir John Tophall wishing me a speedy recovery and promising me a cheque for a pound.'

While not unappreciative of this beneficence, I couldn't help reflecting that the other two 'bundles' in his study would have to reach the ceiling if we were to reach our target. He must have seen through me, for he whispered:

'Father Neil, will we ever make a *true* Christian of you?'

I put my nose in a cup of coffee to prevent myself becoming ironical again.

He turned his attention to Mrs Pring. 'Herself is being considerably quiet.'

'She is pleased to have you in the way again, Father.'

'Not at all. Her silence is but a ruse for drawing attention to herself.' Mrs Pring smiled as if to say, I was right after all. 'There, y'see, the cow's tail is on the swing.'

'There's no fun in being miserable, is there?' said Mrs Pring. 'Did you know, Father D, you won the bottle of whiskey in the raffle?'

'Faith rewarded,' he commented. 'But that is the first time I have ever won a thing in a raffle.'

'And the last,' she said. 'You bought the only ticket.'

'With my money,' I said. 'But it doesn't matter.'

'I will give you your sixpence back, Father Neil.'

'No need. Dr Daley gave me a sixpence and walked off with the bottle.'

At that moment, Fr Duddleswell came across a big envelope that caused him to release an exultant cry:

'*That's* the bit of charity I have been waiting for.'

He slit the letter open and admired the contents for a moment before holding up a cheque. It was from the Moon-

81

light Insurance Company to the tune of £600. My eyes had
never before settled on such a valuable piece of paper.

'You mean,' I gasped, 'you insured the Bazzar against a
downpour?'

'I do the same every year, Father Neil. In fact, because of
me excellent record, the premium this year was only £10.'

'Cheaper than a marquee, you mean?'

'Mind you, Father Neil, we only received £600 because the
Bazaar was completely washed out.'

'Rain, O Blessed Virgin, rain.'

'The Holy Mother can always be relied on, can she not?'

'You talk about faith,' said Mrs Pring shrilly, realizing he
had outwitted her. 'You're an old fraud, you are.' And she
stamped out.

Fr Duddleswell looked at me and shrugged in astonishment.

'Father,' I put it to him, 'how *can* you talk about faith in
God when you fall back on an insurance company?'

'It *is* faith, Father Neil,' he insisted. 'God answered me
prayers exactly, did He not?'

The truth came to me in a flash. 'You mean you prayed for
rain?'

'Surely. For a deluge. Why do you reckon it happened so?'

'Even though you pleaded with the congregation to pray for
fine weather?'

'*Perfect* weather,' he corrected me. 'And it was. Look.' He
held up the cheque again.

'But, Father, you *led* the people in prayer, even the orphans
and widows.'

He rested his head on his hand. 'When we pray, Father
Neil, we do not all have to pray for the same thing, surely.
We must leave the Lord a choice, like. And He decided in me
favour. Which is very fitting, seeing I am in charge here.'

Mrs Pring knocked and announced a visitor. Billy Buzzle.

'Are you improved, Fr O'Duddleswell?'

'No, Mr McBuzzle,' said Fr Duddleswell, finding from
somewhere a husky voice not in evidence before. 'Suddenly
very much worse. I am soon off again to me fever-hut.'

I told Mr Buzzle we had managed to reach our target
without him, after all.

'You could have fooled me,' he said. 'What did it rain on
your Bazaar, then, pennies from heaven?'

Fr Duddleswell asked, 'How is your good dog Judas, Mr Buzzle?'

'Pontius.'

'Indeed, Pontius.'

'Not a drop of rain dampened this road,' said Billy. 'You know you were blankety-blank lucky.'

'Mr Buzzle, would you be gracious and come back another time when I am recovered?'

'If you like,' Billy said. 'But I brought you this.'

From his inside pocket he fished out a big buff envelope and dropped it on the table in front of Fr Duddleswell. Then he left.

'What's that?' I asked.

Fr Duddleswell poked it suspiciously with his knife. 'An envelope?'

'What's in it?'

Mrs Pring said, 'What do Bookies usually put in envelopes? That's his winnings.'

Fr Duddleswell slit open the envelope and tipped the contents on to the table. Once more, my previous financial standards of comparison were overturned. There, spread out before me, were more fivers than I had ever seen.

'How much, Father, six hundred?'

'And thirty. I get me stake money back as well, you follow?'

'You laid out thirty on a downpour?'

'I was desperate to show Billy there is no ill will between us.'

'There probably is now.'

'Not at all. Could you not see his respect for me has rocketed skyhigh?'

'Thirty pounds,' I whistled.

'It seemed good odds at 20–1.'

'Very good.'

'Mind you, Billy thought he had me over a barrel. Remember it had not rained for nearly four weeks.'

I tried to absorb this new piece of information. 'So altogether you've made a profit of twelve hundred.'

'More,' he said reluctantly. 'There are all these contributions of the faithful to be added to that.'

'*Faith*-ful?'

He missed my point, I suppose, for he went on, 'The good

people will be *so* pleased we reached our target after all their efforts and prayers. Had we failed, it might have weakened their trust in the Almighty no end.'

I dropped irony and told him straight what I thought of his subterfuges and Mrs Pring said 'Hypocrite'.

It had some effect. 'Of course, while God likes help when helping people, gambling is a heinous sin.' And he thumped his breast. '*Mea culpa, mea culpa, mea maxima culpa.*'

'And these, Father, are the wages of sin.'

'Father Neil, I will not try to hide from you the fact that your parish priest for all his saintly exterior is a *terrible* sinner. I will undeniably end up in hell like the chappie in *The Mikado* who cheated at billiards.'

'How was he punished?'

'Oh, he was condemned to a fiercely guarded dungeon,'— here he began to recite while making the appropriate gestures over the table cloth:

And there he plays extravagant matches
In fitless finger stalls
On a cloth untrue
With a twisted cue
And elliptical billiard-balls.

'D'you know, Father Neil,' he said, with a twinkle of unrepentance in his big blue eyes, 'sometimes I ask meself if I have any faith at all.'

V *The New Assistant*

'Tony Marlowe's the name, Father.'

'Pleased to meet you, Mr Marlowe.'

'This is my wife, Rena, and our two girls. Mary's eight and Joanna's five.'

It was early Friday evening. I had been standing alone, smiling inanely at no one in particular, at the back of Tipton Hall. We hired it out once a week for family get-togethers. I was wanting to be sociable and it came as a relief to have a friendly group come up and speak to me.

'You're our parishioners, I take it, Tony?'

'Been here all my life. Rena's the foreigner. From Glasgow. The girls have picked up the accent. You'd hear it if only their tongues weren't tied in knots.'

The girls, clinging to their mother, twisted their legs and giggled.

Tony said, 'Why don't you pop in and see us some time, Father?'

'Yes, and join us for a cup of tea,' said Rena in a strong Glaswegian accent. 'We'd be pleased to see you at *any* time.'

'I'd like to do that. Where do you live?'

'Our flat's over our shop, the grocer's shop on the corner of Calvert Street.'

'I know it,' I said. 'And how's trade?'

'Too busy at the moment, Father,' Tony replied. 'My chief assistant has just gone down with an attack of chronic bronchitis and I can't get a replacement for love nor money. The job's tough, and if that weren't enough, nobody wants to work Saturday afternoons any more.'

I remembered that chance conversation when, after the midday Mass on the Sunday following, a broad, squat, venomous-looking character appeared, cap in hand, in the sacristy.

'Archie Lee,' he announced, as I was taking off the green

85

chasuble.

I thought I'd better give him the benefit of the doubt and shook his hand A very gnarled hand it was, too, like the branch of an oak.

'What can I do for you, Mr Lee?'

As I was saying it, I felt he was mentally picking my pocket. He was in his fifties, unshaven, poorly dressed.

'I need a bit of 'elp, Father.'

'Well, Mr Lee ...'

'*Archie.*'

'Archie. In this parish, we have a very well organized conference of the St Vincent de Paul Society. If you have any genuine needs, I'm sure ...'

'It's not money I'm after, Father.'

'Not money?'

'Not money,' he said.

'What then?'

'I need a job.'

'Is that so hard to find?' I asked, as if *I* managed to get a new one every week. 'What's wrong with the Labour Exchange?'

'No use, Father. Even when they get me a job, which ain't often, I can't seem to keep it for long.'

'Been "inside" have you, Archie?' I asked knowingly.

Archie bowed his head. 'You won't tell no one will you, Father?'

'Wouldn't dream of it.'

'In strictest confidence, yeah?'

'Word of honour, I'll treat it,' I said, taking a leaf out of Fr Duddleswell's book, 'as if it were a confessional secret.'

Archie positively purred with pleasure. 'This is 'ow it is, Father,' he confessed. 'I've been inside many a time in me life. More inside than out, if you grasp my meaning?'

I nodded.

'But 'onest to Gawd, Father,' Archie said, signing himself, 'six months past, I promised meself I'd go straight and I 'ave, I really 'ave.'

'I'm glad to hear it,' I said, as I removed the last of my Mass vestments. I was intrigued by Archie; he was the first convicted criminal I'd ever come across. I hoped the encounter would prove beneficial to my ministry.

'Been a bit of a challenge, Father, I can tell yer. When people 'ear you've got a record, they don't wanner know. Grasp my meaning? And I get shot out in the snow on me ... on me back, time and again.'

'People split on you, do they Archie?'

Archie pursed his lips and sighed as if the situation was often desperate. 'I struggle on, Father, because ... well, it ain't fitting to be crooked all yer life, is it? But you wouldn't know about that sort o' thing, I s'pose.'

I hastened to assure Archie that understanding was my *métier*.

'What about 'elping me get a job, Father?'

It was then I remembered Tony Marlowe's words about being short-staffed in his grocery shop.

'How strong are you, Archie?'

'I once lifted a safe weighing near three 'undred pounds on me own.'

'Did you have to do that, Archie?' I asked, displeased at the example he had chosen to illustrate his strength.

'Yeah. Yer see I couldn't break the bloody ... the thing, Father. Shall I give you a demo'? See that safe there'— he pointed to our parish safe in which we stored the chalices and the Sunday collections—'tell me where yer want it put and I'll oblige.'

'No need, I assure you, Archie,' I said, as I moved over to the safe, heaved it to and turned the key.

'You don't 'ave to lock up on my account, Father. I could open it with a toothbrush if I chose, but as I told yer, these days, I'm straighter'n a corpse on the end of a rope.'

'I'm sure you are,' I said ashamedly. 'One more question, Archie.'

'Fire away, Father.'

'Do you mind working on Saturday afternoons?'

'Never done it, not since I left gaol. But I'll try anything if it's gonna keep the wolf from the door.'

'All right, Archie, I'll see what I can do. I know a grocer who's looking for an assistant in his store. If you'd care to come to the presbytery at three o'clock I'll tell you if he'll take you on.'

'That's real Christly of you,' was Archie's parting remark.

After lunch I phoned Tony Marlowe and told him I had a prospective assistant for him who could start whenever he liked and who didn't mind working on Saturday afternoons.

'What's he like, Father? Give it to me straight.'

'Seems honest enough,' I hedged.

'Is he sharp at figures?'

'I know he's handled a lot of money in his time,' I said. 'And you can take it from me he's as strong as a carthouse and as willing.'

'I tell you what, Father. I take your word for it he's okay. I'll give him a week's trial. He can start tomorrow morning at eight o'clock.'

'Thanks a lot, Tony.'

'My pleasure. But do stress that to begin with it's only for the week.'

I promised to do that. When I spoke to Archie later that afternoon, he was overjoyed at the opportunity of proving himself.

'And yer didn't let on about my record, Father?' Before I could chastise him for doubting me, he said. ' 'Course you didn't. I won't let yer down. What's past is over an' done, ain't that right? You can rely on Archie.'

Next morning, I took it into my head to visit the Marlowe family and at the same time check on whether Archie was behaving himself.

It was about 11.30 when I set foot in the shop. Archie was busy filling two tall shelves with cans of Heinz Baked Beans. When he saw me, far from looking apprehensive, he greeted me with a big trusting smile.

'Nice to see yer, Father.'

'You, too, Archie. I've come on a parish visitation to see the Marlowes.'

'Mr Marlowe!' called out Archie.

Tony had a small private office at the back where he kept his accounts and dealt with travelling salesmen.

'Hello, Father,' he said. 'I've got a traveller with me at the moment. I'll tell Rena you're here.'

Rena came to collect me. 'Come upstairs, Father, and I'll get you a cup of coffee.'

In the sitting-room, Rena told me that Tony's impressions of Archie were so far very favourable.

'He works hard, he's friendly with the customers and what's more, he seems to be an honest bloke.'

'That's fine,' I said.

'Yes, there's this old lady—always in here and a real pest she is—well, she was picking and prodding our tomatoes when she dropped her purse without noticing it. Archie saw what happened and gave it back to her. She had £15 in it, she said.'

We chatted on for about twenty minutes sipping coffee, when suddenly there was the sound of someone charging up the stairs and Tony burst into the room.

'Fr Boyd,' he blurted out, 'there's someone on the telephone. I think you ought to hear what he's got to say. I've switched over the extension so you can listen in.'

With that, Tony rushed down the stairs again.

Wondering what this was all about, I picked up the phone as I'd seen Private Eyes pick it up in films. Through the earpiece I heard a door slam and Tony's breathless voice, 'I've just seen a salesman off the premises, sir. Now we can talk in peace and quiet. Perhaps you wouldn't mind repeating what you said before.'

'Nobody can overhear us, I take it?'

'Nobody,' said Tony, obviously not thinking it worthwhile to mention me.

'First my name,' came from a very cultured voice at the end of the line. 'I'm Peregrine Worsley and I'm a retired accountant.'

'Yes, Mr Worsley.'

'I hope you don't think I'm prying into your personal affairs but I couldn't help noticing as I chanced to be strolling past your place an hour ago that there was a fellow, seemingly in your employ, whom I have come across before.'

'That was probably my new assistant.'

'Would he answer, by any chance, to the name of Archie Lee?'

'He would.'

The caller sighed aristocratically. 'I didn't think I'd made a mistake. You see, Mr Marlowe, it is my unpleasant civic duty to appraise you of the fact that Archie Lee has a criminal record.'

I was glad I'd taken the precaution of putting my handkerchief over the mouthpiece, otherwise *two gasps* of horror

89

would have assailed Mr Worsley's ear.

'A *long* criminal record,' the caller emphasized.

'Anything really serious?' Tony managed to get out.

'Theft.'

Tony said almost to himself: 'I'll have to make sure he keeps away from the cash desk.'

'I'm afraid that's not all, by any manner of means. Archie Lee has been incarcerated thirteen times and four of them for robbery with violence.'

'Oh my God!' exclaimed Tony as if he was about to make an act of contrition on my behalf. 'G.B.H.'

'I beg your pardon?' questioned the imperturbable Mr Worsley.

'Nothing, sir. Grievous bodily harm. That's quite another matter, isn't it?'

' 'Fraid so,' drawled Mr Worsley. 'I'd rather not say any more about this frightful business over the telephone. But, Mr Marlowe, if it'll put your mind at rest and dispel any suspicion in your mind that I'm just a nasty anonymous caller intent on blackening a man's character, I'll willingly come and see you face to face.'

'Perhaps that would be better, sir.'

'More *honourable*, I feel. What time might your assistant be going to lunch?'

'Mondays we close from one till two.'

'May I come along, then, say about 1.15?'

'Certainly, Mr Worsley, sir. I'll make sure the coast is clear.'

After the call, I prepared myself for Tony's justifiable annoyance.

'How *could* you do this to me, Father? If news of this got out, don't you know what this would do to trade? Imagine, having a violent criminal working in my store!'

I expressed heartfelt sorrow for my fault but in general terms.

'I suppose,' he said softening, 'you didn't realize Archie had a long record.'

'I did,' I admitted.

'Then how *could* you, Father?' said Tony, stamping his foot and puffing furiously at his cigarette.

'I knew and I didn't know, Tony.'

Rena came to my rescue. 'The seal of confession, Father?'

'Something like that.'

'I'm sorry, Father,' said Tony, gentle again. 'The problem is what to do.'

Rena reminded Tony of the time he'd got drunk after a Cup Final at Wembley and thrown an empty quart-sized beer bottle at a pal. It missed and went through the big plate-glass window of Woolworths.

'Yes,' admitted Tony, 'I was "interned" for a while for that.'

'You were lucky you didn't hit him, Tony,' Rena added, 'otherwise you'd have been doing porridge for six months or more.'

Turning to me, Tony said, 'What Rena's trying to say is that I turned violent once and was given a second chance.'

'This isn't quite the same thing, is it?' I said, siding with Tony. I felt I owed him something. 'That was an isolated incident when Tony'd had too much to drink.'

'I agree, Father,' Tony said, glad of support. 'Archie Lee's been bent all his life, so it seems.'

'Once a crook ...' Rena said.

'I'm not his fairy godmother, love, am I? Suppose Archie snatches an old lady's handbag and clouts her on the head, the magistrate'll say to me: 'Did you know the accused had a prison record?' *I* couldn't take refuge in the seal of confession, could I?'

I turned my head away at the unintended rebuke.

'Think,' continued Tony, 'how my reputation and the business would suffer. There'd be a headline in the local rag. I can just see it: "Grocer Employs Violent Ex-Con". And, hell,' he contributed as an afterthought, 'some nosey reporter's bound to dig up the fact that I've been in the nick myself.'

'That settles it,' Rena said with a trace of irony, 'he'll have to go.'

'Let's wait till Mr Worsley arrives,' I proposed. 'He may be able to advise us what's the best course for all concerned.'

At one o'clock Tony dismissed Archie for lunch and soon Mr Peregrine Worsley put in an appearance. He was a stately figure, indeed: polished black shoes; well-creased, pin-striped trousers; black herring-bone jacket with grey silk tie and a rolled umbrella despite the perfect summer's day. When he removed his bowler on entering the room he revealed a bald head as shiny as his shoes.

I took an instant dislike to him. Archie for all his rugged ways, was much more to my taste.

On seeing me, Mr Worsley turned to Tony. 'Called in the strong arm of the Church, eh? Good show. I presume you have told the Vicar of the state of the game.'

Tony assured him I was well briefed.

The visitor hitched up his trousers as he sat down and said, 'A most distressing visit, what, distressing to me and much more so to you.'

'We're grateful to you for taking the time and trouble to come,' said Tony.

'My card,' he said, flourishing a visiting card on which I read at a glance, Peregrine A. Worsley, C.A. and an address which ended Chambers, 'You may care to look at my credentials.'

'No need, sir,' said Tony, waving the card aside so that Mr Worsley returned it to his well-stacked wallet. He stroked his neatly trimmed moustache and adjusted his horn-rimmed spectacles with their very thick lenses.

'I assure you,' Mr Worsley said, returning to the point, 'it's no trouble. I've retired altogether from accountancy. If, in any minute particular, I can ameliorate this wicked world one whit, my life will be complete.'

'To go back to Archie Lee,' began Tony in his blunt way.

'In the presence of your gracious lady and the local vicar, I'm not at leave to catalogue all the misdemeanours of the said Archie Lee. All I can prudently remark on at this moment is his cold-blooded brutality.'

'He seems so gentle,' I said.

'Your kind-heartedness, sir,' replied Mr Worsley, 'is a credit to your cloth. Is it not right that you, a professional humanitarian, should defend the criminal?'

'In only meant,' I added, 'that every one of God's creatures is entitled to a chance.'

'You are enhancing, sir,' said Mr Worsley, 'my opinion of the Church you represent with every utterance. *A* chance, I grant. *Several* chances, that too I will allow. But how many chances? That is the question.'

'Seventy times seven,' I proposed.

'Sir, I feel altogether humbled in the presence of such magnanimity. But, I beg, can the Almighty Himself pardon an unrepentant sinner?'

I thought, 'This Mr Worsley has theological insight as well as expertise in accountancy.'

'No, He cannot,' I conceded.

Mr Worsley now proceeded without interruption. 'Do believe me when I say I am not judging Archie Lee. Many others are employed for *that* purpose by His Majesty's Government. These unsocial habits he has acquired are traceable doubtless to upbringing, environment or personal misfortune. Which of us ought not to bow the head and say: "There but for the grace of God ...?" But I must not trespass on your territory, Vicar, must I?'

I begged him to continue his admirable discourse. He was perfectly willing to oblige.

'We should attempt to reform the individual criminal, that is true. But must not our chief priority be to protect the interests of the great innocent British public?'

'Exactly what I think,' said Tony.

'Now,' Mr Worsley said confidentially, 'let me come clean, as the saying goes, and confess to you my indubitable bias. I happened once to be in a bank in Sunbury, drawing out some money, when in charged the energetic Archie Lee. I was able to witness at first hand the man's barbaric behaviour. He hit one of the customers over the head with a ... sandbag.'

Tony winced.

'I remonstrated with him,' said Mr Worsley, 'and he threatened to "cosh" me too if I didn't "shut my something trap".'

We all exhibited, in varying ways, our disproval.

Mr Worsley went on: 'As you may imagine, my lips were straightaway sealed, but not by any means for ever. The police, naturally, caught up with the miscreant; and that I followed the case very closely I have no need to assure you. I went to court myself in order to "open my trap" and give evidence. Indeed, I was in court the very day that Archie Lee was sentenced.'

'What did he get?' asked Tony.

'Nine months that time. In my opinion, far too humble a sentence for the iniquitous crime I'd seen him commit.'

'What to do now?' asked Tony despairingly.

'Can there be any dispute?' said Mr Worsley, who seemed to know his way around such cases. 'Surely you should dispense with his services forthwith.'

'But on what grounds?' said Tony. 'And what if he decides to turn on me?'

Mr Worsley appealed to me: 'Couldn't you lend a hand, Vicar?'

'I'd like to,' I said, 'but he might think I was the one who betrayed his confidence and lose faith in religion altogether.'

'A sound argument,' conceded Mr Worsley, to my considerable relief. 'You are, reverend sir, if I may put it thus, so wise for a gentleman of such tender years.'

'I've got an idea,' said Tony, snapping his fingers, 'if only you'll give me a bit of help, Father.'

Back at the presbytery, I waited for signs of movement in Fr Duddleswell's bedroom. As soon as he emerged puffy-eyed from his siesta, I invited him into my study to discuss the problem of Archie's sacking. I omitted to say I had been the one to recommend Archie to Tony Marlowe.

After he had heard me out, Fr Duddleswell gave his opinion: 'There is something very fishy about this Peregrine Worsley.'

I hadn't liked the man, I granted, with his archaic use of language and ingratiating compliments. But he seemed trustworthy enough.

'Not at all, Father Neil. In the first place, he gave his address as something "Chambers". Now, there's places aplenty in Kensington and Chelsea and Victoria with that kind of high falutin' name but none such in Fairwater.'

'Which means?'

'It means he's an outsider. He did not just "chance" to be strolling past Tony's store. He must have come of set purpose. Second point: Mr Worsley claims to have seen Archie Lee working in a grocer's shop on the very first morning he takes up his employment. First morning, mark you! What a coincidence, Father Neil! And why, in heaven's name was an accountant interested in what is going on in a grocer's shop? And, for good measure, what splendid eyesight our conscientious gentleman must have.'

'In fact,' I contributed, 'he wears bi-focals.'

'And he claims he saw Archie working in Tony Marlowe's

but did not ring up for a whole hour. Did he take that length of time to look up Tony's number in the telephone directory, or was he perhaps hoping Archie would blot his copybook in the meanwhile? Mr Worsley does not tell a very plausible tale, d'you reckon?'

'What can he be up to then?'

'I'm my view, he's shadowing Archie everywhere or perhaps employing a private detective to do it for him. What his motive is, I cannot tell for sure. Could be was frightened out of his wits when Archie threatened to cosh him and he has had it in for Archie ever since?'

'And now he won't let Archie hold down a steady job?'

'Seems so, but 'tis only an educated guess. 'Tis something out of the ordinary, I'll be bound.'

'But Mr Worsley did take the trouble to come in person, Father.'

'Even that might only be his way of exerting moral pressure. Tony's a nice lad but easily swayed, you follow? He might be disposed by nature to give Archie a chance to make good but not when a respectable, establishment figure like Mr Worsley starts prying and showing disapproval. No, I feel Mr Worsley was pulling out all the stops to get Archie Lee dismissed.'

'And he succeeded.'

As Fr Duddleswell got up to go, he said, 'Father Neil?'

'Yes?'

'It was not you by any chance who found Archie that job?'

'It was.'

Fr Duddleswell slumped down again. 'You did not tell me that,' he said uncomplainingly.

'You didn't ask, Father.'

'A mental reservation?'

I swallowed hard but didn't reply.

'You have one disadvantage, Father Neil, you know that? You have a nut made of glass.' And he recited a verse from *The Mikado*, altering the words, as he sometimes did, to suit himself:

> I know you well,
> You cannot tell
> A false or groundless tale—
> You always try

95

To tell a lie
And every time you fail.

When he had finished, I said, 'I knew he was an ex-con, but not that he had a record of violence.'

' 'Twas too risky anyway, lad.'

I thought for a moment before declaring stubbornly, 'But if we take that attitude, how are we any different from Mr Worsley?'

'Do you not see, Father Neil, that *because* a priest recommends a man for a job, the prospective employer does not vet him as he is entitled to do. *We* can employ an ex-con if we like but we ought not to foist him on another.'

'That's true,' I said. 'Chaps like Archie then'll have to go on following falling stars. But I'm sorry, I made a mistake. You wouldn't have done anything so stupid.'

'I probably would at that,' he said, slowly nodding his head.

'You would?'

'I was only telling you what I *shouldn't* do, not what I *would*.'

'You'd have gone against your better judgement?'

' 'Tis often, Father Neil, the only decent way to behave. Seeing what a lot of Pharisees we are, what great confidence can we put in our better judgement?'

'So I did right, after all?'

'No, young man, you did abysmal wrong.'

'Like you would've?'

'Correct. You asked me advice and I have to say, as any older and wiser mortal should: "For God Almighty's sake, never follow *my* example." ' He shook his head in despair of himself. 'Tea in ten minutes.'

Then he upped and went.

I felt slightly better after that. Except that, for Tony's sake, I had committed myself to aid and abet Mr Worsley in his campaign of victimization. How I disliked that bald-headed accountant with his immaculate attire and fat wallet. Why did he have to pursue Archie so ruthlessly, making him pay ten times over for his misdeeds and provoking him to a life of crime?

In my mind I went over Christ's parable of the Pharisee and the publican. The Pharisee was named Peregrine and it was

Archie who kept banging his breast with a jemmy and muttering, 'Lord, be merciful to me, a sinner.'

At 4.30 precisely, I phoned Tony. He had arranged to have Archie in his office at that time.

'Fairwater 2321,' said Tony, when he picked up the receiver.

'Hello, Tony, it's me, Fr Boyd.'

'*Hello*, Jim,' said Tony breezily. 'Nice to hear your voice again. And so *soon*. I thought your bronchitis would last a month or more.'

I grimly held on to the receiver, wondering whether this fractured conversation was morally permissible.

'That's mighty good news, Jim. You mean the doctor said, he actually said, you can come back to work tomorrow? Great! I look forward to seeing you at 8 o'clock. And, Jim, give my love to the wife and kids.'

Then Tony hung up on me and my family.

At 6.30, Tony rang me again. 'Thanks for your help, Father.'

'How did it go?'

'Like a charm. He took it without a murmur when I explained he wouldn't be needed any more.'

'I'm so glad. I feel I was mostly to blame.'

'Never you mind, Father. Do you know, I think he suspected someone had ratted on him. Didn't complain but looked real crestfallen, he did, as if this has happened to him before.'

'Poor Archie,' I said, for I had a curious fondness for the crook.

'I felt really sorry for him myself. As the wife says, you can't help being a wee bit on his side.'

'You couldn't have done anything else, Tony. Too much of a risk.'

'Sure, Father, but I'm only saying I felt Archie really has turned over a new leaf, that's the sad part. There was the purse he gave back, and another thing ...'

'Yes?'

'Well, when I paid him his wages—£10 as we'd agreed—I said, 'Look here, Archie, I'm awfully sorry to put you to this inconvenience, you having to find another job in midweek and all, here's an extra couple of quid to make up,' you know what he said?'

97

'What?'

' "No deal, Mr Marlowe. We agreed £10 and not an extra farthing will I take." And he *wouldn't*. Ever known a crook turn down two quid when it's been handed to him on a plate?'

'Thanks for ringing me, Tony,' I said in conclusion. 'All's well that ends well.'

Naturally, things hadn't all ended as far as I was concerned. I was troubled lest Archie thought I'd given him away. The day before, I'd taken his address in Begnall Street and I was sorely tempted to call on him and enquire how he was. But I was frightened he might thrown me out or, worse, ask me to find him another job 'under the seal', as it were. On balance, it seemed better to let matters rest. But three days later, I was walking in the High Street when I ran into Archie. My feelings were mixed. I didn't know whether to flee or commiserate with him for losing his job or accuse him of not telling me the truth about his record of violence.

Archie was all smiles. 'Come and join me in a cup o' char, Father?'

I agreed and we sat down in a little café in a side street. I offered to pay but he wouldn't hear of it.

'Be my guest,' he said.

Seeing his pacific mood, I decided to get something off my chest. 'Why didn't you tell me you had convictions for G.B.H.?'

'Why should I, Father? I'm not violent no more. I'm not a thief no more. Why should I tell all and sundry I've got me a record of crime?'

'I'm not exactly all and sundry, Archie.'

'True, Father, but you couldn't 'ave put me in for a job if you knew, could you?'

'No.'

'There y'are then. You weren't to know I'm now gentle as a lamb.'

'One thing, Archie,' I said, conceding the force of his argument.

'Yes, Father?'

'*I* didn't split on you.'

'I know that, Father. It was a bloke called Peregrine Worsley.'

'Has he split on you before, then?'

'Father,' replied Archie, ''e's doing it all the time.'

'I *am* sorry,' I said, my hackles rising again at the thought of Peregrine Worsley, Pharisee.

'Nothin' to be sorry about, Father. 'E's my best pal. We're confederates, always working 'and in glove.'

'You mean this was all a con trick?'

'Nothin' like *that*,' said Archie, horrified. 'Let me explain, Father. Perry used to be an accountant earning five or six grand a year. But 'e got 'isself into 'ot water, embezzling a few thousand more, see? So 'e joins me in a job at a bank in Sunbury. 'E was only trying to straighten 'isself out so 'e wouldn't 'ave to lead a life o' crime. 'E was supposed to be my decoy, only he opened 'is big gob when 'e shouldn't 'ave and nearly ruined everythin'. In the end, we got nabbed, thanks be to Gawd, and put away together.' He looked up from his tea cup. ''E told you all that, I suppose.'

'Not exactly in those terms,' I said with understandable annoyance.

'Anyways, Father. This is 'ow we earns our keep now. I reg'larly get a week's wage for one day's work, sometimes with luck, for 'alf a day.'

'But, Archie,' I cried, very vexed, 'I resent being *used* like this. Don't you realize you've implicated *me* in your crime?'

'Crime, Father?' asked Archie, aghast. 'But where's the crime? We didn't even tell lies.'

'Did you enjoy the roast beef, Fr Duddleswell?' the busty young waitress asked.

'Indeed, I did, Nelly. Me compliments to the cook. If he is in today.'

I was lunching with my parish priest in the restaurant of The Clinton Hotel, a small place with a few tables and a bar, which had something of the atmosphere of a village pub. It was a little luxury we indulged in from time to time to give Mrs Pring 'a holiday from the kitchen sink and ourselves a respite from her stirabout', as Fr Duddleswell put it.

I was dimly aware of Fr Duddleswell asking Nelly if she had managed to buy the house she was after but I was examining the Menu for a dessert and failed to pick up Nelly's reply.

'Father Neil.' I jerked my nose out of the Menu. 'Did y'hear what Nelly said?' I shook my head. 'Nelly's got a flat.'

At this moment Nelly was leaning over the table sweeping up the crumbs with a silver brush and pan. Her capacious bust was but a few challenging inches from my eyes, monopolizing the whole horizon, so to speak. Mesmerized, I could only repeat stupidly, 'Flat? Flat? I don't know what Nelly was shaped like before, Father.'

Nelly gave me the stony eye, straightened up and asked, 'Anything to follow, Fr Duddleswell?'

' 'Twould be difficult to follow that, Nelly,' he replied with a grin. 'The roast, I mean.' He looked across at me. 'How about you, now? Something exotic, Father Neil. Like, say, a hot cup of coffee.'

I closed the Menu and handed it to the waitress. 'Thank you, Father.'

'The cream is extra, Father Neil,'

'Black will be fine,' I said.

Fr Duddleswell touched Nelly's wrist. 'Fetch me curate a black coffee and one with cream for me, Nelly, if you would.' As Nelly was adding his Menu to mine under her arm, he said, 'I think Fr Boyd would appreciate a bowl of strawberries.'

I gave a grateful gurgle which he acknowledged before touching Nelly's wrist again. 'Without cream.'

'Strawberries for you, too, Fr Duddleswell?'

'For me, no.'

'I thought you liked them,' Nelly said.

'I do, Nelly, indeed I do. But the price has risen alarmingly of late and they are far too expensive for the both of us to be eating them.'

As Nelly went on her way, Fr Duddleswell held up what was left of our bottle of Nuits St Georges. 'More wine for yourself?'

'Just a little, Father,' I said, not expecting the fraction of an inch which was all I received.

'Just a little,' breathed Fr Duddleswell, 'for your stomach's sake, as the Apostle counselled Timothy.' He then filled his glass with the remainder. 'Cannot have you abstaining altogether,' he said, 'else Nelly will suspect you of being a Methodist preacher.' In his estimation, that was a slander impossible to live down.

He glanced sideways before putting his left hand to his mouth in what he took to be a surreptitious movement. From behind the barricade, he muttered like a gangster, 'Over there, lad.' He indicated two elderly ladies coming to the end of their meal at an adjoining table. 'The two Miss Flanagans.'

'Catholics, I presume.'

'They turn up more regularly at Mass than Jesus Himself.'

The ladies must have caught his eye because he smiled courteously and acknowledged them. 'Miss Flanagan, Miss Flanagan.' I half-rose and joined in with 'Misses Flanagan.'

Nelly brought my strawberries. 'Coffee coming up, Gentlemen.'

Fr Duddleswell, in one of his more mischievous moods, remarked, 'I do not for the life of me know how someone shaped like Nelly will fit into a flat.'

If this was some sort of a game, I wasn't playing. I dug into my dessert.

' 'Tis a strange thing, Father Neil, the association of ideas.

Some are good, and some of 'em are bad.'

A meticulous observation, I thought.

'A good association of ideas, now.' Plucking a strawberry from my dish before I could rap his knuckles with my spoon, he held it aloft by the stalk. ' 'Tis when you look at a strawberry and it reminds you of the Sacred Heart of Jesus.' He swallowed it.

I had heard him crack that one before. To humour the likeable old chap I asked, 'And a bad association of ideas?'

As if he had prepared and rehearsed it well in advance, he drew from his inside pocket the relevant gaudy 'holy' picture and held it up for me to see. ' 'Tis when you see a picture of the Sacred Heart and it reminds you of a strawberry.'

Poised to bite such a hallowed object, I set it down slowly on the dish. Right, so it was war.

'I was thinking, Father.'

'Very daring of you, Father Neil.'

'What did you do with the money from the Bazaar?'

'The money from the Bazaar?' he echoed, as if it were news to him there'd been a Bazaar. 'Why, of course, 'twent into the fund for the church hall.'

'All of it?'

'All of it?' he said in a kind of minor key. I nodded. 'All that was donated by the insurance company, that is.'

'And the rest?'

'Oh, the offerings of the faithful, too, naturally.'

'Naturally. And Billy Buzzle's contribution?'

'The faithful were very generous in our hour of need, wouldn't you say?'

I looked at him without blinking.

'Billy Buzzle's contribution? Well, I could not advertise that, could I?'

'I'm not suggesting you stashed it away in a private account in Zurich,' I said. The red wine was making me belligerent.

'There is no *secret* about it, Father Neil. 'Tis gone into the Wallington Building Society where it brings us in a good three per cent per annum. The interest goes towards the expenses of the church.'

'Precisely, and in my view we ought to spend some of that money.'

Fr Duddleswell who, as Mrs Pring observed, was tight as a reefknot with parish funds, his bell apart, looked agitated. 'What on?' he asked.

'You know the mikes in our church.'

'Mike O'Leary, Mike O'Donnel, Mike ...' It was a brave attempt.

'The microphone mikes,' I said.

He was very much aware he was being got at. 'Ah, yes? Polish off those strawberries, now, and do not be wasting parish funds.'

I refused the hint. 'I think you need a new loudspeaker system. The one we've got gives off a terrible hum. The congregation can't hear you. Not even your appeals for money.' The last part registered, at any rate.

As Nelly arrived with the coffee, I added, 'You also need new confessionals, Father.'

'Nelly,' he said, 'what did you lace those strawberries with?'

With a puzzled expression, poor Nelly went back to her work.

'Father Neil, what is wrong with the confessionals we have?'

'They're made of cardboard. Not sound-proof. I read in an old parish magazine that they were put up during the First World War.'

'Things were better made in the old days.' He spoke with a dreamy nostalgia.

'In war-time, Father, there are always economy measures and the confessionals must have been one of them.'

'Have they not served the parish well these last forty years?' I paused dramatically.

'Well, have they *not*?'

'Someone who shall be nameless, Father, walked past your confessional and heard a penitent confess to ... adultery.'

Fr Duddleswell nearly choked on his wine. ''Tis not possible.'

'You mean there's no adultery in your parish?' I asked with a kind of tipsy irony.

'Keep your voice *down*, Father Neil.' He caught the eyes of the ladies again and smiled sickly. 'Miss Flanagan. Miss Flanagan.' From behind his hand again: 'I mean nobody, but *nobody* could possibly hear what is being said in my confessional.'

103

'Father, with respect,' I said, 'could it be that your hearing isn't as good as it was?' Before he could object, I added, 'And to be honest, Father, mine isn't all it should be, either. I'm going to Dr Daley's soon to have my ears syringed. I'm finding difficulty in hearing what penitents say to me these days. I keep having to tell them to speak up.'

''Tis hard to credit that what is said in ...'

'Mrs Conroy, Father.'

'What about Mrs Conroy?' he snapped.

'Mrs Conroy, the butcher's wife, and the undertaker,'

'The undertaker is Mr Bottesford,' he said, reduced to a whisper.

'Rumour has it that Mrs Conroy and the undertaker are ... you know.'

'Father Neil, you are talking in riddles like the prophet Daniel. Know *what*?'

I swallowed a strawberry with a gulp. 'Having an affair.'

''Tis news to me,' said Fr Duddleswell, biting his lip and tapping with his foot.

'If you *have* heard of it in confession your lips are sealed, I know. You can't say they're committing adultery ...'

'Keep your voice *down*,' he interrupted me angrily. Another polite nod and smile to the ladies. 'Miss Flanagan. Miss Flanagan.'

I insisted on completing my sentence. 'And you can't say they're not.'

'I *am* saying they are *not*.'

'Father,' I said in a hoarse whisper, 'I'm not asking you to pass judgement on allegations of a parish scandal. I realize I'll never know if what you're saying now is a mental reservation or the plain, unvarnished truth.' Before he could edge in, I continued, 'Even if you say it's the plain unvarnished truth, that too may be another quite legitimate mental reservation to defend the seal of confession as best you can.'

'What is the point of all this?'

'It's this. The scandal, justified or not, has gained ground because parishioners suspect that the walls of our confessionals have ears.'

Fr Duddleswell missed the last bit. He was distracted by two men who had come in through the back door and were making a bee-line for the bar. As they brushed our table, they said in unison, 'Afternoon, Fathers.'

Fr Duddleswell recovered quickly from what must have been a nasty surprise. 'Fr Boyd, this is Bottesford, the undertaker.' I shook hands with the big, burly man who wore a black tail-coat and carried a topper. 'And this,' Fr Duddleswell went on, 'is Mr Conroy, husband of Mrs Conroy.' Realizing the inappropriateness of such an introduction he tried to cover it up with, 'And the best black-market butcher in the business.'

Mr Conroy, smiling at the compliment, tipped his straw hat and took my hand. 'Liking the parish, Father?'

'It's more interesting,' I replied, 'than I can possibly tell you, Mr Conroy.'

Mr Bottesford took advantage of the chance meeting to criticize one aspect of my parochial performance so far. 'You've not put any custom my way as yet, Fr Boyd.' He handed me a black-edged card. 'My motto is: "Go to the Lord, with Bottesford". Ten per cent reduction for deceased Catholics, as you'd expect.'

'Do not let us keep you gentlemen,' hinted Fr Duddleswell, and the butcher and the burier went to the bar for a quick jar.

'They seem good pals,' I said guiltily.

'The best, Father Neil. They are both in the meat-trade, in a manner of speaking. The butcher would surely know if he was drinking with a man who undressed his prime joint.'

I acknowledged the force of that.

'Mrs Conroy,' he went on, 'is very silly even as women go but she must realize that if she went into the undertaker's parlour she would suffer a fate far worse than death.'

'I'll have to tell Mrs Pring there's ...'

He cut across me. 'I knew it was she.'

Anxious for a change of topic, I asked, 'Is Mr Bottesford married?'

'He is. But his two children left home long ago and his wife just ran off with a commercial traveller.' He drained his glass. 'So he has a lot to be thankful for.'

He jerked his chin at the last of my strawberries. 'Did you by any chance intend to eat that?'

'I don't think so, Father.'

He grabbed and swallowed it. 'We will motor back to the church to experiment, like.'

He rose, said a quick grace and pointed to Winston Churchill's picture hanging on the wall a few yards from our table. 'Astonishing man, Father Neil.'

I drained my cup and got to my feet. 'Yes, Father.'

'He has brains,' said Fr Duddleswell, shaking his head with incredulity, 'to lick the Hun and still not enough to become a Catholic.'

'Time for the news, Father Neil.'

It was ten minutes later and he had me standing in the pulpit with the heavy old-fashioned mike round my neck.

I looked down the church at him. 'My dear brother in Christ,' I began in as muffled a manner as I could manage.

'Get on with you, lad.'

'My text is: "Father Noah hogged the wine and became drunk and lay naked in his tent".' The church's emptiness made my voice echo and re-echo. The indistinctness of my contribution was beyond question.

Fr Duddleswell was scratching his head. ''Tis right what you say, Father Neil.'

I cupped my hand to my ear. 'What did you say, Father?'

He beckoned me to leave the pulpit. When I joined him, he was muttering, 'It sounds as mixed up as a woman's motives or an Irish stew, and no mistake.' He enlisted my help once more. 'Now, into me box and confess your sins.' Seeing my unwillingness, he said, 'I promise to keep whatever you confess under the seal.' As I entered, he called after me, 'And do not forget to admit you gobbled up all those strawberries when there are millions starving in India.'

I knelt down and fairly bellowed in my clearest accents, 'Bless me, Father, for I have sinned.' Since he didn't tell me to stop, I shouted on, 'It's twenty years since my last confession. I stole the sweet rations of the children in the orphanage. I didn't wash my feet last month. I committed adultery.'

Fr Duddleswell gave a sharp tap on the box.

Lingering lovingly on each loud syllable, I cried, 'Did you hear my A-DUL-TER-Y?'

Another tap and a crisp command. 'That is enough, Father Neil. 'Tis quite enough, d'you hear me speak to you?'

I emerged from the confessional with a sense of a job well done. The smile vanished immediately from my face when I saw who was kneeling piously in the rear bench.

Fr Duddleswell said, 'Miss Flanagan. Miss Flanagan.' And this time, I thought it polite to add, 'Miss Flanagan. Miss Flanagan,' on my own account.

In a soft voice, Fr Duddleswell said, 'Your sins àre a deal more entertaining than your sermons.'

One of the ladies stood up. In a loud stage-whisper: 'Would you mind hearing our confessions, Fr Duddleswell?'

'Delighted, Miss Flanagan, delighted.' To me, he said, 'God forgive me for being such a hypocrite. Into the house with you. Cannot have you hovering in the vicinity of me confessional. These two old dears may have been handing round more elderberry wine.'

He entered his box and turned about to face me. 'If I am not out by supper time, fetch me me nose-bag here.'

He gave the gentle whinny of a horse and slammed the top half of his box.

Back in the presbytery, I told Mrs Pring about my ears. Immediately she came to my room armed with a spirit lamp, a spoon and a bottle of olive oil.

She sat me down and draped a towel round my neck. 'I'll spoon-feed your ears with olive oil to loosen the wax that's blocking them,' she said.

As she went about her work, I apologized for letting her down. I admitted mentioning her name in connection with Mr Bottesford and Mrs Conroy. She shrugged it off as of no consequence. Fr D had to learn somehow.

'You did actually hear what Mrs Conroy said in confession, Mrs P?'

'No.'

'No?'

'Mrs Davis, my friend who's an assistant in Woolworth's, she heard.'

I was shaken to discover that what I had relayed to Fr Duddleswell in good faith was only an unsubstantiated rumour. When I told Mrs Pring that only a few minutes earlier we had seen the butcher and the undertaker having a friendly pint together she uttered a dire warning about what she would do to 'that hussy Mrs Davis' next time they met. I agreed it would be kind to put the record right.

'I went to Fr D for confession,' said Mrs Pring dreamily.

'Only once.'

'So did I,' I said. 'But that was brave of you, Mrs P.'

'Not really. I told him exactly what I thought of him. That's the only time he's ever forgiven me.' She broke off. 'Hold your head to one side, please.' I obliged. 'Don't forget your convert is coming for her first instruction this afternoon.'

'What's she like?'

Mrs Rollings, she explained, was married to the baker. Wilf was a cradle-Catholic and they had twin boys aged eight. As to Mrs Rollings herself, Mrs Pring suggested, 'Fr D's handed her over to you because he considers her unteachable. And for once in his life, he may be right.'

'Any idea why she wants to become a Catholic?'

'Strictly between you and me, Father Neil?' I nodded. She bowed her head conspiratorially. 'I think she wants to become Pope.'

A last scalding of my ear with olive oil, a plug of cotton wool and she was done just as Fr Duddleswell appeared.

He eyed her with disfavour. 'If 'tisn't Saint Joan of Arc herself with her heavenly voices. Our very own furtive fly on the confessional wall.'

'I only tried to help.'

'Woman,' he said, 'if you milked a cow 'twould come out curdled.'

'I said,' repeated Mrs Pring, 'I was only trying ...'

'Indeed,' broke in Fr Duddleswell, 'you are *very* trying, but I am not here to discuss the secrets of the confessional with the likes of you.' And he started shooing her out.

Mrs Pring pouted, picked up her equipment and exited with a sigh.

When I apologized for having spoken too hastily, he replied:

'Not at all. I heard every wicked thing you uttered in the blackness. Tell me, now.'

I had already done some research and drew a pamphlet out of my pocket which he snatched from me.

'There's a firm near Westminster Abbey,' I said, 'which sells neck mikes that work off a battery. They're light and you only need one. You can wear it all through Mass, whether you're at the altar, in the pulpit or moving along the altar rails distributing Communion.'

'The price?'

'A hundred pounds,' I said, adding quickly, 'but the congregation will hear your appeals to pay for it.'

'I will think on it. And the confessionals, like?'

'Sixty pounds.'

'Each?'

I nodded. 'Sound-proof and installed in a week.'

'Sixty pounds each,' he mused.

I could see he was impressed by the relative modesty of the outlay. 'Not much is it, Father, to safeguard the seal of confession?'

'Mind you,' he appeared to say, 'we will have to make stringent economies to pay for them. No more living riotously like the Prodigal Son on Nelly's strawberries.'

What with my plugged ears, once we got off the topic of mikes and confessionals I found difficulty in understanding him. I gathered it was something to do with strawberries. Recalling his stress on economy at The Clinton Hotel I said innocently, 'Nelly's strawberries? Without cream, Father.'

I saw his shocked look and lip-read him saying, 'What d'you mean by that?'

'What did you mean, Father?' What could he have seen in such a harmless remark?

'*I* meant strawberries, Father Neil.'

'And *I* meant cream.'

'You did?'

'I did.'

'Then there is no quarrel between us.'

If there had been I would not have known what it was about.

He held the pamphlet up. 'I will keep this and peruse it at me leisure. And remember, Mrs Rollings is visiting you this afternoon. She is a very good woman and that really is her only fault. Since she is your very first convert, I will be on hand, this once, to offer you me ... condolences.'

Mrs Rollings, eager, inquisitive, highly-strung, perched on the edge of her chair as she made ready to interrogate me.

I explained to her the difference between mortal and venial sin; how mortal sins like murder and rape ruptured communion with God whereas venial sins like white lies or stealing sixpence diminished friendship with God but didn't demolish it altogether. Next, I told her that in this sacrament the penitent is obliged to tell the priest all his mortal sins, their number and species.'

'What's that mean?' she asked in a quavering voice.

I explained that the penitent has to say exactly what sort of mortal sin he's committed—murder, abortion, large-scale theft—and how many times he's committed it.

'Catholics have to keep a strict count of things like that?'

'Pardon?' I said, taking the cotton wool out of one ear.

'A strict count?'

'Yes.' And I put the plug back in.

'If a murderer or a raper or a crook confess their sins, are they forgiven?' I nodded. 'And if they die they go to heaven?'

I was pleased to tell her that God is very merciful.

'May be,' came back Mrs Rollings, 'but Heaven don't sound very safe for children. Catholics have to confess regular, I suppose, because of all those rules to break. Sunday Mass, no meat on Fridays, etcetera. They must find mortal sins easier than normal people.'

I made no comment on that.

'Tell me about yourself, Father.'

'Myself?' I repeated, slightly panicky.

'Yes, do *you* go to confession?'

'All priests go to confession every two weeks.'

'Nuns. too?'

'Every eight days.'

'Go on,' she said. 'What *do* they get up to, locked in behind them high walls? More often than priests. Those nuns must have very strong urges.'

'Even the Pope confesses regularly,' I said in the nuns' defence.

'Really, she whistled. 'But *you*, Father, do you prefer going to confession or hearing them?'

'It all depends,' I hedged.

'On?'

I refused to be drawn. 'It all depends.'

She had too many lines of enquiry to pursue to bother about one cul de sac. 'If I became a Catholic, Father, would I have to confess all my sins to you?'

'All your *mortal* sins.' I added hurriedly, 'That's if you have committed any, of course, Mrs Rollings.'

'Will you settle something for me, Father?'

'If I can.'

'The other day, I heard one of mine arguing with the other about this: if an altar boy puts poison in the priest's wine and tells him so in confession just before Mass, has the priest got to drink that wine?'

It was an old chestnut. 'I've heard of that case,' I said.

'What's your answer?'

'There are several opinions,' I said professorially. 'One solution is to say the priest mustn't break the seal of confession for any purpose whatsoever.'

'So he drinks it and dies?'

'Yes. Another suggestion is that since the altar boy has poisoned the wine and refused to tip it away, he's not going to confession with the right intention. He's going not to confess his sins but simply to gloat over the terrible trouble he's causing the priest.'

'So?'

'Since he's not making a real confession, so this argument goes, the priest could either denounce the self-confessed altar boy assassin or secretly empty the wine down the drain and refill the cruet.'

'But what do *you* think, Father?'

'I think a priest should always choose to uphold the secrecy of the confessional.'

'Then you'd drink the poisoned wine?'

'It'd be safer,' I said.

'Safer?'

'For the sacrament, I mean. Above all else, we must protect the seal of confession.'

Mrs Rollings seemed enthusiastic about the whole thing. 'I'm very interested in this confession business.' That pleased me until she dipped down to the personal level again. 'Have you been a priest long?'

'Two or three months.'

'How old are you, then?'

Reluctantly I admitted I was getting on for twenty-four.

'And you're not married?'

'Catholic priests,' I told her, 'aren't allowed to marry.' I hoped that might impress her.

'What use are *you* in confession, then?'

I took out an earplug to make sure I had heard her correctly.

'How can you say people mustn't use birth control,' she asked, 'when you're ... well, you don't practise marriage?'

There was a knock on the door and Fr Duddleswell, bleary-eyed from his siesta, appeared. He sized up the situation in an instant.

'I thought you were free, Father Neil, but I see you are a prisoner.'

'Come in, Father. *Please* come in. Mrs Rollings was just asking about contraception.'

' 'Tis forbidden.'

'I know,' she said, 'but why?'

'Because 'tis a grievous sin, that's why.'

'I see,' said a cowed Mrs Rollings.

'Another thing, Mrs Rollings,' said Fr Duddleswell. 'Do not use that word "why?" too often, like.'

That word was on the tip of Mrs Rollings' tongue when she bit it off and said, 'No, Father.'

' "Why" is a nasty little Protestant word, you follow? Catholics, now, say, "*Credo*, I Believe," to whatever the Pope says. If you want to ask "Why?" go ask the Anglican vicar to instruct you in unbelief and he will let you "Why-why-why?" to your heart's content.'

Poor Mrs Rollings was like a flat dose of salts after that. All she could say was, 'But you *are* bound to keep secret what you hear in confession?'

'Mrs Rollings,' replied Fr Duddleswell, softening towards her, 'a priest has to protect the seal at all costs. Suppose you come to me in confession. Am I permitted to tell your husband who is next in line what you have revealed to me? Or may I tell Father Neil here? Indeed, I may not.' He pursed his lips for emphasis. 'Not even if you have confessed to squandering your whole week's housekeeping money on a bowlful of strawberries.'

A week later, Fr Duddleswell and I were standing in church in front of a new, solid-looking confessional bearing the name FR CHARLES DUDDLESWELL. It had two lights, red and green, for engaged and free.

'There, now, Father Neil, what d'you think of her?' I drew in my breath in the manner expected of me. 'Inside with you and put her to the test.'

He said that or something like it. I couldn't be sure because a combination of wax, olive oil and cotton wool had qualified me for a deaf-aid on the National Health.

I spoke some less reprehensible sins this time and considerably softer. Still he banged on the box. I just made out the word 'Louder'. I tried to give value for money. I only stopped when he opened the door and yelled, 'The all-clear has sounded. Lazarus, come forth.' Plainly, he had ordered me more than once to dry up.

Outside, he said something which I made him repeat. 'Father Neil, I am mighty glad you have mended your ways.' I smiled and he mouthed slowly, 'WHAT THE HELL IS THE MATTER WITH YOU?'

I outlined my predicament.

'Deaf?'

'I couldn't hear my own confession, Father.'

To that I think he said, 'Saved you scandalizing yourself, at any rate.' He mouthed again, 'GO SEE DR DALEY AND HAVE YOUR EARS SYRINGED.'

I nodded. 'What about buying the new mike, Father?'

He cupped his hand to his ear. 'Pardon?'

'The new mike, Father.'

'SPEAK UP, LAD,' he enunciated clearly, 'I AM HARD OF HEARING, YOU FOLLOW?' He relaxed to tell me, I guessed, that he *had* decided to purchase the new mike.

To make sure, I said, 'Pardon, Father?'

His final remarks were unmistakable. 'Bloody heavens, Father Neil, go see Dr Daley about those ears straight away. Talking to you is almost as ruinous as talking to Mrs Pring.'

Dr Daley, portly and bald, was as Irish as a sprig of shamrock. On his shelf, that Saturday afternoon, was a bottle of whiskey, the worse for wear, and an empty glass. A lighted cigarette was wedged in the corner of his mouth.

'The first ear done,' he said, as he surveyed the yellow debris floating in the small enamel bowl he held in his left hand. In his right was an enormous brass syringe. 'Enough wax there to build three tall beehives in Connemara.'

He was speaking in a kind of monologue, apparently under the impression that I couldn't hear a thing. This wasn't so. I was only completely deaf in spasms now. Some of what he said got through to me, including:

'You are deaf as an adder for the moment, Fr Boyd, which is why I'm going to make my confession to you.' He gestured to the bottle. 'A drink of poteen, Father? Of course not. Mind if I do? The drought is upon me, you see.'

He poured himself another treble and raised his glass to me. 'Cheers, Father.' He drained his glass, without removing his cigarette, in one gulp. He put the glass down with a crash and took up the syringe in a trembling hand.

'Without the hard stuff, I'd be a bundle of nerves.' At this, he launched the brass torpedo into my other ear. 'The ears of my soul are deaf to the Almighty's entreaties to give up the drink. Sweet Jesus, but it is impossible—keep yourself still, Father—to straighten the twist in an old stick, and that's the truth. Charles, our revered parish priest, has sounded the fire-alarm at me often enough and raised the ladder to the burning building. But it's no good, you see. I will surely end up with flames licking all round me and not so much as a friendly spark to light my fag with.' He shone his torch in my ear. 'In a minute of two, the bubbles will burst.'

Then nothing. But I had heard enough already. I was sad for old Dr Daley and his unavailing efforts after his wife died to give up the booze. I was worried about my hearing, too. The doctor had rid me of half a dozen large pellets of wax. What was the meaning of this uncanny, inner wall of silence? I wondered whether he had shot right through my eardrums and deafened me for life.

Then followed two small explosions in quick succession, one in each ear. It was as if a sound-proof door had suddenly been thrown open on to Piccadilly Circus at the rush hour.

'They've popped, have they?' roared Dr Daley.

I nodded and rubbed both ears in amazement. Every sound was considerably magnified with electrical clarity.

'Try combing your hair,' he suggested.

I put the comb through my hair and it made a noise like giants crawling through a field of straw.

Dr Daley proceeded to reward himself by filling his glass to the brim.

'For a day or two, Father, before you adjust, your electric razor will scream at you like a pneumatic drill.' He paused to steady his glass. 'I have it on prescription, you see,' was his explanation. 'And you'll be able to hear the circulation of your blood, as well as everyone else's in a three mile radius.'

Dr Daley knelt with a wobble, signing himself and making sure he didn't spill a drop.

'Now, give me your blessing, Father.'

I felt he had earned spiritual rewards of every sort. As I stood over him, gratefully, he bowed his broad, flat, wrinkled head.

That evening, as Fr Duddleswell was serving supper, there was a small, elegant box on the table beside his plate.

'Before I waste me precious breath,' he said behind his hand, 'tell me if you are still deaf or no.'

'I hear you painfully well,' I said.

He wanted to know where I had been that afternoon. The men had come to fix the loudspeaker system in the church. I told him of my visit to Dr Daley's.

'Well oiled?' he asked.

'He was.'

'I know *he* was,' he said. 'I was referring to the wax in your ears.'

He proudly opened up the box to reveal the new, miniature mike.

'There she is, Father Neil. Light as a feather, clear as a bell.' He lifted it up and fitted it round his neck. 'It works like a charm. Audible to the deaf and the dead.' That rang a bell. 'Where is Mrs Pring?'

I listened for a moment and enlightened him. 'At the back door, having words with Mrs Davis from Woolworth's. Mrs Pring is giving her a piece of her mind.'

'Which she can ill afford,' said Fr Duddleswell, absorbed in the microphone's beauty. He awoke from his reverie to strain his own ears. 'How did you know that, Father Neil?'

Without waiting for my reply he went to the door and called, 'Mrs Pring!' As the lady of the house came running, he growled, ' 'Tis the Charge of the Heavy Brigade.'

'Speak, Lord,' said a breathless Mrs Pring, 'for thy servant heareth.'

'Father Neil, there is nothing like a dutiful woman to cheerfullize the place. Now, Mrs Pring, I have decided in view of the vile thieves abounding round here to keep this new microphone on me mantelshelf instead of in the sacristy. You may go.'

Mrs Pring stood there amazed. 'Where to?'

'Do not tempt me, woman,' he replied.

Mrs Pring almost intoned, 'May God in His mercy stretch out His hand to you, Fr Duddleswell, and strike you down.'

'I am more determined than ever,' he returned, 'to save up and send you to America.' As Mrs Pring made to leave for a destination of her own choosing, he called after her:

'Oh, and, Mrs Pring. I will be saying the two early Masses tomorrow morning. I do not want Father Neil to oversleep himself. When you get up, would you mind tapping on his door with your tongue?'

Next morning, I rushed downstairs and almost collided with Mrs Pring as she returned from the eight o'clock Mass.

'How did the new mike sound, Mrs P?'

'Terrible.'

'Terrible?'

'For the first time in years I could hear every word of his sermon.' As I bent down to do up the last few buttons of my cassock, she reflected ruefully, 'It's a good job that man doesn't practise what he preaches. I couldn't stand it.'

I opened my arms wide in the ritual gesture. 'I could hear his *Dominus Vobiscum*,' I said, 'even through the roar of my razor.'

In church, the benches were beginning to fill up. I was relieved to see I wasn't late. No one was waiting outside my confessional. I entered, sat, removed the cotton wool from my ears which I still wore as a protection against noise and started to recite my breviary.

'Bless me, Father, for I have sinned.' It was a woman's voice. I was surprised because I hadn't heard a penitent come in. I raised my right hand and was about to give the blessing when another gave it: Fr Duddleswell. '*Dominus sit in corde ... in nomine Patris et Filii et Spiritus Sancti. Amen*. And how long is it since your last confession?'

I knew my hearing had improved within the last few hours but I wasn't prepared for anything like this. I could distinctly hear what was going on in Fr Duddleswell's allegedly sound-proof box forty-five feet away.

The penitent said, 'Two weeks, Father, and these are my sins. I told a few white lies.'

'No such thing,' said Fr Duddleswell, 'all lies are black, as well you know.'

'I told a few little black lies.'

It was impressed on her that lies of whatever hue are never *little*, either. I stuffed the cotton wool back in my ears but it made no difference. While it was instructive to witness the master at work, I could hardly listen in good conscience to the penitent's confession when I was in no position to grant her absolution.

'I gave short change in the shop, Father,' the lady said.

'How long is short?'

'Only the odd threepence and sixpence on a joint, Father.'

That was when it hit me that the penitent was Mrs Conroy, the butcher's wife. Having identified her, I was entitled even less to sit there listening to confidences not meant for me. I pushed open the door of my box, intending to return to the house. Immediately I did so, I became aware of the electric atmosphere in the church.

Fr Duddleswell was still wearing the portable mike and had forgotten to switch the thing off. Either that or the whole congregation was also graced with supra-sensitive hearing.

Fr Duddleswell was saying, ' "Only" is the divil's own word, me dear. You will have to make restitution, will you not? Let me ponder, now.'

While he pondered, the congregation started turning with varying emotions towards Fr Duddleswell's box. Some laughed and some frowned. One lady had her handkerchief over her mouth while her rosary was dangling from her hand, another pressed her fingers in her ears. A child was standing on a bench holding a toy train and pointing in Fr Duddleswell's direction.

'The best thing for you to do, I'm thinking,' decided Fr Duddleswell, 'is to undercharge a few customers this week. That was you will make up for what you overcharged them last week. Will you do that for me, now?'

I spied Mr Conroy outside Fr Duddleswell's box, still as a stone, his jaw almost to his chest, while from within came Mrs Conroy's voice:

'I promise you, I'll do that.'

'Anything else?' asked Fr Duddleswell, with the slight world-weariness of the skilled confessor.

By this time, I was creeping on tiptoe round the back of the congregation, heading for Fr Duddleswell's confessional. I was careful to genuflect slowly at the centre aisle. Apart from anything else, it gave me a few more precious seconds to reflect on what I ought to do.

'I added three pounds to my housekeeping from my husband's takings, Father.'

Mr Conroy's face registered annoyance at that but he recovered somewhat when Fr Duddleswell told his wife she must give that back, too.

'Anything else bothering you, me dear?'

'Yes, Father. I thought Thursday was Friday.'

'Where is the sin in that?'

'Well, I ate meat thinking it was Friday, so I don't know if that was a sin or not.'

Fr Duddleswell was subject to no such uncertainty. 'If you intended to sin, you sinned.'

I had reached Mr Conroy. I gripped his arm and told him to accompany me. 'We'll turn the switch of the loudspeaker off,' I told him. 'That way, we won't interfere with the confession.'

Out of the corner of my eye, I saw Mr Bottesford the undertaker higher up the aisle first sidling and then positively scuttling towards us. He almost knocked me and Mr Conroy flat.

'Morning, Father,' he said to me in passing, and to Mr Conroy, 'Sorry, Bill.'

As we advanced up the aisle, Mrs Conroy was saying, 'It was only an ounce or two. And it *was* chicken.'

'So?' asked Fr Duddleswell.

'Chicken's not really meat, is it, Father?'

'It is so,' Fr Duddleswell insisted, as I began to examine the loudspeaker by the side of the pulpit. I only wished I had been present when the system was installed.

'But chickens come from eggs, Father.'

'I am long aware that chickens come from eggs, me dear, even though the Church has not yet defined which of 'em came first. Is there some point to all this?'

When I told Mr Conroy there wasn't a switch on the loud-speaker he begged me to pull the wire out. I saw there was no alternative. I pulled and pulled. Instead of snapping, the wire kept coming.

'Chickens come from eggs, argued Mrs Conroy, 'and you can eat eggs on Fridays.'

'If fish laid meat balls you still could not eat meat balls on Fridays.'

In desperation I asked Mr Conroy if he had a knife. No. I asked a lady in the front row if she had any scissors and she fished me a pair out of her handbag. As I held it aloft in triumph for Mr Conroy to see, Mrs Conroy, unaware of our efforts to preserve what was left of her honour, was still insisting that chicken isn't meat.

'Look,' said an exasperated Fr Duddleswell, 'd'you sell chicken in your shop?'

'Yes.'

'Then chicken is meat.'

'But we sell eggs, too, Father.'

'For the purposes of confession,' said Fr Duddleswell, coming the heavy, 'the Pope has decreed that chicken is meat.'

Mrs Conroy capitulated. 'Then bless me, Father, for I have sinned.'

'Was there something else?'

I thanked God we would never know, for at that moment I cut the wire. Mr Conroy and I sighed with the sense of a job well done. We had caused some material damage but that was easily repairable. The main thing was we had not meddled with the sacrament of Christ's forgiveness. As I instinctively held out the hand of comradeship to Mr Conroy, Mrs Conroy said:

'I'm still thinking, Father.'

My comrade and I looked at each other aghast, then at the *second* loudspeaker. We genuflected to the Blessed Sacrament at the centre and stood beneath the speaker. It was much higher up than the first, with no wires visible from below. If I stood on the butcher's shoulders I might just about reach it. Contrariwise, I might fall and break a leg.

'Get a chair, quick,' I said, and he started desperately looking round for one.'

Then, the crushing blow. In a voice which dipped with self-consciousness but was still perfectly audible all over the church, Mrs Conroy said, 'I committed adultery again last week, Father.'

'With a gentleman,' Fr Duddleswell put it discreetly, 'you say, not your husband?'

This was too bad. I gave up any idea of looking for chairs and wires and set off, running on tiptoe, in the direction of Fr Duddleswell's box.

'With the undertaker, Father,' said Mrs Conroy.

'I do not wish to know what your accomplice does for a living.'

'I didn't mean to do it.'

'Not mean to?'

'He induced me,' whimpered Mrs Conroy. 'In the cemetery, Father. Didn't seem quite right somehow, Father, under the yew tree with all those grave stones looking on.'

Fr Duddleswell was not put off his task by the beautiful outlook. 'How many times?'

'Twice times twice, Father.' She paused before adding, 'And once, almost, Father.'

'Which means?' asked a puzzled Fr Duddleswell.

'They started to shut the cemetery gates, Father.'

'I see.'

I was now outside Fr Duddleswell's box, well aware it was far too late to mar his model interrogation. Even then it cost me an effort to intrude on someone's confession. I plucked up the necessary courage as Mrs Conroy had her final word:

'He said he didn't want to stay in all night as well as all day, Father.'

I flung the door open. There was Fr Duddleswell sitting, wearing a long white alb, purple stole and the new mike. I was met by two large eyes quite horse-like in their astonishment.

I went for the microphone cord round his neck, but since I still had the scissors in one hand, he could not make out whether I intended to strangle him or cut his throat.

'Are you out of your *mind*, Father Neil?'

I snatched the cord from him without a word.

Shall I ever forget Fr Duddleswell's look of horror as it dawned on him that for the first time in his long and venerable priestly career he had broken the seal of confession?

VII *The Bethrothal*

' 'Twill be a bit of a farce, I am warning you in advance,' said Fr Duddleswell. 'But, as you will discover, there are times when charity demands we go along with the whims and fancies of the faithful.'

The reason for this caution was the betrothal of a young Sicilian couple who came from the families Bianchi and Christini. The Bianchis lived on Fr Duddleswell's side of the parish, the Christinis lived on mine.

'I'm glad it's a joint effort,' I said. 'I don't speak a word of Italian.'

'Neither do they,' Fr Duddleswell said. 'When they are together, they speak an impossible dialect but they will probably take pity on me and converse in half-English and half-Italian.'

It was such a fine summer's morning, we chose to walk; and first to go to the Bianchis, who were providing the bride.

'This,' said Fr Duddleswell, 'will be an occasion the like of which you have never seen. Sicilians are marvellous Christians but impossible Catholics, except for important celebrations.'

'Christenings, weddings, funerals?' I suggested.

'*And* the big feasts like Christmas, Epiphany, Easter. For the rest, churchgoing is left entirely to the ladies. Do you know, Father Neil, when I once said to old Bianchi, the head of the family, 'Why do you not come to Mass every Sunday?' he replied, "We is *Cattolici non fanatici*".'

I smiled hoping I'd understood the joke.

' 'Tis a strange thing, Father Neil, but some Italians who never go to Mass in their lives leave pots of money in their will for Masses to be said for them when they die.'

'Illogical,' I said.

'There was one chap I knew, name of Zeffirelli, who left

£1,000 for Requiems, all at the lowest rate of five shillings a time. Kept an African missionary in stipends for over a decade.'

'Ten years of black Masses!' I said sympathetically.

'The poor fellow probably needed every single one of 'em, Father Neil. Otherwise he would have been locked up in Purgatory, like, till the place shuts. Now back to this betrothal business. Tomfoolery or no, 'tis important to them. The Sicilians came to England from Messina in 1908, or the original stock did. Survivors of the earthquake. The eldest, Signor Bianchi, was only a lad when he last saw his native land. The same goes for old Christini. But you would never guess it. They speak but pigeon-English and keep to customs which most likely died out in Sicily before the First World War.'

I was enjoying the walk. The sun was climbing the blue sky and its golden glow made me feel it was good to live in our part of London. I loved the red buses; the plane trees dotted about in surprising places; the quiet, mysterious mews in which tiny houses nestled—no more than stables really but very expensive—with red, yellow or green doors and bright brass knockers; the old tall, gas-lighted lamp-posts; the patient road sweepers with their wide, black, bristly brooms.

From out of a kind of happy mental mist, I heard Fr Duddleswell expanding on the subject of the Sicilian betrothal.

Gelsomina Bianchi and Mario Christini had been to the same primary and secondary school. We were to witness the 'arranging' of their marriage. The pretence was they had never set eyes on each other. It would certainly be thought a '*scandalo*' if they had gone out together or held hands. The planning was left entirely to the heads of the family.

'I will try and explain things as we go along,' Fr Duddleswell said. 'Remember "*va bene*" means "okay". You can travel all over Italy with that if you keep varying the intonation. Two other phrases, perhaps: "*Grazie tante*" means "thanks" and you respond to that with "*prego*" meaning "don't mention it".'

We were met at the door of a large mansion-type house by Mrs Angelina Bianchi, a distinguished greying lady with a parchment-like face.

She greeted Fr Duddleswell with "*Buon giorno, padre*" and knelt to kiss his hand.

Without another word, Signora Bianchi conducted us to a

large inner room where the male Bianchis were assembled. All five of them, seated around a table, rose to their feet.

Signor Bianchi, seeing me, exclaimed: '*Ah, due preti*, two priesters,' (he translated after a fashion for my benefit.) 'O what a beautiful *augurio*!'

As head of the family he introduced us to his sons who came forward in turn to bow and kiss our hand, Giorgio, Letterío, Domenico and Peppino. To each of them I gave a smile and said "*va bene*". Afterwards, I felt as though I'd been flavoured all over with garlic.

'And this,' said Fr Duddleswell introducing me, 'is Padre Neil Boyd.'

Signor Bianchi responded with, '*Gli amici dei nostri amici sono i nostri.*'

'The Signor says,' interpreted Fr Duddleswell, 'Our friends' friends are our friends.'

That put my head in a whirl but I took it as a compliment and bowed politely and said, '*Grazi tante, signor.*'

'*Prego*,' exclaimed Signor Bianchi delightedly, '*parla bene Italiano il Padre Boyd.*'

'No speak Italian,' I said in a panic. 'No *va bene*.'

'You is English Englishman?' asked our host.

'Yes,' said my interpreter, jumping to my rescue. 'I Irish Englishman not Padre Neil.'

The Sicilians looked at me wonderingly as if they didn't know the Pope allowed English Englishmen to be ordained as priests.

'Padre Neil,' said Fr Duddleswell, 'is twenty-four years old. Of good parents, *buoni Cattolici*. He has three brothers and two sisters.'

'Ah, *buoni Cattolici*,' emphasized Signor Bianchi, showing his big yellow teeth in approval. 'And now *una preghiera, per piacere, Padre.*'

I gathered we were expected to open the proceedings with a prayer. Everyone turned towards the wall where I saw what I took to be a pair of horns and, nearby, a shelf with a red votive lamp alight under an old print of the Madonna and Child. The Virgin was bejewelled and smiling against a rural background and wearing a golden crown. The Child was at her breast also crowned, and in his hand were three ears of corn symbolizing, I supposed, fertility. In the ornamented silver picture frame were sprigs of lavender.

Fr Duddleswell intoned the *Pater Noster* and *Ave Maria* which all present rattled off in Latin. And then, '*Nostra Signora di Custonaci.*'

'*Prega per noi,*' all responded. I said, 'Pray for us.'

As we sat down, Fr Duddleswell explained to me that Our Lady of Custonaci was the patron saint of Sicilians.

'That peecture ... over the sea come ... from Alesandria,' said Signor Bianchi.

Giorgio, the eldest son, a real *mafioso*-type if ever I saw one, fat, greasy and black, added, 'It was pain'ed by San Luke *evangelista*, but the faces is pain'ed by the Gabriel Archangelo.'

Letterio took up the story: '*La Madonna di Custonac*' *preserva* us from drought and *pestilenze* and *terremoto*, 'ow you say? earfquike, and from the *milioni* of locusts.'

When Domenico contributed his piece, I realized I was listening in on a Sicilian saga, like the Jewish Passover, in which all the males had a traditional part to play.

'On the *festa* of *la Madonna*,' said Domenico, 'nobodies swears on the island.'

'A truly *grand*' *miracolo*,' put in Fr Duddleswell without a smile.

'*Davvero, Padre,*' said Domenico. 'No stealings, also, and even the thievers are *buoni Cattoloci* for one only die.'

Finally, the youngest, Peppino, a fine-looking young man, took his turn: 'This is why the wedding has been fixed a year ahead for next 25th August, the *festa* of the *Madonna di Custonaci.*'

Peppino's English was easily the best of the five, which I presumed was due to the fact that, having lived all his life in London, he couldn't escape English influences altogether. But for some reason his brothers seemed not to approve of what he'd said. They glowered at him. I wondered if he had spoken out of turn when it was old Signor Bianchi's privilege to name the wedding date.

The patriarchal Signor Bianchi then clapped his hands and in came his wife smartly, carrying a tray with a flask of red wine and seven beakers.

'Please,' said Signor Bianchi, holding the tips of his fingers together in prayer, 'please to take to drink a cup of marsala.

It do mucha good to the spireets and the *stomaco*.'

After a few swigs, the bargaining began.

Signor Bianchi asked with ample gestures:

'*Quanto,* 'ow mucha for the *compana*?'

Fr Duddleswell said, 'The bell? It *costa* five shilling.'

Signor Bianchi thought about that for a bit before nodding.
'*Va be*,' he said, and signalled to Giorgio to write it down,
'*Scrive, Giorgio,*' which he did in a big leather-bound family
album. 'And the *organo,* padre?'

'One pound ten shilling.'

'*Misericordia! Troppo,* padre.'

'*Not* too much,' Fr Duddleswell insisted, waving the palm
of his right hand from side to side.

'A li'l bit *troppo*,' pleaded Signor Bianchi.

'*Va bene,*' conceded Fr Duddleswell, 'one pound only.'

I had never witnessed simony at such close quarters before.
I confess I was too fascinated by the whole mercenary process
to be as scandalized as I should have been.

'Flowers for the *sanctuario,* padre, *e confetti*?'

'Confetti?' exclaimed Fr Duddleswell in a shocked tone.
'*Dio mio! Impossibillissimo!* Flowers, *sì,* confetti, *non.*'

'Padre, padre,' said Signor Bianchi in a perfect whimper,
his joined hands stretched out before him in imprecation.

Fr Duddleswell sipped his wine, pouted and said:

'*Un po' di confetti.*'

'*Grazie,* padre.'

'*Prego,*' said Fr Duddleswell, and, holding his left finger
and thumb together to make a circle, repeated, '*Un po,* only a
lettle beet.'

Signor Bianchi turned to Giorgio, '*Scrive* a li'l beet,' and
then to Fr Duddleswell, ' 'Ow mucha?'

'Two shilling.'

'*Scrive,* Giorgio, two sheeling.'

So the bargaining went on to the accompaniment of gestures
so magnificent I could follow most of what was said without
difficulty. Each time agreement was reached, the glasses were
clinked in salute and a toast drunk.

Then came the momentous question of the cope Fr Duddleswell was to wear at the wedding.

Domenico said, 'The golda cop, padre, we musta haf the
golda cop. That is what says our *adorata mamma*.'

Fr Duddleswell slowly shook his head discouragingly.

There was alarm in Signor Bianchi's eyes. 'For Gelsomina, padre. For our *carissima* Gelsomina.'

Fr Duddleswell maintained his stubborn stance.

''Ow mucha, padre?' Our host's shoulders slanted forward as if, should the need arise, he would part with all he possessed for such a favour.

'Too much, Signor Bianchi.'

'Plen'y mucha money?'

'*Sì, signor.*'

'Fiva pounds? I expect with anxiousness your *responso.*'

'*Va bene,*' said Fr Duddleswell grudgingly.

'Three pounds, will that be enough?' asked Peppino hopefully, and, for no reason I could fathom, aroused again the silent wrath of the fraternity.

'Three pounds?' mused Fr Duddleswell. '*Va bene.*'

'*Scrive, scrive,* Giorgio, t'ree poun's for the golda cop.' Signor Bianchi was triumphant. 'All feeneeshed.'

And all the brothers cried out, '*Evviva.*'

Giorgio, on his own behalf, said, 'Padre, you pay the seesters in the *convento* to pray for our Gelsomina?'

'*Certamente,*' replied Fr Duddleswell.

'We give our Gelsomina,' Giorgio said, 'lots of indulgénces, t'ousands of days of indulgénces.'

He made it sound as if the Church's system of indulgences was a protection racket invented by the Mafia.

Another clap of the hands from our host and his wife, right on cue, brought in biscuits and sugared almonds and a huge decorated flask of chianti.

For the next half an hour, it was all '*grazie*' and '*prego*', as they filled my glass whenever, like a fool, I drained it.

I remember Signor Bianchi saying in exultant mood, 'Ah, Padre Duddleswell, the *matrimonio*, is it not the only vendetta blessèd by the Church?'

'The only *vendetta benedetta*,' said Fr Duddleswell with an uncustomary giggle.

'*Sì,*' said Giorgio, 'when I marry my Teresa, my *mamma* she say to me, "Giorgio, why you wanna marry tha' *signorina*? If you be married, you will not love any more tha' lady".'

The *mamma* smiled like the Mona Lisa, but tradition forced her to hold her peace.

'Women,' Giorgio went on, 'don't be thinking of nothing but the *bambini*.'

'The *matrimonio*,' Letterío said, 'is like what is called in Sicilia, *"una tassa sull'ignoranza"*,' and, translating for my benefit, ' "a taxes on the *stupidità*". But, Padre Neil,' he said, looking at me fixedly, 'I advertise you not to never pay in your 'ole life this taxes.'

At this everybody laughed and I said a trifle unsoberly: 'I no pay *no* taxes.'

'It is mucha better,' Domenico said, 'to be free as the salt.'

'*Grazie, cara*,' Signor Bianchi said pointedly to his wife, motioning her to leave. 'You too mucha busy to remine.'

I inferred from this the talk might become too indelicate for women's ears.

'I wanna you,' said Signor Bianchi confidentially to Fr Duddleswell after his wife had departed, 'I wanna you to be telling Signor Christini my Gelsomina is very gooda girl for 'is boy.'

Fr Duddleswell nodded agreement.

Signor Bianchi went on: 'My Gelsomina is pura as the Madonna but not pregnated in the slightest, *capisc*'?'

'*Capisco*. I understand,' said Fr Duddleswell.

'*Scrive*, padre,' insisted the proud father, '*scrive*,' so that Fr Duddleswell had to take out his diary and write in big letters: 'Gelsomina is not pregnated.'

'In the slightest,' said Signor Bianchi, concluding his dictation, and he made Fr Duddleswell write that down too.

'But *after* the *matrimonio*,' said Fr Duddleswell with a wink.

'Then,' Signor Bianchi said, 'plen'y pregnated.' This seemed to jog his memory for he added: 'The benediction at the *matrimonio*.'

'Yes?' asked Fr Duddleswell.

'In Italiano, yes? If to don't bless in Italian, per'aps no *bambini*.'

'To make sure, the *benedizione* will be in *Italiano*.'

Signor Bianchi sighed with the pleasures of grandpaternity to come.

'Now to see the bride,' he said.

He clapped his hands and this time his wife led in Gelsomina. The shy young woman was about nineteen, with long

127

black hair and dark lashes. Blinking to clear my vision of a pink haze, I saw she was pretty, though she moved in a slightly lame fashion and had a definite cast in her left eye.

'Padre Duddleswell,' urged our host, 'you tella Signor Christini our Gelsomina is *bella* also *pura*. She worth all the mucha money I you pay for the *matrimonio*. I no wanna 'im to robba me of my Gelsomina for nuttin'. *Capisc'*?'

'*Sì,*' Fr Duddleswell assured him, 'and I tella that to Signor Christini.'

'Now, padre, *un fervorino* for Gelsomina.'

I gathered Fr Duddleswell was expected to preach a little sermon to the future bride.

'Gelsomina,' said Fr Duddleswell, sipping his chianti, 'Gelsomina ...'

'*Un fervorino, per piacere,*' repeated our host.

'Gelsomina,' said Fr Duddleswell, 'do not quarrel the first time.'

Everybody applauded and Fr Duddleswell expanded his thought thus: 'Do not quarrel the first time with your *marito*, your husband. If you do, it will never end. If you do not, it will never begin.'

Such priestly wisdom brought a gasp of appreciation from all the male Sicilians present and a plum-like blush to the face of the bride.

Signor Bianchi drove home the point. 'Gelsomina, Padre Duddleswell is to you telling to don't be quarrelling.'

Fr Duddleswell blessed Gelsomina and she left, limping a little, with her mother.

Our business at the Bianchis was nearing its end. It was agreed that Giorgio would represent the family and come to the presbytery at eight o'clock to seal the contract with the representative of the Christinis. With many exchanges of *addio, arriverderci* and ''appy days', we staggered to the door.

When we made the fresh, scented summer air, I began to sober up.

'Lovely people,' enthused Fr Duddleswell, even their religion does not seem to do them any harm. They *liked* you, Father Neil.' And ignoring the passers-by, he proceeded to sing:

For you might have been a Roosian
A French or Turk or Proosian
    Or perhaps Sicili-an.
But in spite of all temptations
To belong to other nations
    You remain an Englishman
    You remain an Englishman.

There were many questions I wanted to ask him. 'What about those horns on the wall?' I said for a start.

'Their religion does not much interfere with the superstitions either, I'm afraid, Father Neil. They are first and foremost *Siciliani*, are you with me? Those horns are on the wall to ward off the Evil Eye.' Seeing I had only the vaguest notion of the Evil Eye, he explained. ''Tis a subtle, malign influence which they break up by hanging horns on their walls or wearing them on their persons. Made of coral or mother of pearl.'

'Where is this evil influence supposed to come from?'

'Ah, Father Neil, many Italians think that Pius IX himself, their beloved *Pio Nono*, had the Evil Eye.'

'Really!' I exclaimed in horror.

'Yes, indeed, even some cardinals, when they had an audience with His Holiness, used to make horns at him with their fingers under their robes.'

'That's true?' I asked incredulously.

'True as true. I would not joke on so serious a matter. And do you know how the Sicilians account for Britain's victory over the Nazis in the war? 'Twas due, they say, to Winston Churchill foiling Hitler's Evil Eye with his Victory sign.'

It took me some time to recover from the insult to the Holy Father. When I did, I said, 'I didn't like that bargaining over holy things.'

'Father Neil,' tut-tutted Fr Duddleswell, 'what a puritan y'are.'

I accepted the rebuke as meekly as a Christian should.

'Father Neil, if only you had troubled to add up all the "charges", you would realize they come to £10 exactly, which is the standard fee for all weddings of this sort.'

'But the indignity of it.'

'Indignity, my eye!' he said, still doubtless the worse for

drink. ' 'Twas to save the old man's dignity I dealt with him in the way I did, the traditional Sicilian way, you follow? He needed to assure the Christinis that he paid a notable price for the wedding and his own family that he struck a good bargain. I saved his lovely old Sicilian face on both scores.'

'And the gold cope?' I spoke more diffidently this time.

'I wear it at all weddings without exception.'

'Do *they* know that?'

'Of course they know it. They are not fools.'

'I'm not sure anyway that I approve of arranged weddings, Father. It might be all right for Asians and Sicilians on their medieval island, but here, in the middle of the twentieth century ...' I broke off in a chianti-induced scorn.

'I will talk to you about that later,' he sighed, as if I'd never learn. 'For the present, let us conclude the pact with the Christinis, shall we?'

The Christinis lived in a semi-detached house on Eastside.

'We were expecting you intensely,' said the petite Signora Christini at the door.

Here we go again, I thought.

Signor Christini, though in his sixties, had a full head of black hair and an enormous brush for a moustache. He looked like a benign bandit. After seeing me, he promoted Fr Duddleswell to Monsignore as a mark of distinction.

The Signor had only two sons present—Mario, the groom, was kept out of sight—one was Enrico, the other Umberto.

Once more, a litre of marsala was produced and I regretted I had drunk so much on our first port of call.

Fr Duddleswell extolled the beauty and innocence of Gelsomina in the kind of terms usually reserved for the Blessed Virgin in her litany.

'Gelsomina is as *pura* as a pine tree,' he almost sang, '*innocente* like the spring, and the eyes .. the eyes are the eyes of Dante's Beatrice.'

'And she walks with *dignità*?' inquired the eldest son, Enrico.

'She walkas,' responded Fr Duddleswell, with a touch of sibilance, 'soft-foot like the stars in the skies of night.'

'She no walka under them stars with other men, Monsignore?'

'*Fedele sempre*, always faithful she 'as been and willa be,' said Fr Duddleswell, becoming more and more ample in tone and gestures, '*fedele* to Mario, 'er 'usband.'

'*Va be*,' said Signor Christini, much relieved. '*Scrive*, padre, "*sempre fedele*."'

Fr Duddleswell wrote this in Enrico's big ledger and it reminded him to take out his diary and read: 'Gelsomina is not pregnanted in the slightest.'

Signor Christini was fully satisfied, especially when Fr Duddleswell said: 'He paid plen'y much money.'

In came Signora Christini with biscuits, sugared almonds and chianti, and, in time, we were allowed to see Mario, a nice, quiet, ordinary-looking lad a few years my junior.

To him, Fr Duddleswell was made to repeat his injunction, to equal acclaim, about not quarrelling.

When we left, Enrico promised to be at the presbytery at eight o'clock. For my part, I couldn't get home soon enough to rest my fiercely pumping head on a pillow.

That evening, Giorgio Bianchi and Enrico Christini arrived at the presbytery together. Now almost recovered, I was awaiting them in Fr Duddleswell's study.

'Come in, George, you too, Henry,' he said.

I was pleased that this time the Sicilians shook my hand and didn't lick it all over.

Giorgio said: 'It really was frightfully good of you, Fr Duddleswell, to help us out again as you did this morning. Splendid show.'

Instead of being knocked sideways by the extraordinary change in Giorgio's accent, Fr Duddleswell answered calmly, 'Not at all, George, pleased to be of help.'

'I don't know how you manage it, Father,' put in Enrico in the same cultured tones, 'but be sure your efforts on our behalf are highly appreciated by the entire family.'

Once again, Fr Duddleswell shook off the praises being showered on him. 'I have made out two identical documents in Italian, if you would both sign and countersign them, I'm sure your fathers' minds will be put at rest.'

After the signings, Fr Duddleswell added his own name, stamped the parish seal on the papers, shook hands with the young men—they each gave him £10—and walked them to the door. I remained behind scratching my head.

When Fr Duddleswell returned, I thought it about time I stood up to him. 'So it was another game, was it?'

'Game. Not at all. Serious business.'

'But what about that nonsense in their homes, all of them talking like Italian organ-grinders.'

'Respect makes them adopt the language of their fathers. Remember, with Sicilians the family is the only country they recognize and they are usually very loving families.'

'The Bianchi boys didn't look too lovingly on Peppone.'

'That,' said Fr Duddleswell, 'was because Peppone was getting careless. His bad English was not nearly as good as his brothers. They feared their father might become suspicious.'

'And all that writing down of the bargains, that too ...'

'That too was for their father's sake. You see, neither Signor Bianchi nor Signor Christini can read or write. They are both what Italians call "analfabeti".'

'Why, then, was everything written down.'

'Ah, well, Father Neil, the Sicilians do not trust the spoken word, not even that of a priest. Words pass without trace, you follow? Like the wind. Only when they are written down do they have faces; the fathers can see them, even if they cannot read them.'

'And all that sickly stuff about Gelsomina's beauty.'

'I thank God she is not a deaf-mute,' he said. 'At least she has the qualities of the best Italian *campagna*, warm, soft and fertile.'

'And her virtue?' I droned on.

'That was genuine enough, Father Neil, believe you me. If Gelsomina were found to have gone with another man, the Christini boys would have to attempt to murder her.'

'Murder her?' I cried. 'How horrible!'

'Father Neil, I did not say the *would* murder her, only *attempt* to murder her, which is the exact opposite. Sicilians attempt murder as often as Englishmen attempt suicide. It is of the essence that they fail.'

I put my hands over my eyes and pressed hard.

'I've drunk too much red wine,' I said, meaning it as a criticism of my mentor. He did not appear to notice any rebuke.

'You see, Father Neil,' he continued unperturbed, 'the Sicilians are true *mafiosi*, like.'

'You can say that again,' I said, opening my eyes.

'You evidently do not understand that term as the Sicilians do. For them, *mafiosità* is equivalent to being a real Christian, you follow? They have another equivalent term, *omertà*, manliness. I once came across a young Sicilian chappie who slit the throat of his young wife from ear to ear because he suspected her of infidelity. *Omertà* demanded it of him. If he had not done it, his wife would have lost all respect for him, even though *she* knew she was guiltless. Well, now, the police, who fail to understand such things, called me in as interpreter, and do you know what the young man said? No? He said, 'I did not meana to kill 'er, only to mortally wound 'er for a few seasons.' Which is what he did. The young lady survived and they are very happy together as far as I am aware. Honour was preserved all round.'

My suspicions were roused so much by now, I asked, 'And *was this* an arranged marriage?'

'In a sense 'twas, Father Neil, and in a sense ...'

' 'Twasn't.'

He was reluctant to continue till I spurred him on.

'Well, Father Neil, even the sons are not cognizant of this. But Mario and Gelsomina have been going out together for the past eighteen months.'

'You don't say!'

'Tuesdays and Thursdays, when all the menfolk go greyhound racing, Gelsomina's mamma was supposed to take *her* to a dancing class and Mario's mamma should have accompanied *him* to singing lessons so he could learn to sing like Caruso.'

'That was no good?'

'Terrible. I tried Mario in the choir. Sings like a frog.

'No, Father, I mean the women didn't do what their husbands expected them to do?'

'What an original idea, Father Neil. No Sicilian does what he is expected to do, otherwise they'd never be able to trust each other. No, the mothers made a twosome at bingo and

Mario took his Gelsomina to the Picture Palace.'

Again, I covered my eyes with my hands, feeling I was ageing far too quickly. Then I stood up shakily to take my leave.

'It seems to me,' I said, 'we have been engaging, you and I, in a piece of gross deceit.'

Fr Duddleswell firmly but kindly raised his hand and, with a sigh, laid it on my shoulder. 'Remember this, Father Neil, the whole of life is a farce and a deceit.' Before I could interrupt, he said, 'How else could we be content, now? The women deceive the men ...'

'And,' I contributed, 'the men deceive the women.'

'They lika to thinka so,' said Fr Duddleswell, with an impish smile. 'Mosta times, they are happy enough to deceiva themselves.'

VIII *Crumbs*

When I tried to explain to Mrs Rollings the sublime Catholic teaching on the Eucharist, she showed scant interest.

'The bread becomes the body of Christ,' I said.

'Can you tell me somethin', Father?'

'I'll try.'

'At Mass, why do you make a circle with your index fingers and thumbs?'

'After the consecration,' I explained, 'the bread is not bread any more but every particle of it is the body of Christ. That's why we have to handle it with the utmost reverence and make sure no fragment falls to the ground.' I spoke quietly in order to convey the Catholic's awe at the Eucharist.

'Now I know,' she put in, revelling in the flawless logic of Catholic practices, 'why you always sweep up all the crumbs afterwards and swallow them.'

When my ordeal was nearly over and she was going out the front door, Mrs Rollings turned to me. 'One last question, Father.'

'Yes?' It was to be agony to the end.

'You know all that sweeping up of the crumbs. D'you think Jesus did that at the Last Supper?'

'Shall we talk about that next week, Mrs Rollings?'

'What a good idea,' she said. 'You don't mind me asking questions, do you?'

I assured her that I found all her queries very stimulating. 'It makes one examine the roots of one's own beliefs,' I said.

The following morning, soon after seven, the phone rang. Fr Duddleswell was in church making his meditation before Mass, so Mrs Pring yelled out to me to take the call.

'A priest on the line.'

I interrupted my ablutions and picked up the receiver in

my study. 'Fr Boyd, Fr Duddleswell's assistant. Can I help you, Father?'

'Hugo, O.P.'

'O.P.?' I asked, not yet fully awake.

'Order of Preachers. A Dominican. It's like this. I'm leading a pilgrimage from Tonwell, south of the river, to the shrine of Our Lady of Walsingham. What I want to know is, can we celebrate Mass at your place?'

'Of course, Father.'

'There's only a dozen of us. My party's made up of university students who, for reasons beyond me, are keen on carrying a big wooden cross on their pilgrimage.'

'What time will you be here, Father?'

'About eleven, but it might be later.'

'I'll be expecting you, Father.'

Since it was Fr Duddleswell's day off, I caught him as soon as his Mass was over and told him about the call. He wasn't pleased.

'Dominicans,' he snorted, removing his alb with a scowl. 'Unsound to a man—apart from St Dominic himself who popularized the rosary and Thomas Aquinas. They are grubby. They often do not wear their habit or the clerical collar. Some of 'em do not even say their beads any more.'

'Well, Father,' I said, struggling to put the alb over my head, 'it's nice to know that one of them, this Father Hugo, is going on a pilgrimage to Walsingham.'

'In atonement, I should not wonder. Anyway, Father Neil,' he said brightening up, 'I will be off in half an hour, and Mrs Pring's about to visit her daughter in Siddenhall this afternoon. So keep an eye on things while I am away. And a sharp lookout for that Dominican. Don't want any of his hanky-panky in St Jude's.'

Now fully vested, I promised to protect the premises. As he rang the bell to warn the congregation that Mass was about to begin, he whispered loudly:

'I am picking up Mrs Pring at her daughter's place tonight. Back sometime before curfew.'

My duty that day was to stay in the presbytery, answer the phone and the door bell. I was also 'on call' in case any parishioner was taken seriously ill and needed the last rites.

The morning passed off uneventfully. Around eleven o'clock I was expecting the arrival of Father Hugo and his students but they didn't turn up.

Mrs Pring served me lunch before setting off for Siddenhall by bus, and I retired to my room to read *The Life of Christ* by Riccioti.

At tea time, still no sign of the pilgrims. But at five, the door bell rang. Standing there fronting a dishevelled group of young men was a Dominican.

'Hugo, O.P.'

I just had time to glimpse his white stained habit with rolled-up sleeves, his rosary dangling from a leather belt and his big brown boots. On his back was a large grey knapsack.

He pushed past me uninvited. 'Sorry,' he said over his broad shoulder, 'we're a bit late.'

'I expected you before midday, Father.'

'Got held up. A couple of the lads had trouble with blisters.' He removed his knapsack and turned round to face me. He had ruddy cheeks and, though not yet middle-aged, a shock of steely grey hair. 'Aren't you going to invite them in? They're Catholics.'

'Of course,' I said. 'Please come in.'

About ten university students, mostly bearded, trooped in, leaving a large wooden cross leaning against the lintel of the door.

'You don't *still* want to say Mass, do you, Father?'

'Why not?'

'It's five o'clock.' My protest didn't seem to register. I said, 'We're not allowed to say Mass in the evening unless ...'

Father Hugo raised his right hand and made a dusting movement to silence me. 'We'd like to start without delay if it's all the same to you. We've a long way to travel before nightfall.'

'The church ...' I stammered. 'I'll come with you and show you where the vestments are and the chalice and ...'

'No need for all that palaver, Father. Haven't you a room here where we can celebrate together in a family way?'

He was opening the door of Fr Duddleswell's study. I raced to stop him. 'You can't go in there. That's the parish priest's ...'

Already Father Hugo was trying the door of the parlour. He threw it open. 'Just the job.'

He looked approvingly at the large, polished mahogany table planted centrally on a threadbare Wilton carpet.

The students followed him like a bearded tide and proceeded to move the chairs from the sides of the room towards the table.

If only Mrs Pring was here! 'Father Hugo,' I objected, 'you can't possibly ...'

He obviously could. 'Like the Last Supper, don't you think?'

Breathing heavily, I decided to make the best of a bad job. 'I'll go into the church and get you vestments and an altar stone. Fr Duddleswell keeps one in the sacristy.'

'We've got everything we need, thank you, Father.'

Father Hugo was drawing an old tin mug out of his knapsack. Could *that* be his chalice? One of the students pulled a small brown loaf from a paper bag. Could *that* be the altar bread?

'What about vestments, Father?' I whimpered.

My last hazy impression of the parlour was of the Dominican seated squarely at the head of the table surrounded by a group of medieval peasants.

I almost crawled upstairs to my room. How could I explain *this* to Fr Duddleswell? Below, a guitar struck up and I heard the strains of a popular folk song. What a din for only a dozen people! I hoped the neighbours wouldn't complain. I contemplated phoning the Vicar General and asking his advice but I feared he might insist I put a stop to it. For all my size I didn't feel equal to that.

After forty-five minutes of music punctuated by long silences, there was a clatter of chairs and footsteps. The celebration was at an end. I rose from prayer and raced down the stairs in time to see the students leaving. They were picking up their belongings and four of them were struggling with the cross.

Father Hugo stretched out a large, firm hand with 'Thanks for your hospitality, Father,' and I shook it without enthusiasm. 'We'll pray for you at Walsingham.'

'Thank you,' I said, 'thank you very much.'

But he was already on his way, his knapsack bumping up

and down on his back like a grey-clad child. I'll need all the prayers I can get, I thought.

I closed the door and went with trepidation into the parlour. The students had left the room as they found it. Except that all over the mahogany table were strewn the remains of their sacred repast. The bright evening sun, shining through the garden window, turned the polished surface into a huge golden paten and everywhere, particularly where Father Hugo had been sitting, were little piles of crumbs from the Hovis loaf.

I had never been in such a panic. The body of my Lord and God was scattered all over the table.

Heretic! No other word was ugly enough to describe my loathing of that Dominican who had left me to cope with this wretched situation. I closed my eyes and sank to the ground to implore God's guidance. He did not forsake me. I soon jumped up and went to the sacristy where I rounded up a couple of candles, a clean linen purificator and an empty ciborium from the safe.

Back in the parlour, I lit the candles at each end of the table, put on a white stole and proceeded, with the purificator, to brush the sacred particles into the ciborium. It took me some while because, in the bright sunshine, every speck of dust became visible on the polished table-top and it was difficult to distinguish it from the body of the Lord.

I had completed my task and stepped back to survey the table when it entered my head to look down at the carpet. Horror of horrors. Sacred particles everywhere. Already I must have ground Christ underfoot any number of times. I stood petrified from fear and devotion.

I couldn't, in all reverence, use Mrs Pring's old brush and pan with which she cleaned out the kitchen grate. Then I remembered that only a few days before, Mrs Pring had acquired a new vacuum cleaner, a Hoover. This would suck up all the sacred particles and then I only needed to take out the paper bag and make a sacred bonfire of it in the garden. After that, no traces of the Dominican's infamy would remain.

I took off my shoes, walked gingerly out of the parlour and returned with the Hoover. I plugged it in and, starting from the door, proceeded to vacuum the carpet. In ten minutes the task was complete. Even with the lamp from my bicycle, I couldn't find any more particles on the floor or on the soles of my shoes.

Not being in the slightest bit mechanical, I had never examined a Hoover; but it occurred to me that I ought to turn it upside down. When I did, I received the sharpest shock of all. Why hadn't I realized there were *brushes* underneath? There, caught in the bristles, were countless holy crumbs. It would take me hours to remove them and even then I couldn't be sure of complete success.

Once more I sank down desolately on my knees. It was six-thirty. Fr Duddleswell was bound to return by ten-thirty because diocesan regulations said all priests had to be indoors by eleven and he was always on the safe side. There seemed nothing I could do but keep lonely vigil by the Hoover—a most unorthodox tabernacle—until he returned and sorted out the mess.

In my misery, I acknowledged I had brought this calamity upon myself. Fr Duddleswell had warned me forcefully enough about the hanky-panky Dominicans get up to. In conscience, he would be forced to write to the Vicar General, requesting him to remove me from St Jude's and suspend me from priestly office. The Vicar General would inform Bishop O'Reilly who would haul me over the coals for an unexampled act of folly: allowing the body of Christ to become inextricably enmeshed in the brushes of a Hoover. I could just see my old Professor of moral theology being summoned to propose 'the more probable' moral solution to this improbable dilemma.

I began to wish I'd never been ordained.

Kneeling there in sunlight and candlelight, I suddenly saw red. Why should I be victimized for the blasphemous behaviour of a brother priest? Why should my career be nipped in the bud for no fault of my own? Why should I have to endure ridicule for the rest of my priestly life for attempting to rectify a grievous wrong?

I made my decision. I'd wait until the sun had declined further, and then bury the Hoover in the garden.

There was, I had noted, a tool shed in the garden containing a fork and a spade; there was also plenty of space beyond the far hedge for digging in. The hedge would protect me from prying eyes especially when dusk fell.

In the meanwhile, I remained kneeling beside the Hoover which I both hated and revered. I kept promising God that I would pay back over the months the price of the Hoover—Mrs Pring said it cost £12 with all the attachments—by putting money in the Poor Box.

In the dining-room, the clock struck eight-thirty. Time for me to remove my jacket and start digging.

In the garden, beyond the hedge, it was darker than I had expected. After several days of unblemished sunshine, a storm was brewing and dark clouds were scudding overhead I planned to dig a trench two feet deep, two feet wide and just over four feet long to accommodate the Hoover; and time was short. As I perspired, mosquitoes came in waves to pester me and the rain lashed down. It must have been about 9.45 before the hole was big enough. All the time I was praying that Fr Duddleswell wouldn't return before my task was done.

I went back indoors, put on my white stole of office and covered it with my jacket. I grabbed the Hoover in one hand and the ciborium in the other.

At the scene of operations, I used the purificator to sweep the particles from the ciborium into the hole before gently laying down the gleaming Hoover on its side. The waste of such a grand piece of equipment hurt me deeply, but what choice had I? I piled on the fresh earth until it looked like a newly dug grave. Now all that remained was to cover up my traces.

I put the tools back in the garden shed, and replaced the ciborium, the stole and the candles in the sacristy. Then I ran upstairs to get out of my drenched clothes.

I was running the bath when I heard Fr Duddleswell's car drive up ten minutes ahead of schedule. I stepped into the tub with a sigh of relief.

A couple of minutes later, I heard a loud and now familiar tread on the stairs. Surely Fr Duddleswell wasn't going to bed so soon? Why wasn't he finishing his breviary in his study as he usually did? Why was he, yes, making straight for the bathroom door?

Was there some incriminating evidence I had overlooked? I started to splash and hum loudly 'I'll Sing a Hymn To Mary' as nonchalantly as I could. I pitched it far too high and sounded falsetto.

There was a loud rap on the bathroom door and Fr Duddleswell called out, 'Is there something wrong, Father Neil?'

'No,' I returned. 'Why do you ask? I'm only having a bath.'

My racing mind told me he couldn't possibly have seen 'the grave' so soon especially as it was raining and dark. Perhaps the neighbour, Mr Buzzle, had informed him there was a suspicious character digging at the end of his garden or Mrs Pring had noticed her Hoover was gone. Must be important for him to interrupt my bath.

'That is all right, then,' said Fr Duddleswell. ''Tis only that Mrs Pring said you have not eaten the supper she left you. We were asking ourselves if you were unwell, like.'

'Never felt better, Father,' I lied brazenly. 'I had an enormous lunch and I thought I'd leave myself with a snack before I turn in.'

I heard Fr Duddleswell walk away mumbling to himself:

> A tenor, all singers above
>> (This doesn't admit of a question)
>>> Should keep himself quiet,
>>> Attend to his diet
>> And carefully nurse his digestion.

I sighed so heavily with relief the water rose and fell in the bath. Then his footsteps approached again.

Hell, what now? I thought.

'By the way, Father Neil. Did that foreign priest turn up for Mass this morning?'

I thought swiftly and made a couple of 'monumental' reservations.

'He came, Father, but he didn't celebrate Mass this morning, after all.'

I was was right not to call that evening charade a Mass.

'Highly delighted, so I am. You never can tell what antics those Dominicans are likely to get up to.'

It wasn't until the next day that Mrs Pring reported that

her Hoover was missing. Fr Duddleswell had just said, 'Father Neil, I repent me of what I said yesterday. About the Dominicans. Must not judge the whole crew by one of two mutineers.'

His U-turn on the question of clemency failed to impress me.

Then in came Mrs Pring. 'Strange,' she said, as she was plying us with coffee and toast. 'I've searched even the mice holes for my new Hoover and not a sign of it. I do believe someone's pinched it.'

'Poppycock,' said Fr Duddleswell, 'how could anyone have pinched it?'

'The latch wasn't on the side-door yesterday. P'raps a beggar looked through my kitchen window ...'

'The latch *should* have been on, Mrs Pring. 'Tis your business to *see* that 'tis on.' Turning to me: 'You did not notice, I suppose, any shady-looking characters hanging around the house yesterday.'

'No one,' I replied, sad that Mrs Pring was being blamed for my misdeeds. 'It can't have walked far.'

She said, 'There's thieves around here as could steal the milk out of your tea.'

Fr Duddleswell had a more amusing hypothesis. 'I should not be at all surprised, Father Neil, if that Dominican had something to do with it.'

'Very likely,' I said.

Later that morning, while Fr Duddleswell was out on his rounds, Mrs Pring told me, 'That Dominican is on the line again.' My big chance. I thought, I'm really going to give him hell.

Before I could unburden myself of bile, Father Hugo apologized for having to leave in one unholy rush to keep up with his schedule. He had meant to say sorry for leaving the parlour in such a frightful mess.

'I should think so,' I said, gathering myself for a prodigious outburst.

'The lads hadn't eaten for hours and they insisted on finishing their sandwiches before they started up again.'

'Sandwiches,' I gasped, 'Is that all?'

'Yes,' he said, 'but what else could there be?'

I didn't elaborate. Instead, I put the phone down in a daze.

IX *In the Swim*

' 'Tis complaints-time, Father Neil.'

Fr Duddleswell had invited me to his study and settled me in comfortably before giving me this information.

'Complaints-time, Father?'

'Indeed. You have been several weeks with us at St Jude's now, and have you any complaints?'

'About you, Father?'

'Well, I was thinking more ... Complaints about anything. Meself included, I suppose.'

I was brief and to the point. 'No, Father.'

'That is *nice* of you,' he said smiling, as if he was surprised at me giving him a clean bill of health. 'Of course, if at any time in the future you find anything even slightly complainable in me behaviour you will be sure to ...'

'Tell you.'

'I would be gratified. How about Mrs Pring, like?'

'She hasn't complained about you either, Father.'

'Then she must have worn her tongue threadbare an' all. No, Father Neil, I was meaning, have you noticed anything strange about *her*?'

I reflected for a moment to show I was trying. 'Not really.'

'Come, come, Father Neil, have you been blindfolding your ears altogether? You must have remarked her speech-defect.'

I had to confess I hadn't.

'Surely?' he said, with the twinkle that characterized him when he spoke of Mrs Pring. 'She cannot stop. She has a tongue on her the size of Southend Pier. Many a time have I beseeched her to take up the bagpipes so I can get a few inches of peace and quiet around here.'

'She works very hard, Father,' I said weakly in Mrs Pring's defence.

'She has a strong snout on her for digging, I grant, but after twenty years of her I realize that however hard you scrub a crow 'twill never turn into a dove.'

I could hardly say I had realized that before I even thought of it.

'Well,' he went on, 'I cannot tempt you or twist your arm into a complaint? No? A pity since ...'

I anticipated him. Biting my nail, I asked, 'You have a complaint against *me*?'

'Do not bite your thumbnail, lad,' he said hurriedly, 'you may need it for the boiled potatoes, as me father used to say. No, 'tis not so much a complaint against you as against your preaching. D'you know the words of the famous song about Fr O'Flynn,

> Powerfullest preacher, and
> Tinderest teacher, and
> Kindliest creature in ould Donegal.

'No, Father.'

'I have just told them you. Now what is wrong with your preaching.'

I hazarded a guess. 'Everything?'

'You *could* put it like that,' he said, bowing once or twice. 'Why, tell me, do you *read* your sermon?'

I explained the obvious: nerves, inexperience, fear of forgetting what I want to say.

'The trouble is, Father Neil, when the good people see you reading in the pulpit, they think 'tis a pastoral letter from Bishop O'Reilly and promptly fall into a dead faint in the pews.'

I agreed that my sermons did seem to have that sort of effect.

'Another thing,' he said, laying it on with a trowel, 'you mumble.' Involuntarily, I gave him a demonstration of my talent then and there. 'You should open your mouth.' He showed me—and it was like the opening of a farmyard gate. 'Wide, Father Neil, so the congregation can see the darns on the inside of your socks.'

I started chewing imaginary gum to show willing.

'And, remember, Father Neil, should they snore you in the face, give 'em hell. Like the old Irish preacher, 'The lions will roar at yez, the serpents will hiss at yez, the owls will hoot as yez, and the hyenas will laugh you to scorn.' 'Tis such a wonderful consoling doctrine,' he murmured, ''twould awaken the dead from the long sleep. Finally,'—I had been thinking that, like hell, this would never end—'why do you preach so short?'

I explained, reasonably it seemed to me, that I stopped when I had nothing more to say.

He was a mixture of the amused and amazed. 'You do not need to have something to say to go on preaching, Father Neil. That is the art of it, surely. Besides, if you run out of words, take a dictionary with you into the pulpit.'

'Is three minutes too short, Father?' In the seminary, we were told *that* was the attention-span of most congregations today.'

'Not only too short,' he said, despising modern theorizing, ' 'tis terribly dangerous. The good people who come in late, which is the most of them, will miss Mass altogether. And worse, they will miss the collection.'

The prospect of losing two or three pounds sterling every time I preached the word of God had staggered him.

He asked me what I intended preaching about next Sunday. I told him.

'Jesus walking on the water? Beautiful theme. Make it plain to the doubters below you, mind, that He was not using water skis, a surf board or a raft. Nor was He treading water or merely walking in the shallows.' He paused to offer an apology. 'But you would have said that anyway, I am thinking.'

'I'm not sure, Father.'

' 'Twas a great miracle to prove our Blessed Lord was God and gravitation had no pull over him, you follow? The rest of us mortals have to swim like St Peter. When *he* tried to walk on water, did he not sink like a rock?' He laughed at that. 'Our Lord's own pun, you recognize? "Peter", "Rock".' I nodded. 'Why did he not swim, now?'

'Jesus? Perhaps he couldn't.'

'Do not speak heresy in me presence, Father Neil, even in fun. In any case, I was referring to St Peter. Even I have been known to do the hundred yards when pressed.'

'Thank you very much for all your help,' I said, straight-faced.

'Think nothing of it, Father Neil. I like to give encouragement when I can. Oh, and by the way, we have Councillor Albert Appleby coming to tay this afternoon.'

Mrs Pring had already told me that Mr Appleby, a Catholic, was the Mayor-designate of the Borough of Kenworthy.

'Great honour for the parish,' I said.

'Indeed, 'tis so. I have only one or two little bumps to iron out with him.'

I volunteered to absent myself from tea if he preferred to talk to the Councillor privately.

'Not at all, Father Neil,' he said. 'You will have to deal with Mayors yourself some day, so you might as well have a lesson in the best way to go about it.'

At a quarter to four the front door bell rang. Mrs Pring answered it and I heard her knock on Fr Duddleswell's study.

' 'Ello, Farver.'

I was struck immediately by the cockney voice which did not match what I had assumed was a Yorkshire name.

'Hello, Bert, welcome and heartiest congratulations.'

The words of the two men tailed off as they went into a huddle before tea. When Mrs Pring rang, I was already stationed in the dining room, waiting. For five more minutes, muffled voices could be heard coming from Fr Duddleswell's study.

'What's he like?' I asked Mrs Pring.

'Impossible creature,' she retorted.

'Why was he elected Mayor, then?'

'Oh,' she chuckled, 'I thought you meant Fr D. Mr Appleby's lovely. Been on the Council for years and helped hundreds of folks. Brave, too.'

'Really.'

'Yes, twice mentioned in despatches in the First World War. Fr D won't blow him over easy with his breath.' The thought pleased her. 'Mind you, Fr D's proud as a fallen angel that St Jude's is providing the Mayor after all these years.'

She then gave me an outline of the week of celebrations before the swearing in of the Mayor. There was to be an athletics meeting, a ping-pong tournament, finals of the area darts tournament and musical evenings in the park. The climax was to come on the following Saturday with a lunchtime carnival, a swimming gala in the afternoon and a big entertainment with prize-giving in the Town Hall at seven in the evening.

Just then Fr Duddleswell led in the Mayor-elect, grey-suited, medium height, with white crew-cut hair. He looked about fifty-five.

I was introduced and felt the firm grip of the Mayor-elect before the three of us sat down to a bright assortment of bread and jam and iced cream cakes. Mrs Pring began to pour.

'Look at all those mounds of edibles,' said Mr Appleby. 'She could have fed all Ireland during the famine, could Mrs Pring.' He and she were clearly old cronies.

'Small wonder, Bert,' said Fr Duddleswell. 'She has sixteen ration books including one for a cat that died and another for a dog named Rufus that never lived.'

'Don't praise me in his presence, Councillor,' advised Mrs Pring. 'Not unless you want to do him an injury.'

'In this house, Bert,' Fr Duddleswell said lightly, 'I see to it as a good Christian should that no broody hen is allowed to crow.'

'A kind word from him,' said Mrs Pring in the same vein, 'would have to break a tooth.'

The parish priest leaned over the table. 'Be careful of the charitable woman's sponge cake, Bert. Have a bite of that and you will disprove an old English proverb.'

'Which one, Farver?'

'That you cannot take it with you when you go.'

We all laughed at that but it seemed to me that beneath the tranquil exterior, a tension was building up.

'You have done us real proud, you know that, Bert,' said Fr Duddleswell. 'Our first Catholic Mayor.'

'Elect, Farver. Mayor-elect.'

Fr Duddleswell ignored the qualification. 'All the more glory for St Jude's, Bert, because everyone knows your family are staunch Catholics. *Roman* Catholics first and foremost.'

As the mayor-elect bit into a slice of bread and jam so as not to have to reply, I sensed that was the first shot in a fierce campaign.

'And what might your duties consist of, Bert?'

'Opening garden-fêtes, bazaars, dances, schools, etcetera.

148

A regular bottle-opener, you might say.'

Mrs Pring and I smiled at the modest witticism. Not Fr Duddleswell. 'And attending the occasional service?' he rejoined.

'The odd one or two, Farver. In my official capacity, of course.'

'Ah, Bert,' sighed Fr Duddleswell. 'Even Anglican services?'

'The Church of England *is* the Established Church, Farver.'

'So I am told. Established by Good Queen Bess nearly four centuries ago.'

'Oh?'

'In fact, she was excommunicated by his Holiness the Pope for so doing. But do go on, Bert.'

Mr Appleby tried to. 'The inauguration is always 'eld . . .'

'Not in St Luke's Anglican Church?'

'You know it always is, Farver.'

'But, Bert, we have never had a *Catholic* Mayor before. We have no precedent for it, have we, now? Why should a Catholic be installed in an Anglican church with an Anglican minister presiding and prayers being said in *English* so God Himself cannot follow a word? 'Twould break me heart.'

Mrs Pring said, for my benefit only, '*I'd* sweep up the sawdust.'

To avoid taking sides, having consumed four slices of bread and jam, I turned my attention to the cream cakes.

Bert Appleby, as if to prove he was not a war veteran for nothing, grouped his forces for a counter-attack.

'Did I or did I not read in *The Catholic 'Erald* that under canon law the Church lets Catholic bridesmaids attend Protestant weddings?'

'Under certain circumstances,' Fr Duddleswell conceded grudgingly. 'But 'tis a strange wedding surely where you would be invited as a bridesmaid.'

'The same *principle*, Farver, applies to Mayors acting in their official capacity.'

'There are other conditions, too,' said Fr Duddleswell.

'Such as,' continued Mr Appleby, who had done his homework, 'that 'e don't give interior assent to what's going on? I know as well as the next man it's wrong to say so much as the Our Father with non-believers.' Getting no further response, he said, 'In fact, I'll be a-fingerin' of my rosary in my pocket.'

'Praying for the conversion of the Vicar?'

'That, too,' replied Mr Appleby, wisely riding high on the wave of sarcasm.

'You see, Bert,' urged Fr Duddleswell in a pastoral tone, 'Anglicans are outside the one, true Fold and so in peril. Good people, I know that. God loves 'em for sure. But they are too much like us, you follow? Do not they have Holy Communion even, so it looks no different from the true body of Christ.'

'But,' argued Mr Appleby, 'they receive their Eucharist with bread *and* wine like at the Last Supper. They don't fool no one.'

'*You* may not be deceived by all this, Bert, but think of the simple faithful. Do you want them to stray from the straight and narrow because of you?'

The last point appeared decisive. After a moment's thought, Mr Appleby, disconsolate, said, 'I'll 'ave to make the sacrifice, won't I?'

'All Catholics have to make sacrifices, Bert,' said Fr Duddleswell, softening, 'especially professional people, the likes of you and me. After all, Catholic chemists and barbers are not allowed to sell contraceptives and that cannot be good for business, can it?'

'I'll 'ave to resign then since I don't want the rest of the Councillors making fun of me.'

Fr Duddleswell only seemed to hear the second half of Mr Appleby's remark and, to counter it, launched his final offensive. 'Was not Jesus Christ Himself ridiculed and crucified because He was a Catholic? You cannot imagine *Him* attending a Protestant Church, now.'

He paused, as if the reference to resignation had just sunk in. 'Who said anything about *resigning*? You have not even taken office yet.'

'What use would I be as Mayor if I can't do the job? I'll just 'ave to inform the Council it's not possible to 'ave a Catholic Mayor in this Borough.'

'Not possible?' gasped Fr Duddleswell.

'Councillor Biggins will gloat, o' course. 'E always says us Catholics 'as to jump to attention when the priest gives the order.'

Apart from the chink of crockery and my munching and gulping, no sound for fully two minutes.

Mrs Pring could stand the strain no longer. 'Ring if you need more tea,' she said, and left.

'A fine woman, that,' said Mr Appleby generously.

'Y' think so,' returned Fr Duddleswell, his mind not really on it. 'I would trust her with me life but not with anything important.'

Silence again until Fr Duddleswell, as if confessing he had overplayed his hand, pleaded, 'Bert, would you not let me give you a dispensation?'

'Thank you kindly, Farver. But Catholic Mayors, like our colleagues the barbers, 'ave to make sacrifices.'

'By not becoming Mayors? Look, Bert, the Earl Marshal is a Catholic and he is in charge of the Coronation Service in Westminster Abbey when the monarch is crowned Head of the Church of England.'

'Praying for the King's conversion?' said Mr Appleby, intimating that he wasn't entirely on the retreat. 'Nah, I can't pin my conscience on another man's back. *You* can't get married, *I* can't be Mayor.'

'A compromise, Bert?' asked Fr Duddleswell hopefully.

'A drop more tea, please? asked Mr Appleby, pleasantly holding out his cup. 'A compromise? Not with my faith, surely?'

'No.'

'Nor with my conscience.'

'No.'

'Well then,' went on Mr Appleby,—'a nice cup of tea, this.'

' 'Tis thin but drinkable, I reckon.'

'I dare say I could prevail on the Council to 'old the in-augurals in St Jude's ...' Fr Duddleswell began to smile with relief. 'But at a small cost, mind.'

'How much?'

'Not in money, you understand.'

'So?'

'I'd 'ave to convince the Councillors, especially Mr Biggins, you 'aven't got me in your cassock pocket.'

'And how do you propose to do that?'

Mr Appleby put his cup down. 'By getting you to take part

part in the swimming gala.'

'I could hand out the prizes, you mean?' asked Fr Duddleswell apprehensively.

'That's *my* job.'

'Not by swimming in the Clergy Race against the Anglicans and Methodists?' The very prospect pained him.

'Not the Methodists,' said Mr Appleby. 'They've pulled out because one of their ministers was recently attacked by the Word of God.'

Fr Duddleswell asked what he meant.

'He dropped the Bible on his toe, Farver, and broke it. So without you, no race.'

'Impossible!' cried Fr Duddleswell. 'I would sink faster than the Rock of Ages. D'you want me to get my death?'

'You can't swim, Farver?'

'He *can*, Mr Appleby,' I said, 'he told me so this morning.'

Fr Duddleswell pointed accusingly at the food on the table. 'Jesus Himself would sink in the waters if He had to eat *that*. No, I am not able for it. I am out of shape. I have got too much shape, if y'like.'

'He's being modest as usual, Mr Mayor,' I said.

Fr Duddleswell looked at me blackly. 'Thank you, Father Neil,' he said most ungratefully.

'It's nothing, Father. I like to give encouragement when I can.'

Mr Appleby asked me if I could swim and I told him it was my only accomplishment. 'Good,' he exclaimed, and proceeded to tell me that the Clergy Race was a medley with three ministers to a team.

'There we are,' put in Fr Duddleswell. 'I only have one assistant.'

'I've a friend at the Cathedral,' I volunteered. 'He swam for Reading before he went to the seminary. Fr Tom Fleming.'

'Bert,' sighed Fr Duddleswell, 'I may be a bit old-fashioned ...'

'Yes, you may be, Father,' I said in his support.

'But,' he continued, 'you cannot expect to expose me ...'

'Your what?' asked Mr Appleby quickly.

'Me soul and belly. Me cloven hoof.' More irritably, 'Me nipples and things.'

'What things?' asked Mr Appleby, expecting an answer.

'Don't you know, Bert, I bulge in all the wrong places. Well, *almost* all the wrong places. Besides, d'you want me to put sinful thoughts in damsel's heads?'

'I'm sure Mrs Pring won't even notice,' Mr Appleby said soothingly. 'There, there, Farver. Only a couple of lengths from you, and St Jude's will 'ave its first Catholic Mayor.' He smiled broadly. 'One of them small sacrifices us professional Catholics 'ave to make from time to time.'

Later that evening, I was drinking a cup of cocoa in Mrs Pring's kitchen. She was horrified to hear that Fr Duddleswell had agreed to swim in the Gala.

'Father Neil!' The voice came from afar.

'He's either giving birth or dying,' said Mrs Pring. 'That man was made on a conveyor belt and he will insist he was hand-carved.'

The voice came nearer. 'Are you *there* Father Neil?'

'If only I could buy him for what he's worth,' said Mrs Pring 'and sell him for what he thinks he's worth I'd make a fortune.' I laughed and Fr Duddleswell heard me. Mrs Pring didn't mind. 'I only hope our Water-Baby doesn't end up a stiff 'un from a heart-attack.'

The subject of her solicitude bellowed from the other end of the corridor, 'I'd be much obliged if you would be after keeping to yourself your untutored opinion on me state of health.'

'And who'll lay you out if you cop it, tell me that?'

'You should humour him, Mrs Pring,' I whispered.

'Let his back go on itching, I say.'

Another outburst. 'Leave the lad be, before I shoot you to shivers.'

'Trot along, little doggie,' said Mrs Pring kindly to me.

'Herself is that plausible,' said Fr Duddleswell when I found him, 'she would put wooden legs under hens.'

In his study, he was at leisure to tell me more about the race. Each member of the team had to swim two lengths, the first swimmer free-style, the second backstroke and the third breaststroke. The senior curate of St Luke's, d'Arcy,—a late vocation, now nearing fifty—was a former Oxford blue and a force to be reckoned with in spite of his years. The new junior curate, Pinkerton, was listed to swim the backstroke. He was such a fat fellow and he smoked so much, Fr Duddleswell reckoned he would float better than he would swim. The Vicar, Percival Probble, D.D., rather fancied himself at the breaststroke.

'Now, Father Neil, I am morally obliged to take on Probble. Besides which, 'tis the only stroke I can manage. What will you opt for yourself?'

I chose backstroke. Tom Fleming, I said, would swim the first leg, being a whizz at the crawl.

'My problem,' said Fr Duddleswell, 'is getting meself fit in time for the race.'

He had made enquiries and discovered that Bollington Hall, the local swimming baths in Trickle Way, could be hired to private persons out of hours for a modest fee. 'Ten shillings per hour, in fact,' he said. 'The mere price of a respectable Mass stipend.'

'Out of hours,' I said warmly. 'I fancy a late-night swim.'

'Dare say you do, but I have arranged for us to go from 6 to 7 a.m. so as to be back by 7.30 for the first Mass. But, remember, Father Neil, the morning hour has gold in its mouth.'

'Six to seven,' I repeated.

'You said you like swimming, boyo, and what could be better than taking to the clear air before the sun is orange ripe?' He must have seen a shadow of reluctance flit across my face. 'You do want to accompany me, I suppose?'

'Of course, Father.'

'Must practise so the Protestants do not get the better of us.'

'I agree with that,' I said.

Bollington Hall was an old grey-brick, glass-topped building which school children frequented after classes and at weekends.

Inside, the baths, with narrow paved sides, ghostly light and twenty-five yards by ten of still, glassy water smelling strongly of chlorine, echoed with our early morning footsteps.

Mrs Hetty Gale the cleaner showed us to our changing rooms. After getting into my tartan trunks, I stood shivering on the brink awaiting the advent of Fr Duddleswell. I decided he should have the privilege of first dip.

Mrs Gale, leaning on her mop, a cigarette wedged in the

corner of her mouth, said to me, 'Do you come here often, Mister?'

'Too often,' I said. 'This is the first time.'

'Nice for me, Mister, to 'ave the company. You've been waiting for that old mate of yours for ten minutes. What's 'e up to?'

'Getting changed.'

'Cor blimey!' exclaimed Mrs Gale. She had caught sight of Fr Duddleswell in a huge white woolly bathrobe, his head squeezed into a silver bathing hat.

Making his way to the shallow end, Fr Duddleswell dipped a big white toe into the water and snorted at the cold belligerence of it before dropping his robe in a single lordly gesture.

From the side, I saw him clad in a one-piece glossy black costume of Victorian dimensions. There was a silver crucifix about his neck and what I took to be a miraculous medal pinned to his chest.

Mrs Gale's mouth was agape, the cigarette dripping from her upper lip. 'O my gawd,' she said, ' 'e's changed into a bleedin' seal.'

The whole pool recoiled as he jumped in. He swam laboriously with much imbibing and swooshing out of water; but he *could* swim. I dived in dutifully to keep him company and it wasn't many seconds before I was pleased I'd come. The early reveille to defend the honour of Holy Mother Church had its compensations, after all.

It wasn't until the following Monday morning when I saw Fr Duddleswell was feeling chirpy about his progress that I dared to broach the subject of his bathing costume.

I put my head round his door. 'Fr Duddleswell?'

'Yes,' he said looking up from his popular tabloid daily, 'who are you? Stop blocking me doorway with your shadow and come in.' I obeyed. 'What can I do for you?'

'Well, Father, it's more in the way of what I can do for you.'

'Yes?' His tone was apprehensive. 'Say on, Father Neil. If you must.'

'You know you said if at any time I had the slightest complaint, I should tell you.'

'Has Mrs Pring been rash with her mouth again?'

'No, Father. It's about ...'

'Meself?' He was shocked.

'Not so much about you as about your swimming costume.'

He wanted to know what possible argument I could have with his swimming costume.

'Have you had it long, Father?'

'You have seen it. As long as possible.'

'By "long",' I explained, 'I meant a long time.'

'Yes,' was his curt reply, and he nose-dived into his newspaper.

I didn't budge. 'Are you thinking of getting another one?'

'They don't make 'em like that any more,' he said without looking up. I was well aware of the reason for their rarity. I said, 'Would you consider buying one of the ... new sort?'

'No.' He read for a few more seconds before closing his paper. 'Father Neil, why should you be wanting me to make concessions to the permissive society? Do we not have enough already of Sodom and Begorrah?'

I waited in order to phrase my remarks well. 'It's actually easier in bathing trunks. More freedom of movement for the shoulders.' Seeing no reaction: 'More chance of ... beating the Protestants in bathing trunks.'

'Father Neil, to be frank with you, I feel 'tis improper for a priest to appear naked as a frog before the grinning populace.' Noticing my discomfiture, he added, 'When he is no longer young, I mean.'

'But Mr Probble, the Vicar. I presume ...'

'I was talking about a *real* priest, you follow? Not about a doubtfully baptized layman of the so-called Church of England. Besides,'—the first sign of weakening—'where would you obtain a pair of bathing trunks sizeable enough to cover my rotundity?'

I asked him for his waist measurement.

'Forty-four at the last count. *Inches.*'

'They do stretch, I know, Father.'

He looked hurt. 'The same tragedy will befall you, Father Neil, when you are my age.'

'Oh, Father, I was referring to bathing trunks not to your ...' I couldn't find the proper word and wasn't taking any risks. 'Rotundity,' I concluded.

'So you think I suffer from rotundity.'

'That was your word,' I reminded him, 'not mine.'

'But if I said I was an idiot would I expect you to agree with me?'

'I suppose not, Father,'

He paused for a moment before saying, 'I could not sit in the palm of your hand, that's for sure.'

'You probably could if you tried, Father.'

My embarrassment brought out the gentleman in him. 'Are there big *black* ones?'

'Big black *what*, Father?'

'Bathing trunks. Not tartan or rainbow ones. Black ones or clerical grey.' I nodded. 'I would not need to be fitted for 'em in a shipyard?'

I took out the tape-measure which I had borrowed from Mrs Pring. 'I'll just check your size,' I said. 'You wouldn't care to remove your cassock?'

'No.'

'Not for a few seconds?'

I *will* not be defrocked, like, even for a few seconds.' As I put my arms round him, he said, 'This is rather like being swallowed by a benevolent octopus.'

Mrs Pring was wrong in her assessment that the five-foot tape measure wouldn't 'reach'. Even so, I did not frighten him by revealing the result.

As I was leaving, he said, 'To be perfectly honest with you, Father Neil, the old costume *was* beginning to feel a bit too tight under the arms of me legs.'

That afternoon, at Fr Duddleswell's invitation, I joined him in his study. I had purchased a pair of pure wool, black bathing trunks in Piccadilly and wanted to know what his reaction was.

Having told me to shut the door on myself he slowly raised his cassock to his hips. Above the shoes, socks, suspenders and broad white legs was the new costume.

'What d'you think?'

I accepted the challenge as best I could. 'Breathtaking, Father.' No other response was possible to such a sight.

'Do you not think I am sort of ... um ... underdressed.'

'On the contrary, Father.'

'*Over*dressed?'

'Just right,' I assured him.

Fr Duddleswell pointed to his legs. 'Me Betty Grables are a bit on the anaemic side, wouldn't you say?'

'A trifle pale. Perhaps.'

'Not surprising, Father Neil, seeing they have lived in the shadow since I was long-trousered at the age of twelve.' Still looking down, he said, 'But it is very obvious in this costume, is it not?'

'What?'

'Me rotundity, me misplaced halo.'

I was firm with him. 'Father, I couldn't disagree with you more if you made me.'

'Nice of you,' he said, 'but in the last three days before this contest, I propose to live off nettles and dandelions, as a treat, like, *and* to take the edges off me circles.'

I explained that since the 'new' variety of bathing trunks had no shoulder straps I had chosen one with a belt. He appreciated the added safety device and only curdled a bit when I told him the price.

'Thirty bloody bob,' he said, paying up with three crumpled ten shilling notes. 'They used to be much cheaper.'

'Inflation,' I said, hastily adding, 'the cost of living, I mean.'

'And there used to be five times the material in 'em. Oh for the good old days, Father Neil.'

Mrs Pring happened to barge in. Fr Duddleswell immediately dropped his cassock. I couldn't be sure whether she had seen his lily-white legs or not.

'Trying on a new set of vestments for low Mass, Fr D?'

'Hold your tongue, woman,' he said reddening, 'and even a wise man will not know you are a fool.'

'What every well-dressed clergyman is wearing this season,' she said sarcastically. She turned to me. 'Oh well, at least you've saved him from one piece of ignom'y. His appearing in the local paper in his old suit along with pictures of bathing belles.'

'Sorry?'

'The Clergy Race,' she explained, 'comes straight after the Beauty Contest.' *That* was why he had parted with his thirty bob. 'If his Reverence strays into the Beauty Contest,' went on Mrs Pring, 'he could come in First, Second and Third.'

'Mrs Pring,' he said darkly, 'would you mind going fast

ahead of your heels before I take me best right arm to you out of the mothballs.'

'Okay, Fr D, I only came to ask about the sherry party after the inaugurals.'

'Two bottles of sweet and four of dry,' he said.

'I didn't expect a floor show in three-D.'

He raised his hand, whether to Mrs Pring or the deity I could not tell. 'Go, before I send hornets upon you.'

'Don't,' she warned. 'You know it's against the law for nudes to move on stage.'

The inaugural ceremony was held at six o'clock on the Saturday evening. Mr Appleby looked neat and distinguished as he walked behind the mace-bearer, wearing his nineteenth-century gilded chain of office.

All the local dignitaries attended. There was the acid-tongued anti-Catholic Mr Biggins with the rest of the Councillors; the local clergy—with wives—including all three Anglicans, the Congregationalist and the bearded Methodist minister.

Looking through the spy-hole in the sacristy, Fr Duddleswell whispered to me above the choir an impertinent greeting for each of them in turn as they processed up the centre aisle. For all his gentle mockery, Fr Duddleswell was proud St Jude's was hosting that distinguished company.

The service, mostly of a non-denominational sort, ended with Fr Duddleswell walking down the sanctuary steps to where the new Mayor was kneeling at a special purple pre-dieu usually reserved for the Bishop. There he made an almighty sign of the cross over him in benediction as if to say, 'Both of us know who's boss.'

After the service, a sherry party was held in the presbytery parlour.

Dr Daley immediately grabbed my arm. He held up his thin glass filled with 'that doleful liquid' and said, 'There is not as much here as would relieve the faintness of a cat. There is nothing stronger, I suppose.'

'Sorry, Doctor,' I said, 'only the landlord's language.'

'It's a poor house, Father, that will not hold another still. D'you drink yourself?' When I said, 'Very little,' he smacked his lips. 'A wise lad. Better to lay your head where you will find it in the morning. Ah, but me darlin' sin is the drink, all right.' He showed me, if not the darns in his socks, at least his tonsils. 'I have this wicked wide throat on me.' He put his head on my shoulder. 'I took a urine test of myself only the other week.'

'Oh, yes,' I said, as if it were a piece of information I received regularly from all my friends.

'Forty per cent proof,' he said proudly.

I asked him, half-seriously, if he ever asked God to help him give it up.

'The drink? I only have the courage to pray for sobriety, d'you know, when I'm drunk.'

'Then I'll pray for you, Doctor.'

'No, no, *no*, Father. If you were successful, would I not have to ditch the drink?'

I was separated from Dr Daley and pitched into a conversation between the Probbles and my parish priest. The Vicar was saying:

'Thank you so much, for that *beautiful* service of inauguration. And the *angelic* choir.'

'Kind of you to admit it, Mr Probble,' said his opposite number.

'It is so good to know,' said Mrs Probble, 'that today Catholics and Anglicans are at last learning to pray together.'

'Madam,' interrupted Fr Duddleswell, 'we were not praying together. I was in charge. You were praying with us but we were not praying with you. 'Tis forbidden to us.'

'That is a very fine distinction,' objected Mr Probble.

'I am glad you appreciate it,' said Fr Duddleswell.

'What Mr Probble is suggesting,' said Mrs Probble, 'is that your attitude appears to be a trifle narrow.'

'Indeed, Madam. Like the road that leads to salvation. But be sure that though I may not pray *with* you, I pray *for* you in season and out of season.'

Mrs Probble said, 'you make us sound like plums and damsons, Fr Duddleswell.' Then even more haughtily, 'But we badly need your prayers, I suppose, being such sinners.'

'May God bless you, Madam,' Fr Duddleswell retorted, 'for your insight and humility.'

'But, my dear fellow ...' began Mr Probble.

Fr Duddleswell naughtily looked over his shoulder before

facing the Vicar again. 'Oh, you mean *me*,' he said.

'Of course, we prayed together,' the Vicar insisted. 'If you and I play soccer together, does it matter who is *in charge* of the football?'

The Mayor, doing the rounds, came in at that point. 'After the swim, are you two Reverends planning a game of soccer, then?'

'If 'tis *my* football, Bert,' Fr Duddleswell said with a grin.

The Probbles moved into quieter waters as the Mayor introduced Fr Duddleswell and me to Mr Biggins.

'The Mayor has been telling me about you, Mr Biggins,' Fr Duddleswell said as he shook hands.

'Nice things, I hope.'

'The truth, like,' Fr Duddleswell replied ambiguously. 'The Mayor was saying, Mr Biggins, you are an unbeliever.'

'I'm a free-thinker.'

'Oh,' whistled Fr Duddleswell, 'free-thinking can be a very expensive thing if by it you lose your soul.'

'Better that than losing my reason,' Mr Biggins said. 'But tell you what, if I'm wrong and there is a God, I'll apologize and stand you a drink on the other side.'

Fr Duddleswell, who seemed to be revelling in the battle of wits, said, ' 'Tis you, I am thinking, who will be needing the drink on the other side, Mr Biggins.'

'Do you still believe in hell, then?'

Fr Duddleswell drew himself to his full height and looked up. 'Mr Biggins, everybody who meets me believes in hell—*after*, if not *before*.'

A few seconds later I found myself confronted by the salmon-faced Mr Pinkerton. His eyes were screwed up to keep out the smoke from the cigarette which he appeared to be devouring rather than puffing.

He stretched out a hand. 'Pinkerton's the name. John Pinkerton. I say that Duddleswell's a rum 'un, eh?'

'You think so,' I said.

'Whenever I see him,' Pinkerton coughed, peering through his slits, 'I thank the Lord for making me a Protestant.'

'You do.' I pointedly fanned away a part of his smoke-screen.'

'Don't you?'

'Yes, Mr Pinkerton,' I grinned, 'I too thank God for making

you a Protestant.'

He stopped chewing his cigarette and drew in a couple of chins. 'Aren't you Tinsy the new Methodist minister?'

'No, I'm Boyd, Fr Duddleswell's new curate.'

A kind of incantation struggled out of his throat. 'O *my* God, *your* God and *everybody's* God.'

We were saved further embarrassment as Fr Duddleswell clapped his hands for silence.

'Mr Mayor,' he began, 'ladies and gentlemen. What a grand occasion is this.' Some said 'Hear, hear,' and other, less reverent but thankful nonetheless for the Amontillado sherry, said, ' 'Ear, 'Ear.'

Above appreciative murmurs, foot-stampings and tapping of the table, Fr Duddleswell continued, 'Fairwater now, at last, has had the good sense to choose a *Catholic* Mayor.' A polite titter greeted this intentionally partisan remark. 'You will be delighted to know that I wrote a letter to this effect to the Palace, Buckingham, not Crystal, you follow?' That put things on an even keel for a moment and someone said 'Good show.' 'No reply,' said Fr Duddleswell, 'and none was expected.'

'I wrote also to Rome and only this morning I received the following message from the Secretary of State to Pope Pius XII.' The boat was definitely rocking as he unrolled and read from a yellow scroll. ' "The Holy Father sends to His beloved son, Councillor Albert Appleby, and the entire district under his charge His Apostolic Blessing," And now, ladies and gentlemen all, I give you a toast.'

We raised our glasses muttering, 'A toast, a toast,' before the ship finally went down. Fr Duddleswell lifted his own glass and said:

'To His Holiness the Pope.'

There was some hesitation and a certain amount of unfeigned distress among the company but I am sure I saw Fr Duddleswell and Mr Appleby wink knowingly at each other.

After 'For 'e's a jolly good fellow,' exclusively in the Mayor's honour, Mr Appleby left in his chauffeur-driven Rolls and the party broke up in a haze of various sorts of smoke, conscious that a fair start had been made to the Borough's week of celebrations.

'Charming, charming,' purred Mr Percival Probble, the

Vicar, as he languidly took his host's hand. 'Till we meet again. Celebrations in water next time, not sherry, what?'

Referring to that tender adieu, Fr Duddleswell said to me later, 'God is me witness, 'twas like shaking hands with a tired sausage. As to that wife of his, she was bright red like a damson in distress.'

Mrs Pring, who had begun to sweep up the ashes and rearrange the parlour after what she called alternatively the 'binge' and the 'debauch', complained, 'They've killed all six bottles and'—here we heard the crunch and tinkle of glass— 'they've gone and bleedin' well broke—begging your Reverences' pardon—five of my best sherry glasses.'

'The wives of the clergy did it, Mrs Pring,' said Fr Duddleswell. 'Out of pique.'

'Oh,' said Mrs Pring disgustedly, marshalling her epithets for a combined attack. 'What a binge! What a debauch!'

When I tackled him, Fr Duddleswell was unrepentant about his stress on the Pope and on the Mayor being a Catholic. ' 'Tis what was expected of me and it pleased them mightily.'

I queried the pleasure it had given to such as Mr Biggins.

'Surely, Fr Neil, you saw how it confirmed them in their bigotry, and no feeling is more pleasing than that of bigotry, or so I am told.'

On the Saturday of the race, I was allowed to sleep in until seven o'clock. When I woke the sun was already bright and everywhere was steaming.

The Gala was to be held in the big open-air municipal baths in the town centre. I had arranged to meet Tom Fleming at the main turnstiles at 1.45 because we were keen to see the earlier races.

Fr Duddleswell caught up with us at three o'clock in the hot and crowded arena. He was flustered and a bit edgy after a curtailed siesta. Mrs Pring had insisted on joining him and he could not see why 'except out of a prurient curiosity'. He was even beginning to call the race 'an unlucky job' and to waver in his resolve to swim in it until I told him how proud Tom and I were to be with him in this 'straightforward contest between the one, true Church and the usurpers.'

At 3.30 the bathing beauty competition commenced, so we decided it was time to make ourselves scarce and prepare ourselves for the race. We three moved as a body towards the changing room area. One of the stewards of the meeting was standing by with a list of competitors and the rooms assigned to them.

Fr Duddleswell made himself known. The steward said, 'Yes, sir,' betraying immediately by this form of address he was no member of the true fold, 'your room is the big one at the end, Number 23.'

'Neil Boyd,' I said, checking in.

Before Fr Duddleswell had trotted out of earshot, the steward said, 'Same room, sir. All the clergy change in Number 23.'

Fr Duddleswell turned back on his tracks. 'That cannot be,' he protested.

'It's a very big room, sir.'

'All right,' said Fr Duddleswell, 'give me a very little room, provided I am on me own.'

The steward shrugged his shoulders. 'Can't, sir. There's over a hundred swimmers and thirty entrants in the bathing beauty contest.'

'For *all* the clergy?' asked Fr Duddleswell.

The steward nodded affirmatively. 'There's a Reverend Probble there now, sir, who has the key to lock up all your valuables.'

Fr Duddleswell, his tail up, said, 'Catholic clergy, *sir*, have *no* valuables.'

With that he led off his small black brood towards Number 23. At the door, he halted, drew a deep breath and signalled to me to knock.

'Come in.' It was the high-pitched voice of Fatty Pinkerton.

When we entered, we saw the three Anglicans already changed and sitting in brightly coloured beach robes. The Vicar was flanked by his two curates. On the right, with military moustache and greying temples, was the former Oxford blue, and on the left, Pinkerton puffing voraciously on a cigarette.

Mr Probble stood up and extended his chipolatas to Fr Duddleswell who tried to find a hold. He glanced at his watch and said, 'You are cutting it fine again, what?'

Tom and I changed quickly under the dreamy gaze of our opponents opposite. It seemed the simplest way to deal with a sensitive situation. I put a towel round my waist, then removed my trousers and put my costume on. Tom was ready when I was. But Fr Duddleswell, having taken off his jacket, was spending a good deal of time trying to balance his linen collar on a peg.

Pinkerton remarked, 'This race is the highlight of the Gala.'

Fr Duddleswell muttered something about not being in the least surprised.

'The locals enjoy it even more than the beauty contest,' Pinkerton said.

'Yes,' took up Mr Probble, 'they only see us normally in clerical garb, collars back to front, lurid vestments and that sort of thing. They're delighted and not a little amused to find that underneath it all we're organically no different from themselves.'

Everyone laughed except Fr Duddleswell who was still trying, improbably, to get his collar to stay on the peg.

Mr Probble, being a gentleman if nothing else, as Fr Duddleswell put it afterwards, sensed that the tardiness with which his Catholic counterpart was removing his plumage had something to to with the presence of the Anglican Church. He handed over the key and suggested to his team that they depart.

Fr Duddleswell, in his relief, went across and shook each of them by the hand promising to see them all very soon.

With the usurpers out of the way, Fr Duddleswell put a towel round his waist and said, 'I suppose you two lads did not bring your breviaries with you.'

Tom Fleming took the hint. 'Would you prefer us to leave as well, Father?'

'Not at all,' Fr Duddleswell said unconvincingly.

'We will if you like,' I said.

'Very well, Father Neil, if the pair of you have something more important to do, you can wait for me outside.'

There, I explained to Tom that Fr Duddleswell was only making a pretence at clinging to properties. At lunch he had told me he would be wearing his costume to the Gala under his trousers, 'just to be on the safe side, like.'

A few minutes later, Fr Duddleswell appeared, locked the door and pocketed the key. As a group we followed our opponents into the open air. Once out of the shade, we felt the burning tiles under our bare feet.

'My godfathers!' exclaimed Fr Duddleswell. 'I am going to get blisters underneath the arches.'

A roar of applause accompanied our arrival on the scene. Fortunately, it was only for the last five girls to reach the final of the beauty contest. I was surprised and far from displeased to find that one of the five was Nurse Owen, a Catholic nurse I had met on my occasional visits to the Kenworthy General Hospital. Her red hair had been let down for the occasion— I wondered how she managed to cram it all beneath her nurse's cap. She was even shapelier than I would have imagined had I dared to imagine.

The crowd was hushed as the jury made their decision in reverse order. Nurse Owen was declared the winner. 'The Catholics,' Fr Duddleswell said in a descriptive phrase, 'out in front again!'

After the Mayor had crowned the Beauty Queen and the photographers had finished, the loudspeaker announced the climax of the afternoon: the medley race, two-lengths apiece, between the clergy of St Luke's (cheers) and St Jude's (bigger cheers).

'The English always like an underdog,' said Fr Duddleswell through gritted teeth.

I suspected his silver bathing hat had something to do with our being the darlings of the crowd.

Mrs Pring appeared, ready to hold our towels and robes.

'Are you a water-nymph,' Fr Duddleswell said to her, 'that you are waiting to wash me shroud on the edge of death's lake?'

Mrs Pring took no notice.

Fr Fleming was to start against Mr d'Arcy. Then me against Pinkerton. The anchor men were Fr Duddleswell and the Vicar.

The opening leg proved to be a surprise for onlookers and contestants alike. In spite of his superb style, Mr d'Arcy lacked stamina. After the first leg, he was down ten yards. Soon it was clear that Fr Fleming would give us a lead of nearly twenty yards. Fr Duddleswell was ecstatic.

I disrobed and was followed by Fatty Pinkerton. He stood beside me sporting a pair of bathing trunks coloured red, white and blue. The crowd cheered a churchman who was patriotic enough to carry the Union Jack on his backside. I thought it was in dubious taste and it made me all the more determined to beat the daylights out of him.

On the backstroke, I saw Pinkerton all the way. I gradually increased our lead. By the time I neared the finish we were nearly a length in front. Fr Duddleswell had only to stay afloat for us to win.

A deafening cheer heralded his entry into the water. I clambered out to find Mr Probble leaning over the side of the pool hoarsely urging on his patriotic but over-ripe colleague. By the time the Rev. Pinkerton had touched and the Vicar had plunged in to the accompaniment of further cheers, Fr Duddleswell, in a flurry of water, had almost reached the turn. He turned well but from then on I began to detect a drop in his stroke-rate.

Fr Duddleswell was nearly level with Mr Probble going in the opposite direction when he stopped moving forward altogether and stared bobbing up and down. Oblivious of the crowd, I raced down the side of the pool until I was in line with him. Above the cheers, I could just make out his cry:

'Help me, Mother of God. Help!'

Mr Probble either heard Fr Duddleswell's yell of anguish or guessed why the gap between them was not being narrowed by his opponent. Before I could dive in, he had moved across and grabbed Fr Duddleswell round the neck and proceeded to swim with him to the side of the pool. I reached down and dragged Fr Duddleswell from the water.

Nurse Owen, still clad in her bikini, was pushing her way through the crowd. I heard her say, 'I'm a nurse. He needs artificial respiration.'

Next moment she was by my side. She was about to begin her work when I caught her arm.

'I'll do it, Nurse, thank you.'

I hadn't the slightest doubt that the local press would be on to this literally in a flash. I didn't want my revered parish priest, after one calamity, to be photographed half-naked as he received the kiss of life from the newly crowned Beauty Queen.

'You're crazy,' Nurse Owen cried, 'the poor man needs help urgently.'

Not heeding her remonstrances, I lowered myself next to Fr Duddleswell. As I dipped my head, he squealed in agony,

'Get off me belly, boy,' and rolled over on to the offended part of his anatomy. When I leaned on that, he cried, 'Stop riding me like a horse in me final convulsions.'

To add to the confusion, Mrs Pring arrived. I had never seen her so agitated. She pulled the bathing hat from Fr Duddleswell's head and handed me a small silver phial.

'What's this?' I asked.

'Holy oil. For the last anointing. I *knew* this would be the death of him.'

'Mrs *Pring*. It's not a heart-attack. He's swallowed too much water, that's all.'

As I knelt down beside the writhing figure—the top of his white bottom peeped above the slipping bathing trunks—I realized my diagnosis needed amending. Fr Duddleswell was moaning, 'Me left leg. The back of it. Cramp. Oh, 'tis agony, agony.'

I massaged where the pain was: a big, stiff ball of muscle behind the left leg at the top. After a few minutes—I lost count of the bulbs flashing in the meanwhile—he was sufficiently restored to stand on his feet to the sympathetic cheers of the crowd. Fr Duddleswell held both hands high like a defeated boxer who had just picked himself up off the canvas. I looked about me for Mr Probble to thank him but he had modestly melted into the crowd.

Mayor Appleby insisted that our party should be driven home in his Rolls. Mrs Pring was so concerned about Fr Duddleswell's health she made us leave immediately. I only had time to gather up our belongings from the changing room before jumping into the Rolls.

No sadder or stranger little group, even at a funeral, ever travelled in more majesty. In the streets, some passers-by, seeing the car with its armorial standard on the front, took off their hats until they glimpsed who was inside. Fr Duddleswell promptly draped a towel over his head.

Back at the presbytery, Mrs Pring ordered him straight to bed. When I had changed I went to his bedroom to offer him my sympathy. He was not there. I found him in his study clad in a clean pair of pyjamas and a dressing gown with a thermometer sticking in the corner of his mouth.

'I am *not* staying in bed, Mrs Pring.' It was obviously not

168

the first time he had said it.

'Keep that thermometer in your mouth,' she commanded, 'and don't bite *that* thing's head off.'

'What is the point of it,' he grumbled, 'the very vision of you raises me temperature fifteen degrees.'

The front doorbell rang and Mrs Pring said she was going to let Dr Daley in.

Fr Duddleswell started to say, 'You didn't call ...' but he intererupted himself with the first sounds and stiffening motions of a sneeze. He held it in check as long as he could but it finally overwhelmed him just as Dr Daley made his entrance.

The doctor did not seem to mind the cloudburst. 'Bless me, Father,' he said, 'for you have sneezed. Now what is this I hear of you, Charles, that you have been at the swimming pool, drinking it dry?'

'Leave us, Mrs Pring,' bade Fr Duddleswell, 'and see to it we are not disturbed.' Then to Dr Daley: 'There is nothing much amiss with me, Donal. I am not killed completely.'

'Take your gown off, Charles, any way.' He obeyed. 'Sit your softy down on the desk there.'

'Do not ask me to go any further with removals, Donal. I have had enough of the striptease.'

'It's all right, Charles,' said Dr Daley, trying to soothe his tattered nerves, 'I have seen worse sights before. In motor accidents mainly, and on marble slabs in the fish shop. But you are about as bashful as a virgin on her wedding night. Put you collar back on if it makes you feel any better.'

Once more Fr Duddleswell protested his rude health.

'Charles, my dear friend, water in the bladder is bad enough but in the lungs it can be terrible destructive. Oh, but I *hate* the water, Charles. It is all I can do to make myself dip the tip of my middle finger in the holy water stoup.' He looked about him for the whereabouts of important things. 'You wouldn't have a dram of the hard stuff locked away anywhere, I suppose?' Fr Duddleswell shook his head. 'Oh, *Charles*, for the sake of the many good, hard-working times we've had together joining hands round the beds of the departing.'

Fr Duddleswell relented. He pointed to the cupboard by the door. 'Help yourself to the mischief, Donal.'

'God bless and keep you, Charles, any way. If I hadn't been baptized when I was three days old I would have refused the honour because of my fear of the water.' He knelt down by the cupboard. 'But you *are* in the dolours today, Charles.'

'And who would not be?'

'It is not every day a man is frightened out of the husk of his heart by the drowning.' He filled his glass. 'Can I pour a Paraclete for yourself, Charles?'

Fr Duddleswell declined the offer. 'True for you. I thought I was about to leave this country for a better. And beneath the airless water me soul shrank within me like a pair of socks in Mrs Pring's washtub.'

'What could be worse than that?' said Dr Daley, growing strangely melancholy as he took his first relieving sip.

'Worse by far is the humiliation, Donal. Will I ever get the better of me shame? I will not.'

'What is your shame, Charles?'

'To start with, them photographers hurling their lightnings at me and taking pictures of me posterity. And now am I smarting till the crack of doom from the indecency of having me life saved by an Anglican Vicar.' He tut-tutted more than a few times. 'He was even too little of a Christian to stand still for me to thank him. And that, mind, after I let him half strangle me in the water to make a hero of him.'

At this point, I left them for my study which I had offered to Tom Fleming as a changing room. We took tea and chatted together for about an hour.

As I was showing him out, Mr Probble, Mr d'Arcy and Pinkerton appeared. They were on a flying visit to see if the incumbent had recovered from his dipping.

It never occurred to me that Dr Daley was still there. I knocked on Fr Duddleswell's door and went in, followed by the Anglican clergy. 'Father,' I announced, 'these gentlemen just dropped in to see if ...'

Fr Duddleswell was still perched in patient misery on his desk with his belly bared to the elements. Dr Daley had interrupted his examination to knock back another drink.

My parish priest made a leap for his dressing gown, and, drowning me from afar with one wave of his wrath, he called out, 'Donal!'

'Yes, Charles.'

'Would you hurry up fast and pour me, too, a double flagon of whiskey.'

X *Father and Mother*

One day when Mrs Pring was busy in my room, she informed me that Fr Duddleswell's parents had emigrated from Cork soon after they were married. The family had lived for a few years in Bath where Fr Duddleswell was born and eventually settled down in London's famous Portobello Road. His father had owned an antique shop there.

According to Mrs Pring, Fr Duddleswell's upbringing accounted for his 'craftiness' and his refusal to take anything at its face value. For my part, I had noticed his tendency to collect 'little items of value' and to smuggle in pieces of furniture which he hoarded in the loft, usually when Mrs Pring was out shopping.

One morning, Fr Duddleswell decided I needed another bookcase for my study and generously agreed to let me borrow one of his precious *'objets d'art'* now growing cobwebs 'upstairs'.

I was holding the ladder for him as he slowly ascended, torch in hand, and raised the trap door into the loft. That was when Mrs Pring appeared, carrying a tray with our elevenses. 'Where is he?' she asked me. I pointed upwards. 'He can't be dead, then,' she said. 'What's he doing in my parish?' Suddenly she raised her voice, 'Come down this minute, Tarzan, do you hear me?'

Fr Duddleswell, his round face already smudged, glowered down from the loft like an angry cherub. 'A deaf man just passed your message on to me.'

'You'll tumble and break your stubborn neck, that's what you'll do,' persisted Mrs Pring. 'And be careful with those steps. They cost two pounds ten.'

'Mrs Pring,' said Fr Duddleswell menacingly. 'd'you not think I would have wed had I thirsted for the advice of a woman? And *are* we man and wife?'

'No, Father D, folly has its limits.'

Fr Duddleswell looked down on her for a moment like an admiring deity. 'Pure Jack Point,' he said. 'Now, Mrs Pring, stand there if you would be so kind and help Father Neil take a hold of the bookcase when I lower it.'

In an echoing voice, he warned us he'd have to hand down an old picture so as to give himself room in the crowded loft to get at the bookcase. I only glanced at the gilt-framed picture which was about five feet by three. It was ugly and overlaid with dust.

'Mother Foundress again,' sniffed Mrs Pring, before placing the picture diagonally against the landing wall.

By now, Fr Duddleswell was ready to lower the heavy mahogany bookcase. When it came to the test, Mrs Pring didn't have Mosaic muscles, after all, and she impeded me from applying mine. Fr Duddleswell, his cassock lifted up and tucked inside his trousers and his sleeves rolled up, had to take most of the weight himself as he gingerly stepped down the ladder.

He had only two more rungs to go when the picture began to slide down the wall. With his last little sideways jump, he put both feet clean through the canvas.

Not that he was in the least distressed by the accident. '*O felix culpa*, I have been wanting to do that for years,' he laughed, 'and never found the courage.'

He paused for a moment, gazed quizzically at the picture as though he *had* regretted the damage he had caused, and promptly forgot about my bookcase altogether.

'Something strange about this picture,' he said, carrying it effortlessly past me down the stairs. 'I am wanting to see it in a better light.'

When Mrs Pring and I reached his study, we found he had placed the picture on his desk and turned his table lamp like a spot light on to it.

'It certainly *is* strange,' I commented on entering. 'Never seen a ghastlier picture in my life.'

The picture represented an elderly haloed nun in the black habit of an earlier era. She was kneeling in front of the Virgin's statue, placidly holding a skull in the palm of her right hand.

Fr Duddleswell, crouching on the floor, said, 'By "strange"

I meant something quite other, Father Neil. I do believe this portrait has been painted on top of something else.'

Mrs Pring placed the tray on the desk beside the picture. I went to pick up one of the mugs of tea. 'Not that one, Father Neil,' she warned. 'The handle came off and Father D fixed it with his patent glue. Take the other.'

Fr Duddleswell, absorbed, told me, ' 'Tis a portrait of Mère Magdalène, Foundress of the Handmaidens of Mary, the good sisters who look after our orphanage.'

I remarked that I thought it was the grave-digger from Hamlet and Mrs Pring, flashing her finger at the skull, said, 'Just imagine, meat must have been even scarcer then than now.'

'Ah,' sighed Fr Duddleswell, still absorbed in his find, 'Mrs Pring, the wanton widow with a mouthful of tongue like the rest of her kind.'

While Mrs Pring went about her dusting, he explained that the sisters had donated their precious portrait of Mother Foundress to St Jude's in the person of his predecessor. That was nearly twenty years ago when the present Superior, Mother Stephen, was first appointed.

'Well, Father Neil, as you will realize, when I took charge of St Jude's, I was in a dilemma. The picture is so awful, I could not leave it there to frighten the women and children, but had I removed it without cause, I would have offended the good sisters or, at any rate, Mother Stephen.'

'Who frightens *him*,' contributed Mrs Pring.

Fr Duddleswell did not deny it. 'She is a formidable, severe lady, Father Neil. Rumour has it,' he said confidingly, 'that as soon as she was born she slapped the midwife on the back.'

'So?' I asked.

'The Lord draws good out of evil, does He not? Fortunately, the Blitz began and took the pressure off me. I made the excuse to Mother Stephen that I would have to remove the portrait of her Foundress to a safer place for the duration.'

'What about *after* the war?' I asked. 'She must have asked you to put it back in the church many times.'

'As many as there are mongrel dogs in Ireland.'

'And your reply?'

'Whatever wins the race into me head. I have said that the copy of the Leonardo which replaced Mother Foundress is much loved by the people. I have said, God forgive me, that an original oil painting of such rarity is a target for vandalism. Some Protestant ruffian might come along and daub it all over with dye or slash it with a knife.'

'Or put his feet through it,' said Mrs Pring.

'I must confess these wicked feet on me took a good measure of sinful pleasure in their fault.' He went to pick up his mug of tea. 'But these accidents happen.' He was left holding the mug handle while the contents were pitched all over the canvas. 'Mrs Pring!' he cried.

'You mended it,' said Mrs Pring, backing away. 'You wouldn't let me throw it in the dustbin.'

Fr Duddleswell, unexpectedly smiling, said, 'You know very well that no nun is allowed by her rules to take tea with us.'

Mrs Pring started to mop up with her duster. When she had got the worst off she left to brew Fr Duddleswell another pot of tea.

He used the interval to tell me of the running battle he had waged over the years with Mother Stephen.

'She is exceedingly holy, Father Neil, so 'tis very difficult getting near her.'

I recognized the type.

'Mother Stephen,' he went on, 'believes she is in the place of Christ, that is why she demands absolute obedience. The nuns are not even allowed to pray for fine weather without her consent.'

'Really!'

''Tis a question for nuns, Father Neil, of following their rules to the death. And the rules of their Order, alas, were drawn up by the Foundress, Mère Magdalène who came from Aix-en-Provence. You would never believe this ...'

'Try me,' I said.

'She was a married woman with a husband and two children when she left home to found ...'

'An orphanage.' He nodded. 'God works in mysterious ways His wonders ...' It struck me I wouldn't have spoken like this a couple of months before.

I put my index finger in my tea and flicked some in Mother Foundress' eye. She took it without flinching but Fr Duddleswell rebuked me for it with mock indignation. 'Have you gone mad, Father Neil? That tea is precious. Anyway, she took the veil.'

'Judging from this picture, she should have kept it over her head.'

'To continue with the present Superior. One of the battles I fought and lost was over dear Sister Perpetua. When Sister Perpetua's father died, Mother Stephen told her she had to make a choice: she could go either to her father's funeral *or* her mother's when the time came, but not to both.'

'Is that really written in the rules?'

He nodded, saying, 'Mère Magdalène.'

'For heaven's sake, why?'

'To show that her nuns, having put their hands to the plough, were not to turn back; to prove they had left father and mother for the sake of the kingdom.'

'Then why not be consistent,' I objected, 'and let *all* the dead bury the dead? Why present poor Sister Perpetua with such a dreadful alternative? You say you lost the battle.'

'That I did, Father Neil. I suggested in the end she went to her father's funeral to console her mother.'

'And when the mother dies?'

'We'll leave that to the angels, like.' Seeing my disgust, he went on, ' 'Tis an old saying but true: "You can drive out nature with a pitchfork and she will slink in the back door." The fact of the matter is that in spite of their inhuman rules, most of the sisters are grand people.'

I agreed they seemed to love the children.

'Indeed, Father Neil, was there ever a happier orphanage than ours? The sisters are devoted to the little ones, so they are.'

'But no thanks to that witch,' I said, flicking another drop of tea in the imperturbable face of Mère Magdalène.

After lunch, we drove off with the canvas to the Portobello Road. We parked and knocked loudly on the bolted door of *Duddleswell's*. Eventually we managed to rouse the proprietor, Fred Dobie, from his slumbers.

Looking through the slats of his fingers at our picture, the good-humoured Mr Dobie said, 'For old times' sake, Fr Duddleswell, I'll give you five shillings for the frame.'

' 'Tis not the frame I have come about,' said Fr Duddles-well.

'It can't be about the portrait,' responded Fred, twirling his big waxed moustaches in disbelief. 'You must be joking. The Egyptians, you know, had the decency to swathe them all over with bandages before they reached that stage.'

Fr Duddleswell explained his hunch. After a microscopic inspection of the canvas at the place where it was torn, Fred confirmed that there was indeed another painting underneath.

'What makes you think that what's below is any better than what's on top?' Fred asked.

'It couldn't be worse,' I said.

'Feelings, Fred, feelings.'

'I've known your feelings before,' Fred said respectfully.

'I want it X-rayed, Fred. Can you do that for me, now?'

'That requires expensive scientific equipment and you know I'm not in the big league.'

'I realize that. I want you to take it to one of your contacts, a real expert, and get an opinion. I will pay all the dues.'

'Including the insurance?' asked Fred.

'On the picture?'

'No,' Fred said with a laugh. 'On my life. If I don't get back to you in a couple of weeks, you'll know she's eaten me alive.'

In the event, Fred phoned the next day begging us to come round immediately.

'Well, Fred?' asked Fr Duddleswell breathlessly on our arrival.

'Mate!' said Fred excitedly. 'Are you in luck!'

'Come on, Fred, out with it, tell us more.'

'I took the picture along to James J. Brockaway. He wouldn't touch it at first till I told him who'd dropped it in.'

'He was a friend of me father's,' explained Fr Duddleswell.

Fred continued, 'Brockaway put it under the lamp and inside five minutes he could tell that underneath that muck is an original by Jean-Paul Tichat.'

'Never heard of him,' confessed Fr Duddleswell, a little disappointed.

'Tichat was a friend or at least an associate of van Gogh and Gauguin.'

'The divil,' roared Fr Duddleswell. '*Now* I place him. He came from ... Holy Jesus, from Aix-en-Provence!'

Fred Dobie was beaming like the Angel Gabriel. 'Jean-Paul was one of the leading lights in the Impressionist movement. He visited van Gogh when he was put in the asylum at Saint-Rémy in 1889.'

'A few months after van Gogh did those self-portraits with a bandaged ear.'

'Yes, and Tichat went to see him. And, in the view of James J. Brockaway, Tichat was in fact the "sitter" for van Gogh's painting which is usually entitled "The Peasant".'

'Know it well,' said Fr Duddleswell, 'lovely picture with cornfield and orchard in the background. But why does Brockaway think the peasant was Tichat?'

'Because of the dating, the established timing of Tichat's visit to Saint-Rémy and also because of the consumptive appearance of the peasant.'

'Explain that last bit, if you would be so kind,' said Fr Duddleswell, wiping the mist from his spectacles.

'Well, Father, Tichat died of T.B. in 1890.'

'So he did, now, God rest his soul, so he did. Only twenty-six or twenty-seven years of age.'

'And,' continued Fred Dobie, 'he left behind him at least a hundred canvases. But they didn't have the good fortune to survive like van Gogh's.'

'But this one has.'

'This one has,' echoed Fred excitedly. 'There are only three others in existence as far as we know. One is in private hands somewhere, one is in New York and the third is in the Pitti Gallery in Florence.'

'I am mystified to know how ...' began Fr Duddleswell.

'How Brockaway discovered so soon that it's a Tichat?'

'Yes,' said Fr Duddleswell. '*No,*' he suddenly exploded in understanding. ''Tis the cat.'

'Dead right, it's the cat. *Tichat* always signed his portrait, not with his autograph, but with a cat, *chat* in French'—that was for my benefit. 'That alone would make the picture invaluable. But there's more.'

'More? Get on with it, then, man,' urged Fr Duddleswell.

'It's the subject of the painting that's so fascinating. It's of a wheatfield with crows.'

'The absolute divil,' cried Fr Duddleswell.

'The composition shows it's very like van Gogh's picture of July 1890.'

'And Tichat died when?'

'On 18th June 1890.'

Fr Duddleswell could scarcely breathe for excitement. 'So 'tis possible van Gogh painted his picture as a kind of memorial to his friend.'

'Entirely different styles, of course,' said Fred. 'Tichat's is all light and the other sombre and heavy.'

'Naturally, but ...' Fr Duddleswell was lost for words.

Delighted at causing such joyous consternation, Fred said, 'Aren't you going to ask me what it's worth?'

'No,' said Fr Duddleswell flatly.

'*I* am,' I said. 'How much?'

'Brockaway tells me someone's been gilding a real lily. It's worth upwards of £6,000.'

'But,' I pointed out, 'Father's put his footograph on it.'

'No matter,' said Fred. 'It'll take a couple of thousand quid to get rid of the top soil and restore the original, but even so.'

'Even so,' I took up, 'it'll bring in a profit of £4,000?'

'That,' said Fred, 'depends on whether Brockaway is right and the picture underneath is in good lick *and* whether there's a ready market for it.'

'And,' added Fr Duddleswell quietly, 'whether the owner is disposed to sell.'

'Say the word, Fr Duddleswell and I'll take a risk. I'll write you out a cheque here and now for four thousand quid. If I sell it for over six thousand, I'll give you half the excess.'

'That is very generous of you,' Fr Duddleswell said reflectively. 'But I really am not sure who owns it.'

'It's not yours?' Fred was astonished.

''Tis and 'tisn't, if you follow me. 'Twas donated by the good sisters to the parish. I do not know at all whether I have the right to sell. You see, the nuns are rather fond of what you call "that muck" overlaying the Tichat.'

'But, Fr Duddleswell,' Fred Dobie objected strongly, 'you can't possibly let that ... that nun stay for ever on top of what is probably a masterpiece. Wipe her off and give the sisters a share in the proceeds. There'll be enough in the sale to divide three ways.'

A huge sigh escaped Fr Duddleswell. 'Never was there an extravagant burst of joy without affliction in its train.' He offered Fred his hand in farewell. 'Thank you kindly.'

'More money for orphans' outings, Father.' Fred could see defeat staring him in the face.

'Grateful, Fred. You are a very kind crook to be thinking of the poor suffering orphans at a time like this. How much am I in your debt?'

'Forget it, Father. It's peanuts. Besides, Brockaway wouldn't charge *you* for an opinion.'

With that, Fr Duddleswell gathered me to him and we beat a hasty retreat.

In the car, my mentor moaned, 'Ah, what 'tis like to have divided loyalties, Father Neil.'

I asked him to explain the reason for his lamentation.

'To be torn twixt love and beauty.'

'That's no clearer,' I pretended.

'I do not want to upset the sisters whom I dearly love, but if I leave their Mother Foundress undisturbed, what becomes of that exquisite beauty hidden underneath?'

'If you ask me,' I said, 'Mother Foundress has been hiding too much beauty for far too long already. It's about time the old witch was knocked off her perch. It's a sacrilege not to.'

'You are absolutely right, Father Neil, but I cannot agree with you.'

'With the utmost respect, Father, I think you're crackers.'

'Do I have to remind you, boy, that I have masterdom in St Jude's?'

'I apologize,' I said, 'provided you realize it's totally insincere.'

He was so upset his driving was becoming erratic. ''Tis true, you see, the Tichat belongs to the world but Mother Foundress' portrait means the world to the sisters.'

'To Mother Stephen, you mean. Are you really so scared of her?'

He was shocked. 'Scared of *her*? Scared of a *woman*? Yes, I am.'

'Bad as that, is she?'

'Father Neil, I have told you that as Superior of the convent she thinks she is the voice of God when in fact ...'

'As parish priest that is your prerogative.' He grinned in

acknowledgement. 'Suppose,' I said, 'you rang her and asked her permission to scrape off the portrait, what are your chances of success?'

'Me chances?' he echoed. 'Slighter than the thin white vest clinging to the inside of an eggshell.'

Next morning, Mrs Pring came into my study. 'I fixed that picture for you, Father Neil.'

'Fixed it,' I said, horrified. 'You don't mean you sewed up the tear in it?'

' 'Course not. I know how valuable it is. Father D's right about me. I have ears on me like sea-shells and more eyes than a dragon-fly.'

She explained that she had telephoned Sister Bursar at the convent to say that Fr Duddleswell urgently wanted to discuss a delicate spiritual matter with the Superior.

I congratulated her on her initiative. 'What reward can I give you, Mrs P?'

'Father D's head on a plate,' she said.

'Mother Superior can't be such an ogre. What's she really like?'

'Like Queen Victoria,' she replied, 'after she's been on six months' hunger strike'

Fr Duddleswell burst in without knocking, clutching a letter. 'Father Neil,' he gasped, 'I have been invited by the Superior to tay at the convent.' Seeing Mrs Pring there, he added, 'You bold, bad woman, this would not be any of your doing?' Her hesitation proved his suspicions correct. 'How many times have I not told you to correct your morals else I will close the front door on your back?'

'That old crow, Mother Stephen . . .' began Mrs Pring.

' 'Tis not for the likes of you to call a holy nun an old crow.'

'That's what you always call her,' retorted Mrs Pring.

'Surely, but I am in sacred orders and 'tis me privilege. Oh,' he broke off sadly, 'I was so hoping for a thorn-free afternoon and now 'tis convent tay and cucumber sandwiches at four.'

'You can rely on my support,' I said, winking at Mrs Pring.

'With how many tanks?' he asked. 'No, I am resolved. Not a bit of me will go. Besides, cucumber sandwiches twist me intestines into terrible knots.'

I applied a touch of psychology in Mrs Pring's presence.

'You're not going to give in to a woman, Father?'

'Ah,' he said with a sickly smile, 'me little hero, me young champion, me wee white calf. You do not know this lady. You have not yet resisted unto blood.'

'So,' Mrs Pring said, supporting me sturdily, 'you're to lie down in front of her, quiet as a mouse under a cat's paw.'

'What you two conspirators did not know,' he hurled at us, 'is that I have been making me own business arrangements.' Mrs Pring and I looked at each other guiltily. 'The only thing Mother Stephen understands is superior force, you follow?'

'You haven't hired Joe Louis?' said Mrs Pring, naming the only boxer she had ever heard of.

'I am speaking of holy obedience. I wrote the General of her Order at Mother House in Aix-en-Provence. I told her truly that Mother Stephen had donated the Foundress' picture to St Jude's and asked if I might suitably dispose of it to the glory of God and for the benefit of the orphans. I am expecting her reply any day.'

Pretending to be shocked, I said, 'You've gone over Mother Stephen's head?' That registered. 'But, Father, that would mean erasing the original and you distinctly said the nuns love ...'

'I was going,' he put in quickly, 'to arrange for a top notch photographer to take a picture of it.'

'Not the same,' I insisted. 'The good sisters can't pray in front of a photo.'

'It makes no difference now,' he said irritably. 'I will just have to face up to Mother Stephen, I reckon. I promised meself anyway I would get the better of that bumpy woman before I qualify for a wooden leg, and the time is now.'

'The older the buck, the harder the horn,' Mrs Pring said, relishing the prospect of the decider between the two best heavyweights in the business.

Fr Duddleswell turned on me. 'As a penance for your conniving with that maid of the melodious voice ...'

'Yes, Father?'

'You will be joining me for tay at the convent.'

Sister Frederick greeted us silently with a bow and we followed her swishing skirts along a gleaming parquet corridor to the parlour. We were shown into a cold, dust-free room stuffed with silence and there abandoned. A bloody statue of the Sacred Heart was its only adornment. There we awaited the Superior, seated like a couple of naughty kids on a park bench.

'A pretty cheerless place,' I whispered conspiratorially, 'specially reserved for visitors?'

'I breakfasted here once,' Fr Duddleswell whispered in return. ''Twas the first time in me life I saw egg-cosies. And somethin' else: they not only gave me two boiled eggs, but also two spoons to eat 'em with.'

'Very hygienic,' I laughed softly, as though we were in a graveyard and I did not want to scandalize the dead.

''Twas a bitter cold morning, Father Neil, around Christmas time. They had kindly lit a fire for me. The table was over there'—he pointed to the centre of the room—'and the cutlery was in front of the fire *warming*.'

There was a knock on the door so slight it could have been made by a sponge, and Fr Duddleswell called out, 'Come in,' and to me he muttered, 'Leave me with the talking. I have got the knack of her.'

Mother Stephen's long, narrow head appeared round the door and intoned, *Laudetur Jesus Christus.*'

'*Semper laudetur,*' replied Fr Duddleswell jumping up, 'may Christ be always praised.'

The Superior followed her head and was followed in turn by Sister Gemma, an elderly nun who acted as the convent Bursar.

'A companion must be present,' explained Mother Stephen. 'It is written in our holy rules.'

'Of course,' said Fr Duddleswell who had evidently made treaties with nuns before. 'Won't you take a seat, Mother?'

'Please be seated, Fathers,' said the Superior. 'Are you ready for your tea?' I soon noted Mother Stephen's sentence-form was often interrogative when the tone was unmistakably affirmative.

'Indeed, Mother,' said Fr Duddleswell, and I seconded him. It occurred to me—and the thought nearly made me giggle—that I had been invited as his chaperon.

Sister Bursar opened the door, smartly clapped her hands and two pretty nuns with down-cast eyes entered bearing a table set for two. They put the table down in the centre of the room and, bowing, retired.

As a spectacle is was nothing short of oriental.

Chairs were set at table for us by Sister Bursar and we were admonished to sit and eat.

'You will not join us, Mother?' asked Fr Duddleswell, purely out of politeness.

'Our rules, Father.'

'Of course.'

I poured out the tea. In that enormous silence, it sounded like an old-fashioned lavatory cistern; and munching the delicate cucumber sandwiches made a churning noisier than a cement mixer.

'Milk, Father?' demanded Mother Stephen from afar.

Fr Duddleswell nodded gratefully. 'May the Almighty God keep the children and the milking hand.'

'You like cucumber sandwiches, Fr Duddleswell?'

'Only this morning I was telling Father Neil here what cucumber sandwiches do to me, was I not?' I nodded. 'October is round the corner, Mother,' he said, directing his words at the Superior with some difficulty, for she had stationed herself like October just out of sight, by the window. He was at a disadvantage and he knew it.

'October? So it is, Father.' She spoke as if she entirely approved the regularity with which the days and months succeeded one another.

'I was wondering if you would like Father Neil to come here to give Benediction on Friday evenings in October. With the rosary, of course.'

'Thank you, Father.'

'Does that mean yes?'

'No, it means no.'

'Ah,' said Fr Duddleswell, 'I thought it might be convenient for you.'

'No, Father.' Her timing, like her life, was impeccable. She waited before explaining. 'Our rules prescribe special devotions, the litany of Mary, prayer to St Joseph and the stations of the cross, throughout October.'

''Twas only a thought,' murmured Fr Duddleswell, and went back to mixing cement.

Out of the corner of my eye, I could see Mother Stephen fingering her rosary beads as if wanting our visit to interfere as little as possible with her supplications for a happy death.

Fr Duddleswell put down his tea-cup on the saucer with a cymbal-like clash and said, 'I have been seeking an opportunity to talk with you, Mother, about the picture of Mother Foundress.'

'We want it back, Father,' said Mother Stephen, quiet but assertive.

'I beg your holy pardon, Mother.'

'We want it back. You see, an eminent Jesuit in Rome, Fr Giuseppe Orselli, has agreed to take up the cause of our Foundress with a view to having her beatified by the Sovereign Pontiff in 1955.'

'But why the need for the picture, Mother, 'tis not miraculous in the normal sense?'

'Something far more important. It is the only one there is.'

'That,' wheezed Fr Duddleswell, with masterly understatement, 'is inconvenient.'

'How "inconvenient"? Has it not been stored away for years?'

'I always intended, Mother ...' Fr Duddleswell began but braked sharply when he recalled what he had said to me a few days earlier.

'As St Francis de Sales put it,' said the Superior, 'God does not count our good intentions, He weighs them.'

I thought that Fr Duddleswell's good intentions in this respect would hardly trouble the scales.

'The Leonardo, Mother ... a masterpiece.'

'Does God concern Himself so much with masterpieces, Father? Can He not make and unmake masterpieces when He wills? Surely God's heart is moved much more by sincere and simple things?'

'Is not a masterpiece, Mother, God's gift to man given through man?'

'Ah, Fr Duddleswell, do you not agree with Thomas à Kempis when he writes, "God does not so much regard the gift of the lover as the love of the giver"?'

'I do, Mother. I do. Indeed, I do. 'Tis why all these years I have treasured the portrait of Mère Magdalène, not for its intrinsic worth only but because of the love with which you gave it.'

He emphasized the word 'gave'.

'*Gave*, Father?'

'Mother, *gave*.'

'But, Father, does not giving imply acceptance?'

'Mother, does not God give His grace even when we refuse it?'

'No, Father, He does not. He offers it but does not give it, otherwise the sinful soul would be in a state of grace which, by definition, it is not. God does not give in this instance because He cannot.'

'D'you compare your Foundress' portrait to the gift of grace?'

'It was meant, Father, as God's blessing on the whole parish.'

'And so it shall be,' said Fr Duddleswell, completely vanquished at theology. 'But I am obliged to tell you a painful fact I would rather have kept from you.'

'Yes, Father,' said Mother Stephen, suddenly starching her habit.

'The picture ...'

'It has been stolen!' cried Mother Stephen.

'No, Mother.'

'*Deo gratias*.'

'It has been in a slight ... accident. Or two.'

'Tell me!' The tone was magisterial.

'I was admiring it the other day when, without a spark of malice, I spilled a cup of tay over it.'

'Oh, no.'

' 'Twas not boiling hot, mind. And I ... I ... I put me feet through it.'

'*Miserere mei, Deus*,' moaned Mother Superior. 'More than ever must we have it back.'

' 'Tis too precious, Mother,' said Fr Duddleswell.

'*Now* you tell me, Father! You lock up our Order's most treasured possession in a cellar ...'

'We don't have a cellar, Mother,' I informed her.

'Fr Duddleswell,' objected the Superior, 'would you kindly tell this garrulous young man to speak only when he is spoken to.'

'Young man,' Fr Duddleswell said severely, 'speak only when you are spoken to. Now tell Mother Superior we do not have a cellar.'

'We don't have . . .' I broke off. 'She knows already, Father.'

'But not *officially*, Father Neil.'

I gave Mother Stephen the information officially. It did not seem to pacify her.

'Fr Duddleswell, you stab our portrait with your feet and then have the impudence to say it is precious to you. What would you not have done with it had you hated it? Do you not know that our humble Foundress always wore a veil so that throughout her years in the convent her features were unknown? The face is on the portrait providentially. It was painted from life by one of our founding sisters less than an hour after Mère Magdalène had expired.'

'Really!' I cried, unable to contain myself despite the admonition. It explained why the portrait made my flesh creep.

Mother Stephen looked at me even more disapprovingly as though I were one of her nuns who had broken the *magnum silentium*, the great silence of the night hours.

At this point, Fr Duddleswell felt it incumbent on him to tell the Superior how he was using the term 'precious' when he applied it to the picture.

'You mean,' said Mother Stephen, after hearing the whole story, 'that our Foundress is to be erased from memory . . .'

'We have no portrait of Jesus,' put in Fr Duddleswell.

'The Holy Shroud of Turin, Father,' I said.

'With that one exception,' Fr Duddleswell added black with rage, realizing I had inadvertently demolished his strongest argument.

'Our Foundress is to be erased from memory so that you can make a few pounds profit.'

'Mother Superior,' exclaimed her protagonist, 'you do me dishonour. I am not doing this for money. 'Tis for the sake of art.'

'Fr Duddleswell,'—the tone was threatening—'I counsel you to lay down your sword.'

'If I give up me sword, Mother, be assured 'twill be point first.'

'I knew I had no choice.'

'None whatsoever, Mother.'

'That is why I have submitted my case for the return of our portrait to the highest authority.'

'To God?'

'To the Bishop.'

Fr Duddleswell went rigid. 'What wickedness, Mother Superior. You have gone over me head. To the Bishop.'

'More, Fr Duddleswell, I give you ample warning. I intend to instruct the sisters and orphans of your irreligious purposes. I will tell them you have, like a pagan, thrust both feet through the portrait of Mother Foundress. And I shall put them under obedience to bombard heaven with their entreaties until we have restored unto us our most treasured possession.'

As we left, full of undigested food, Fr Duddleswell belched and said to me, 'Talk about bringing in the big battalions.'

'D'you think,' I asked, 'that the Lord who loves little chilren can refuse the petitions of His darlin' little ones?'

A week later, the four of us reassembled at Bishop's House. This time we were mercifully spared tea.

'Dear Father and Mother,' said Bishop O'Reilly, as if he were beginning a letter to his parents. 'I have read most carefully and prayerfully the submissions the both of you have sent me. And now, with all the authority of office invested in me by Christ, I have come to this humble and irrevocable decision. That picture—so dear to all of us for diverse reasons—must be accounted the heritage of the entire diocese. As Christ's representative, I pledge myself to do with it as He Himself would wish. And now, if you would care to kneel, I will give you all my apostolic blessing.'

The interview lasted approximately thirty seconds. Never before had I been so vividly aware that the imparting of information is a minor function of language. Stripped of its theological finery, the Bishop's contribution amounted to this: 'Hello. A curse on both your houses. I'm the boss. The picture is mine. I will do what the hell I like with it. Good riddance and the devil go with you.'

All of us, the Bishop included, knew that's what he meant; but obedience forbade us to voice any objection.

As we prepared to leave, the Mother Superior asked the Bishop for 'a word in private, my Lord,' which he granted.

Outside in the street, Fr Duddleswell was fuming. ' 'Tis hopping mad I am. 'Tis kicking badgers out of me toes I am.'

I tried to console him. 'At least he didn't do a Solomon on you and cut the picture in half.'

187

'And then,' he complained, 'that old crow, that mouldy black sausage put me hat out of its shape by breaking all the rules.'

'Not of her Order?'

'The rules of common decency,' he said. 'Now I have to figure out for meself what she is up to. Only God and the Bishop know so far the poison of her. Her wiles are as dark as a brown cow's inside.'

I asked him if he thought the Bishop would let her have the picture back.

'Am I the Voice from the cloud?' he replied. 'All I am sure of is that Bishop O'Reilly knows as much about art as he knows about religion.'

I realized that while he was in that mood nothing I said would bring him any peace.

He consoled himself by venting his feelings about the Bishop with a loud rendering of the song of the King of the Penzance Pirates:

> Many a king on a first-class throne,
> If he wants to call his throne his own,
> Must manage somehow to get through
> More dirty work than ever *I* do.

'But, Father Neil, Father Neil,' he moaned, as we reached the car.

'Yes, Father.'

'Why are women so ... so *deceitful*?'

It was barely four weeks later when Fr Duddleswell came tearing up to my study. 'Fred Dobie's just phoned,' he said. 'He told me to look in today's *Times*. I went out and bought it. *See.*'

He spread out an inner page of *The Times* on my desk and there was a large reproduction of 'A Recently Discovered Tichat'. Underneath, there was a learned article about Tichat's influence on van Gogh and the early Impressionists. Finally, a note that the picture, put up by a private dealer (name unknown), was to be auctioned at Ritzie's the following day.

Fr Duddleswell was ecstatic with relief and joy. 'So the

Bishop did not listen to old Sourpuss, after all. Did I not tell you we could safely leave the decision to our wonderful wise Bishop?'

'No,' I said. 'But are we going to the auction?'

'To be perfectly honest with you, Father Neil, I would sooner miss the Almighty God's verdict on me soul at Judgement Day.'

We arrived very early and managed to find seats in the front row to the right of the rostrum where we whiled away the time by reciting our breviary. The picture on its easel, marked Lot One, disappointed me. The restoration was masterly, it was hard to tell where the canvas had been rent. But the picture itself seemed to me to be swathed in mist, not at all precise and photographic in the way I liked. I confessed as much to Fr Duddleswell.

' 'Tis little wonder, Father Neil, seeing you are only a connoisseur of chocolate and ice cream. Ah,' he sighed, ogling the picture, ' 'tis a beaut, 'tis a gem, a masterpiece.'

'And,' said Fred Dobie, resting his chin and whiskers on Fr Duddleswell's shoulder from behind, 'in a few seconds, 'twill be mine.'

'Quiet, please,' called the auctioneer, banging his gavel a couple of times. 'Lot Number One. "Landscape With Crows" by Jean-Paul Tichat. Reserve price of six thousand guineas. Anyone?' Someone must have given a slight signal. 'Thank you, sir. Seven, eight, nine, ten thousand guineas.' The auctioneer glanced occasionally in Fred's direction where, no doubt, he advanced his offer by a twitch of his moustache. 'Eleven thousand guineas. And a half. Twelve thousand. And a half. Twelve and a half thousand guineas, I am bid.' I was breathless. 'Thirteen thousand. Any advance on thirteen thousand guineas. Gone!' He brought his hammer down no louder than if he were using his knuckles. 'To the gentleman in the second row.'

Once more Fred seemed about to moult all over Fr Duddleswell's shoulder. 'It's not all mine,' he said modestly. 'I'm buying for a consortium.'

'Lot Number Two,' the auctioneer said in the background. 'A Louis Quatorze snuff box. Reserve price of fifty guineas.'

I wasn't interested in trifles.

'I've got a stake in it,' Fred said. 'Shouldn't be surprised if we sell it in three years for double or treble that.'

The auctioneer was droning on. 'Fifty-five guineas. Sixty. Sixty-five. Seventy. Any advance on seventy guineas?'

'That is a mercenary mean attitude, Fred Dobie,' whispered Fr Duddleswell hoarsely.

'Seventy-five guineas.'

'What do you mean?' objected Fred.

I seconded him. 'Yes, what do you mean?'

'Eighty. Eighty-five. Ninety guineas.'

'The nuns adored that picture,' explained Fr Duddleswell.

'So do I,' said Fred.

'Only for the financial rewards 'twill bring you.'

Ninety-five, one hundred. One hundred guineas. One hundred and ten.'

'That's not fair, Father,' I said, as the auctioneer went on gathering in the bids.

'Fr Duddleswell,' protested Fred.

'Be quiet, Fred Dobie. I will be dealing with the divil before I deal with you again surely.'

'*You* be quiet, Fr Duddleswell,' urged Fred. 'Please, Father, the auction.'

'I will *not.*'

'Wait till later,' I pleaded, conscious that people were beginning to stare at us, and Fred added, 'Still, for just one moment.'

'No advance,' called out the auctioneer, 'on one hundred and fifty guineas. Gone! To the young clerical gentleman in the front row.'

'Oh, me guileless friend, me chumpish codling of a curate,' lamented Fr Duddleswell. 'You have just parted with one hundred and fifty guineas that you have not got.'

Fred touched Fr Duddleswell's shoulder. 'Hard luck, Father. You just missed it at a hundred and forty-five.'

'What d'you mean, Fred?'

'From seventy guineas on,' said Fred, 'the only one bidding against him was you.'

Fred offered to pay for the snuff box out of his own funds. He promised to try and sell it in his shop for sixty pounds or so and send us the bill for the difference.

'After all,' Fred said, 'I do own a masterpiece. At least for a year or two.'

'No criticism of your preaching, Father Neil, but I distinctly heard you say in the pulpit, "I think".'

I was on the carpet in his study. 'I did,' I admitted.

'The faithful are not at all interested in what you or I *think* but in what the Catholic Church teaches us is the truth.'

Mrs Pring brought in tea and a couple of letters. 'Second post,' she announced.

Fr Duddleswell slit one of the letters open. 'You know how the Anglican preacher got up in his pulpit one day and said, "Now, as Almighty God says ..."'

'With some degree of justification.' He was too distracted to notice I had committed the unforgivable sin of finishing off one of his jokes.

'Father Neil, that snuff box you foolishly bought at the auction.'

'I'll pay the money back, Father.'

Mrs Pring put in, 'Little by little, as the cat said while eating the herring.'

'There is no need,' said Fr Duddleswell. 'Fred Dobie sold it to an Arab for two hundred and fifty guineas and he sends you a cheque for a hundred.'

'Hurrah,' cried Mrs Pring.

'Empty bags,' he said, 'make the biggest bang.' Then he exploded himself. 'Hu-bloody-rah!'

'He's won the pools,' shouted Mrs Pring.

'As good as. A cheque for £3,000.' He flagged it in front of my eyes.

'This is becoming quite a habit, Father,' I said. 'From the Bishop?' I had noticed the envelope bore the Bishop's crest, '*In Medio Semper*'.

He nodded. ''Tis a token gift from the proceeds of the auction.'

'It'll help in the rebuilding of the church hall.'

Fr Duddleswell didn't reply at once, but at length he said, 'No. It struck me at the auction that there was more than a granule of truth in what the Superior said. The sisters would have revered the portrait of their Foundress. Instead, 'tis disappeared for ever, and greedy mercenaries like Fred Dobie and his associates have acquired the Tichat. *They* only appreciate it for the profit 'twill bring them. There would have been far more beauty in the sisters' eyes than ever these dealers will find in Tichat. I am afraid, Father Neil, I have allowed me aesthetic sense to overcome me love of our holy religion.'

'How can you say that, Father? As a good priest should, you left the decision to a wonderful wise Bishop, and he chose to give the work of art to the nation, to posterity.'

'Perhaps Bishop O'Reilly is short on faith, too, Father Neil. Could it be that he, like Fred Dobie, was only out to make a pretty penny? He sold the Tichat for thirteen thousand guineas. What if he had it restored for two thousand and gave me another three? By my reckoning, he has picked up a cool eight thousand guineas merely by talking to a dealer down the blower.'

'Could be.'

'The least we can do, Father Neil, is to hand over this cheque to Mother Stephen. 'Twill console her some to know that though Mother Foundress died fifty years ago, she is still working overtime in heaven raising money to support an orphanage.'

'Such kindness,' said Mrs Pring, 'such generosity—he's delirious.'

After telephoning the convent, he told me the bad tidings: it was to be tea again in the nuns' parlour that very afternoon.

Once more we were bowed into the spotless reception room. The first thing to greet us was the portrait of Mother Foundress in the place of honour above the fireplace.

'It's impossible!' I gasped. 'Look, Father, there's where your feet went through it.'

'I have heard of experts removing icons *in toto* when one has been painted on top of another but ...,' he smiled knowingly, 'I have never known 'em transfer a rip in the canvas before.'

Just then Mother Stephen knocked and entered, followed by two young sisters who carried in the tea table set for two. This time, as the sisters left, they bowed reverently towards the portrait of Mère Magdalène.

'No Sister Bursar today, Mother?' asked Fr Duddleswell archly.

'Not disposed, Father.'

'Does that mean "unwell" or "told not to come"?'

'I thought, Father, it *might* make her unwell if she came.'

'Mother,' said Fr Duddleswell, as we took our places, 'I was wanting to atone, in so far as I can, for the loss of your beloved portrait.'

My head was in a whirl. The portrait was patently hanging in its gilded frame above the fireplace.

'I have signed the cheque on the back, Mother, so you can put it straight in the convent's account.'

'No, Father.'

'I assure you, Mother, my one aim in all this was to preserve an art treasure for the world. But I am thinking now that perhaps you were right and ... I was right, too, of course, in the wrong way.' Holding out the cheque to her, he implored, 'Please take it, Mother.'

'No need, Father.'

From the folds of her habit she produced a cheque for the same amount.

'But,' I began, then caught Mother Stephen's eye. 'We do not have a cellar in our house, Mother.'

'I think, Mother,' said Fr Duddleswell apologizing for my incoherence, 'we are making Fr Boyd indisposed.' Mother Stephen actually smiled, wolfishly. 'May I tell him, Mother?'

Mother Stephen gave her consent with a nod.

'That portrait up there is a copy, you follow?'

'The only copy of the original we possess,' put in Mother Stephen.

' 'Tis exact down to every detail,' went on Fr Duddleswell, 'even to showing the signs of me pagan footprints. But,' turning to Mother Stephen, 'why did you ask the Bishop to have *them* included?'

'Not to perpetuate your crime, Father, I assure you. But, you see, I did carry out my promise to God to tell the sisters and the children what happened ...'

'That imitation tear is the authentic touch, you mean, Mother.'

'Exactly, more or less. Things were made easier for me because the older sisters have not seen the original for years and their memories are none too good. The younger sisters have never seen it at all. But all of them, the children too, are convinced that their prayers brought Mother Foundress back to us.'

Even though they didn't, I thought. I ventured to say, 'And Mère Magdalène's face is still preserved for posterity.'

'You express yourself so nicely, Father,' said Mother Stephen, not reprimanding me this time for opening my mouth. 'Further, Fr Duddleswell, our three thousand guineas are going towards the beatification process of our Foundress. With that amount of backing, God's grace can hardly fail.'

Heavens, I reflected, if Mother Stephen and Fr Duddleswell had married each other, their offspring would have made Machiavelli look like Micky Mouse.

'For three thousand pounds,' I burst out, 'I could get Fr Duddleswell canonized. Even before he's dead. But isn't that a waste of money, Mother?'

'On Fr Duddleswell, I will not give an opinion. But the honouring of our Foundress will mean more vocations for our Order and so more sisters to look after orphans all over the world.'

I felt properly put in my place.

Fr Duddleswell said, 'If the Bishop paid a thousand guineas for this copy ...'

'It's the most expensive fake in the business,' I suggested.

'And three thousand apiece to Mother Stephen and me,' Fr Duddleswell continued, 'then after the fee for restoration he left only four thousand for himself. I have maligned him.'

'He is only half the scoundrel you took him for,' I said.

'Now, Fathers,' interrupted Mother Stephen, assertively, 'shall we take tea?'

She drew up a chair for herself and, carefully seated with her back to Mother Foundress, she produced from the labyrinthine folds of her habit an enormous tea cup.

Back at the presbytery, Fr Duddleswell coaxed me into his study. 'Delightful, sensitive lady, that Mother Superior.' A burp brought him to his senses. 'Cucumber,' he explained.

'I said, 'No need to swear, Father,' just as I noticed a large-brown-paper parcel on his desk.

Mrs Pring entered with her broom. As Fr Duddleswell cut the string and began to remove the wrapping, she told us, 'It came by Post Office van.'

Fr Duddleswell, snowy-faced, held up a second portrait of Mère Magdalène, indistinguishable from the first.

'Cucumber! Cucumber!' I cried. 'A present from the Bishop?'

Fr Duddleswell shook his head and proceeded slowly to read the attached letter. 'Monsieur le Curé ... Dear Father ... It's from the Mother General in Aix-en-Provence. She thanks me cordially for all the help I am giving her Order and the orphans and ... she states there were in fact five portraits done of the dead Mère Magdalène at the one sitting—and ... and would I like another?' He looked up, his mouth agape. 'D'you reckon that old crow at the convent knew all along her picture was not the only original in existence?'

He handed the picture to me while he picked up the phone and dialled a number. For a moment I thought he was going to have words immediately with Mother Stephen.

'Fred? Fr Duddleswell here. Just to let you know I think we may have acquired another Tichat ... You heard me. Another Tichat.'

In her curiosity, Mrs Pring came closer to examine the picture in detail. She tripped on the carpet and her broom went through the canvas. She herself ended flat on the floor like a plate of porridge.

Fr Duddleswell raised his eyes to heaven but his mind and heart were in the other place. 'Hell!' he yelled before he could contain himself. 'Forgive me, Fred, I was just saying safe home to a fallen woman ... Yes, Fred, by the most ugly of coincidences this one, too, has a whopping great hole in it.'

XI *The Doomsday Chair*

It was a chance remark of mine that turned the breakfast conversation to the topic of superstition.

'It says in today's paper, Father, that a Church of England vicar doesn't believe in the fires of Hell.'

'Then,' said Fr Duddleswell, slitting open a letter as though it were an infidel's throat, 'I hope he has made provision in his will to be buried in asbestos underwear.' He nodded to Mrs Pring at the end of the table. 'A cut of bread, if you would be so kind. Ah, yes, Father Neil, 'tis always the absence of faith that leads to superstition.'

Mrs Pring, her bread knife poised, said, 'The Irish are superstitious enough.'

'Incredible as it may seem, there is something in what the lady says. In me parents' home-town in County Cork ...'

'Will one slice do,' interrupted Mrs Pring.

'Two,' and he proceeded to direct her hand with his wagging index finger. 'Thicker, please. That way the butter ration goes further.' He signified approval of her efforts. 'Yes,' he went on. 'In County Cork, now, there was a superstition among some that if a dog bit you, you should take a hair from his tail and 'twould heal the wound forthwith.'

Mrs Pring was putting the bread on his plate. She touched his head, pretended to claim a hair, and gave me a wink. 'Insurance against an attack of rabies,' she said.

'A feeble-minded feller, name of Seamus Crowe,' Fr Duddleswell proceeded, 'was one day accidentally scratched by a huge, thin mongrel. A *gentle* dog was Rover,' he emphasized, 'but something of a cross between a Great Dane and the Eiffel Tower. 'Twas but a wee scratch on the leg. Even so, Seamus pulled a hair from Rover's tail.'

Instead of continuing his story, Fr Duddleswell crammed

196

his mouth with toast. 'So much for *that* superstition,' he concluded.

'It didn't heal the scratch?' I asked.

'I have no idea. But I do know that afterwards, Seamus Crowe had to make do with four fingers on his right hand.'

'I don't suppose there's much superstition round here, Father.'

'The usual dependence of the weak-minded, Father Neil,' he replied with a glance at Mrs Pring, 'women mostly, on mascots, mediums and fortune-telling.'

'There's one gentleman not far from here,' growled Mrs Pring, 'who thinks he's God.'

Fr Duddleswell took no notice. 'Many who would not dream of coming to church decorate the dashboards and windscreens of their cars with St Christopher medals.'

'Don't you?' challenged Mrs Pring.

'Of course, woman. But I believe in St Christopher.'

'And they don't, I suppose.'

'Certainly they do not. They expect a little bit of unconsecrated metal to assist them,' he said, starting to shake the salt cellar over his fried egg. 'Whereas I rely on the intercession of the saint himself with ... God Almighty!' The last words were more an expostulation that the conclusion of a sentence. The top of the salt cellar had come off and there on his plate was a pillar of salt as big as Lot's wife. 'Woman,' he exclaimed, 'I have told you a thousand times to well screw the top of that salt cellar.'

'You're not superstitious, I suppose,' said Mrs Pring unperturbed.

Fr Duddleswell took a pinch of salt with his right hand and threw it over his left shoulder where Mrs Pring happened to be standing. 'Indeed, I am not.'

Mrs Pring dusted the white crystals from her dress and apron. 'You read your horoscope every day, you can't deny it.'

'Only to find out how marvellously mistaken 'tis. You, now, get St Vitus's Dance if even a stray black cat enters the house lest death should enter with it.'

I went on munching, not very involved, until Mrs Pring, obviously riled, said, 'What about The Doomsday Chair, then?'

Fr Duddleswell put down his fork and leaned on his elbow.

'The age of persecution is not over by any means, Father Neil.'

Mrs Pring explained for my benefit that The Doomsday Chair was a chair in the local public house, 'The Pig And Whistle'. Legend had it that whoever sits on it, dies.

The parish priest sighed and shifted to his other elbow for support.

'Is there anything in it?' I asked.

'As much,' said Fr Duddleswell, 'as you would find with a miscroscope inside that lady's head. 'Tis all dreamed up by the publican, Fred Bowlby. His wife Eileen is a darlin'. She always appreciates a visit, by the way. But Fred is another who would do well to invest in a fire-proof shroud.' With that satisfying observation he resumed eating.

'I thought,' sniffed Mrs Pring, 'that Jesus was the friend of publicans.'

Out of the corner of a crammed mouth, Fr Duddleswell managed to joke, 'The friend of tight men and loose women, eh?'

Mrs Pring didn't let go. 'Last Saint Patrick's Day, Father Neil, Fred Bowlby issued a public invitation. Any Irishman who wanted to, was free to sit on his Chair. Including Fr D.'

Fr Duddleswell didn't care much for my asking whether he had accepted or not. 'I would not be seen dead in Bowlby's pub, you follow?'

'That's the truth of it,' jumped in Mrs Pring. 'He was afraid he'd die. So everyone said, "If the Catholic priest at St Jude's is scared out of his wits, there must be something to that Doomsday Chair." The legend grew because of his Reverence's superstition.'

Once more, Fr Duddleswell put down his knife and fork. His voice was soft but there was menace in it. 'I ... am ... not ... superstitious.'

Mrs Pring turned to address me. 'Do you know, every time he sees a ladder he *has* to walk under it.'

The tiger broke loose in him. 'Woman,' he roared, banging the table, 'I am not superstitious, I tell you.'

The shock wave was considerable. Lot's wife jumped a foot in the air with most of what was on the table. A mirror fell from its nail on the wall and smashed into a thousand pieces on the sideboard.

A stunned silence ensued.

Mrs Pring, without stirring, whispered, 'Fr D, you broke that mirror without even looking in it.'

'Seven years bad luck,' he retorted in the same reverential tone, 'after herself has been with me twenty years already.'

At ten o'clock that same morning I was banging on the black, brass-knockered side door of 'The Pig And Whistle'.

A tense, red-eyed, middle-aged lady, smartly dressed, opened up. She no sooner saw me than she relaxed into a smile. 'The new assistant. I've seen you at Mass, Father.'

Soon we were seated at a small table in the well-kept public bar sipping tea and nibbling biscuits. Several tables were already set out for lunch. I had an overall impression of large bow-windows, gleaming mahogany, polished brass, hundreds of upturned glasses, coloured bottles of spirits hanging downwards like so many udders from the shelving behind the bar. The air was heavy, smelling slightly stale and sour.

'My Fred's still in bed, Father,' Mrs Bowlby said apologetically. ' "The Pig And Whistle" keeps us up very late at nights.'

I smiled understandingly.

'Another cup of tea, Father?'

I pointed to my collar. 'I'm full up to here, Mrs Bowlby.'

'And so am I, Father,' she said in a choking voice, as she reached for her handkerchief.

'Have I said something to upset you, Mrs Bowlby?'

'No, no, Father.' She dried her eyes. 'Forgive me. It's just that I'm fed up to the teeth with ... with that Doomsday Chair.'

Without looking, she thumbed across the floor of the bar. Between the piano and dartboard was a cane chair. It had a gold cushion on it and was chained and padlocked to a fixture on the wall. On the cross-section of the back-rest was a silver plaque inscribed with the words: THE DOOMSDAY CHAIR.

'Time and again,' said Mrs Bowlby, 'I've asked my Fred to get rid of it. He even sells models of it. Look.' There were a dozen wooden models on the bar counter. 'Five shillings each. He says the Chair is good for business.'

'Is it?'

'It does draw in hundreds of tourists a year,' she conceded. 'Americans mostly. They come to see the Crown Jewels and *that*.'

She was in such a highly-strung state I tried to comfort her. 'Is there any harm in that?'

'Precisely my sentiments.'

The voice belonged to the publican who had made his way, very quietly for such a burly man, into the bar. He was wearing a loose pink shirt and baggy tweed trousers. The trousers were supported by a broad leather belt studded with badges and from the belt dangled a large bunch of keys. He was holding his tea mug. 'Fred Bowlby,' he said in introduction, 'you must be ...'

'The new curate at St Jude's, Fr Boyd.'

'Eileen's told me about you. Made quite a hit with the ladies, so I believe.'

'Take no notice, Father,' said Mrs Bowlby, 'he has no respect for the cloth.'

Fred started to pour himself a mug of tea. 'Come to see The Doomsday Chair, have you, Father?'

Mrs Bowlby rose immediately and hurried out clutching her handkerchief. Her back was shaking as if she were in tears.

'Are you off, then, love?' But she was already out of hearing. Fred turned to me. 'She takes it hard, Father. But you Catholics are a superstitious lot, aren't you? What with your medals and statues and incense and dressing up like Masons and kneeling in front of bits of bread.'

'Mr Bowlby,' I said, raising my fist, 'we are *not* superstitious.' Remembering only too well the effect of Fr Duddleswell's fist on the breakfast table, I brought mine down soundlessly beside the tea-pot.

'You do realize, Fr Boyd,' Fred said, testing the warmth and texture of the tea on his tongue, 'Catholic superstition well nigh ruined the beginning of my marriage. Know what my wife made me do all through our honeymoon?'

That question revealed at once Fred's talent for and delight in double-meanings.

'No,' I gulped.

'I thought it was odd at the time, mind, but'—he gave me a knowing wink—'well, you're a man of the world, when you're newly wed you'll go to any lengths to please the little woman. That's why Eileen and me spent all our time in ... churches.' The last word, beautifully timed, brought a self-satisfied smirk to his flabby face.

'Rome,' he went on, when he had recovered from his own joke. 'The Holy Year it was. And in St Peter's Basilica was this big, black, horrible-looking statue of St Peter. The foot was worn smooth by kisses.'

'Italians are very passionate,' I told him, determined to hold my own.

'Eileen said, "For my sake, Fred, give it a kiss." ' Fred nodded amusedly several times. 'Like a coalman's boot. "Give it a kiss, Fred," she says. A bleeding funny honeymoon, I can tell you.'

'*I'm* laughing,' I replied with a Stan Laurel face.

'As I bent down to kiss it, I slipped and my tooth went clean through my bottom lip.' He pulled the pink rim of it down to show me the actual site of the wound. 'After that, Eileen had to do without. Kisses, I mean. "It's all right, love," I said, "I'm off to Lourdes next week for a cure." ' '

'About this Chair.'

'Come and see.' As we walked across, he asked, 'Care for something stronger?' I shook my head. 'A glass of Holy Water?' He apologized before pointing to the Chair. 'There she is Father,'

Above this harmless-looking Chair was a notice board on which were pasted yellow newspaper photographs and press cuttings. I spied headlines like THE KILLER CHAIR and DEATH CHAIR'S LATEST VICTIM.

'When we took this pub over three years ago I found *her* in the cellar. Newspaper cuttings, too, which spoke of a Doomsday Chair. Anyone who sat on it died *inside the week*.'

'Week?' I packed the word with scorn. 'How childish. And that's the Chair, I presume?'

His answer surprised me. 'Dunno, to be honest. Maybe it is, maybe it isn't. In the beginning, it never occurred to me there was anything haunted about that Chair because,' he said sarcastically, 'I'm not that way inclined. I even threw the cuttings in the fire. Then to jog business along in a slack period I got the Chair out, gave it a lick and a polish, and stuck it in the public bar where you see it today.'

He broke off from his story. 'Sure you won't have a snifter?' When I shook my head, 'You might need it.' I let him see he wasn't impressing me any.

'Well, then, Father, for fun I called it The Doomsday Chair. The locals came in, eyed it suspiciously and asked me why I called it that. I told them whoever sits on it dies inside a week and, hell—begging your pardon, Father—not one of them dared sit on the flaming thing. "A free drink," I said, "to any chap who plonks himself down on my old cane chair." And know what?'

'Surprise me.'

'No one would.'

'You said you threw away the press cuttings.'

'Oh, those,' Fred said, pointing to the notice board, 'those are new ones. I tell you. A year or so ago, a posh, red-faced city gent came in here. Six o'clock of a thirsty evening, the whole place bursting at the seams. "I'm not afraid of that non-sense," he said. And he sat down *there*.'

Good for him I wanted to say but didn't.

' "Called your bluff, he has, Fred", all my clients laughed. "Give the brave bloke a pint." "Why not?" I said. "He'll be stiffer'n his rolled umbrella inside a week." *Well*.'

'Well?'

'One sip of his pint of best bitter, he puts his glass care-fully on the table. And drops dead on the spot. Right where you're standing.'

'A heart attack,' I suggested, moving slightly to one side.

'No sign of one before, mind.'

'From Beer To Eternity, so to speak.'

That took Fred off his guard. 'Very jovial' was all he could manage.

'Came to a bitter end,' I said.

'Ha, ha, Father. Must store up these little witticisms for my grandchildren. But,' he turned solemn, 'such a waste.'

'Married with kids, you mean?'

'No, I was thinking of the rest of his beer. No one would finish it for him. Next,' he went on, 'a Jehovah's Witness. Came in screeching "Godlessness, Superstition." '

I said I agreed with him.

'But so do I,' said Fred, touching his heart. 'He sat down on it and wouldn't even take a pint for his pains.'

'And that didn't put a stop to it?'

'Nah, well, it wouldn't, would it? He caught a plane to a big Witness's Convention in Miami six days later and it sort of ... crashed.'

'All killed.'

Fred nodded delightedly. 'It never made the headlines, though, till the third victim.'

I could feel my Adam's apple rise and fall quite painfully.

'Charlie Skinner, a regular, should have known better. Folks used to say, if ever Charlie has a post-mortem they won't find a trace of blood in his alcohol. So, there was Charlie soaking his back teeth for two hours, one double Scotch chasing another down the tunnel, and, I suppose he sat down without realizing.'

I swallowed hard.

'After that, not one of his mates would lend a hand. Charlie staggered to his feet, went out to his car and drove straight in the river. Only three feet deep and Charlie six feet two.' Fred Bowlby wiped his eyes with the back of a hairy hand. 'Drowned.'

'Ironic,' I said.

'*Very*,' returned Fred, cheerful all of a sudden. 'Normally, he didn't take water with his whiskey. His car was a write-off.'

'So was Charlie,' I said.

'And the Coroner's verdict?'

'Dead drunk.'

The smartness of my reply made Fred say admiringly, 'You beat me to it.'

He leaned over the plaque of the Chair, breathed on it and polished it with his sleeve. 'My pride and joy, Father.' He touched his belt. 'I had a special silver lock made for it. Keep the key in my belt here, day and night. Unnecessary, really. No thief is going to break into this pub. Not with the Chair there.'

When I asked for an explanation of the unusual events, Fred feigned surprise. As far as he was concerned there was nothing to explain. A matter of a weak heart, a faulty aeroplane engine and a crowd of idiots too superstitious to help a drunk home because of what might happen to him—and so it did. After that, 'The Pig And Whistle' did rather well. There were newspaper articles, the B.B.C. did a television feature. Orders for the model chairs came from as far afield as Japan, Tibet, and places Fred had never heard of.

I tentatively put it to Fred that he was trading on people's credulity.

'Course I am,' he agreed. 'It's up to religious experts like you and your chief to get rid of credulity, isn't it? And you don't seem to be having much success, if my wife is anything to go by.'

His mercenary and cocky attitude so roused me I responded with what he took to be a trial of strength. 'Mr Bowlby, have *you* ever sat on it?'

'No.' He saw me chuckle drily. 'Not what you're thinking, Father. Cross my heart, that Chair doesn't scare me. But if I did sit on it, I'd have to admit it to my customers, wouldn't I? And I'd be living proof my Doomsday Chair is a dud. Bad for pounds, shillings and pints.'

I nodded, only half convinced.

'I challenged your Fr Duddleswell to sit on it. Offered him a hundred quid.' I started at that and he noticed. 'Oh, he didn't tell you that, then? But he was too superstitious.'

Once more I was obliged to defend Fr Duddleswell's honour.

'Okay,' said Fred. 'Tell him, I repeat my offer. A hundred quid. Any old time. More, if he sits on it—and survives—I'll sit on it myself.' This tickled his fancy. 'Safest bet I ever made,' he laughed.

It was getting to me that I had bitten off more than I could chew. I glanced at my watch. 'I'll have to be going.'

'Before you vanish, Fr Boyd.'

I turned back. 'Yes?'

'Care to try it out yourself?'

'I'm sorry,' I stuttered, 'I don't know what you mean.'

'Have I said something clever?' he leered. 'You're not superstitious, you said. Besides, I bet old Duddleswell would bury you for free.'

I was still searching desperately for some slender theological reason for not availing myself of his hospitality when Mrs Bowlby's voice pierced the silence.

'Fred! What *are* you up to? You're not trying to get our nice Fr Boyd to sit on that dreadful thing. You're not to, do you hear? *Not* to.' She stamped her foot and fled from the bar in tears.

'Catholics!' Fred said, winking at me. 'My offer's still on.' He gestured to the Chair. 'Be my guest.'

I returned to the presbytery too shaken to continue my rounds. Why was I so scared to sit on an innocuous cane chair? What was I scared of? As a Christian and a priest I shouldn't be afraid of martyrdom, but what possible danger was involved in the case of The Doomsday Chair? Perhaps it was my duty to go straight back and sit on it. Perhaps it wasn't.

Fr Duddleswell was in his study. 'You visited "The Pig And Whistle", you say, Father Neil? You saw it, then?'

I nodded casually. 'A load of codswallop,' I said. 'Didn't believe a word of it.'

'In *my* parish,' Fr Duddleswell snorted. 'Under this'—he tapped the offended organ—'very nose. Eileen, Fred's wife, has not had a decent night's sleep in months for worry.'

As nonchalantly as I could, I volunteered the news that Fred Bowlby had offered to let me sit on the Chair.

'He *what*?' exploded Fr Duddleswell. 'Were I not a man of God I would give him a thick lip.' He clenched his right fist in front of his face to show the instrument he would do it with.

'I think St Peter feels the same way about him, Father.'

'Well, did you, Father Neil?' I answered his look of concern with a shy shake of the head. After a moment, he asked, 'As a point of interest, *why* didn't you?'

I cleared my throat and pointed to my chest. 'I forgot to pin on my St Christopher medal this morning.'

Instead of splitting his sides with laughter, Fr Duddleswell slowly raised and lowered his large head. 'Very wise of you, Father Neil. *Very* wise.'

I was so embarrassed I gave him a piece of information I had resolved to keep to myself. 'He repeated the challenge he made to *you*, Father.'

Fr Duddleswell clasped his hands together as if in prayer and closed his eyes. He came out of his trance to say determinedly:

'The elastic of me patience has just snapped. I am resolved to put a stop to Fred Bowlby's caper one and for all. 'Tis me duty as parish priest, you follow?' I pursed my lips in encouragement. 'Very soon, Father Neil, I will have that proud turkey cock going down on his benders and kissing me feet.'

Breakfast time, a few days later. I asked Mrs Pring why she wasn't serving bacon and egg, the usual Saturday morning fare.

'No point in frying up for one,' she replied. 'I don't eat it and his Unholiness has been off his food for a whole week.'

Just then, Fr Duddleswell entered, grunted, said his grace and sank down in his chair. He looked very tired, I thought, as though he had spent the whole night praying. Three tufts of cotton wool on his face covered the spots where his razor had slipped.

If he had prayed a lot, it hadn't done anything for his mood. 'Where to God,' he asked, 'is me blessèd bacon and egg?'

'Ran out of eggs,' said Mrs Pring.

'Ran out of eggs,' he said. 'Any one would think she lays the perishing things.'

As Mrs Pring left, clucking like a hen, he followed her with the words, 'That woman is about as useful as a bicycle without wheels.'

Then he turned his attention to what was on offer. He sipped his coffee. 'Stone cold! What sort of a breakfast is this, then, dead coffee and'—pointing to the toast—'cremated bread?' He sighed deeply and composed himself. 'Me humble apologies, Father Neil. This morning I'm feeling miserable as sin.'

'Not sleep well, Father?'

'Had some difficulty slippin' over the border, that's all.'

I grunted in sympathy.

Suddenly he put his cup down with a crash and looked at me solemnly. 'Keep after supper free this evening, lad.' I nodded. 'Prepare tomorrow's sermon early.'

I waited for further enlightenment.

'I have thought and prayed for a whole week now. 'Tis about time I rooted out this wretched superstition of The Doomsday Chair.' He crammed his mouth with toast. Then, dramatically: 'Even if it kills me.'

During evening confessions, my mind kept returning to The Doomsday Chair and wondering what Fr Duddleswell was up to. After an unusually quiet and strained meal he told me to get ready for the road.

I stepped out of my cassock, put on my jacket and coat and went to join him in his study. The door was open. I found him kneeling on his prie-dieu, which faced the wall, gazing at a crucifix.

'Father,' he whispered, 'not my will but Thine be done. But do not let it hurt, Lord, do not let it ...'

Glimpsing me over his shoulder, he coughed and rose. I apologized for interrupting his devotions. 'I was just putting in a good word for meself,' he said. As I held out his jacket for him, he was saying, 'I am expecting your full support, Father Neil.'

' "The Pig And Whistle", Father?'

'Aye. You are no yellow-belly.' I smiled at the thought. 'You are not one of those priests who are all words and have no faith at all.' Another wan smile. 'You do want to come, of course?'

I was afraid. I desperately wanted to say 'No', but I hadn't the courage to be a coward. 'Yes,' I said, 'I'm coming.'

'Friend of me inmost heart,' he said with relief. 'I knew I had only to drop the slightest hint and you would follow me to the death.'

It was almost eight o'clock. The High Street, after a heavy day's trading, was carpeted with refuse: cardboard, orange peel, empty cigarette cartons. News vendors were still calling out, 'Star, News and Standard, paper-late', and red buses were charging angrily up and down like armour-plated cavalry.

Without a moment's hesitation, Fr Duddleswell pushed open the pub door. There were not too many patrons in at the time. A pianist was dreamily playing 'Galway Bay'.

Fr Duddleswell nudged me. ' 'Tis a most beautiful hymn, Father Neil, but beseech the organist to rest his fingers awhile till I'm done.' Fortunately, the pianist stopped of his own accord.

Gradually word went round the pub that they had company. Even the hardened pub-crawlers must have sensed that something unusual was in the air if two parsons were breathing it; and the chatter and clinking of glasses abated until only Fred's voice was audible.

The landlord was standing, arms akimbo, facing The Doomsday Chair and explaining its history to a man who was wearing a kind of stetson.

'Straight up,' Fred insisted. 'The Governor of California wrote me only last week to ask if he could borrow it. To execute criminals, I believe.'

'Gee is that so?'

'Cheaper in the long run than electricity.'

'Guess it is.'

'Make me an offer, go on,' said Fred. 'Nothing less than half a million. Pounds, naturally.'

Fr Duddlesewell and I threaded through the silent throng to the bar behind which Mrs Bowlby and a well-built platinum blonde were operating. Fr Duddleswell picked up one of the model chairs from the counter.

'That'll be five shillings, please, sir,' said the blonde innocently.

My parish priest withered her with a glance, grabbed a chair and walked to where Fred Bowlby was standing, frowning now, beside the American tourist. There he set the chair down, stood on it rather shakily and turned, white-faced and trembling, towards the crowd. He clapped his hands, unnecessarily, for silence.

'Me dear Brethr ...' He corrected himself. 'Gentlemen ... and ladies. Ladies and gentlemen. Your attention, please.'

At this, Paddy, one of our more notable parishioners, stepped forward, none too steady on his feet. He wore a three-piece suit and a trilby so far back on his head it looked as if it was trying to escape. Each time he said 'Father' he touched his forelock.

'Can I buy ye a drink, Father?'

'Not now, Paddy,' said Fr Duddleswell. Then a thought struck him. 'And why have I not seen you at Mass these last few Sundays?'

'You didn't notice me because probably I was praying with my eyes closed, Father.'

Fr Duddleswell straightened himself and addressed the crowd. 'Now, why should I, a Catholic priest, dare cross the sacred threshold of "The Pig And Whistle"?'

Paddy craned his neck. 'Father, what're ye doin' here for heaven's sake?'

' 'Tis because,' called out Fr Duddleswell, 'I am concerned for the pagan practice being perpetrated in this pub. He who sows the wind'—here Paddy burped loudly on cue—'shall reap the whirlwind.'

'I'll be communicating tomorrow for sure, Father,' said Paddy.

Fred Bowlby attempted to intervene with 'Couldn't we talk this over, Father, in the backroom?'

'I refer of course, ladies and gentlemen, to The Doomsday Chair, so-called. In lieu of anyone better qualified, 'tis up to me, the Lord's unworthy servant, to undertake this task meself.'

Fred tried again. 'Fr Duddleswell . . .'

'The very same,' said Fr Duddleswell mischievously, as if he had just been formally introduced to Fred's customers.

'Father, Father,' said Paddy, twice touching his forelock. 'Keep away from that Chair, else tomorrow you'll be saying a Requiem Mass for the repose of your own soul.'

Fr Duddleswell lifted his voice again. 'Fred Bowlby has generously offered me one hundred pounds if I dare sit on this miserable Chair.'

'I'm upping the offer,' Fred proclaimed out of the blue. 'Two hundred pounds.' That really impressed his regulars. 'Provided,' he added, 'that you *don't* sit on it.'

When the murmurs of the crowd subsided, Paddy was heard to mutter, 'That'd buy me enough of the hard stuff to retire on,' and Fr Duddleswell announced gleefully, 'Fred is afraid, y'see, that I will prove the curse of this Chair is but a confidence trick and 'twill ruin his trade.'

'Never!' cried Fred. 'I don't want you to die, that's all.'

'I am about to sit on it, all the same. This very hour. And at the same hour each evening till one week from now.'

I had called out 'Hear, hear,' before I realized how silly it sounded.

'At the end of the week,' Fr Duddleswell said, 'I will claim the Chair for me very own. Agreed, Fred Bowlby?'

Fred said that if Fr Duddleswell were alive in a week's time the Chair wouldn't be any good to him, so he didn't care who owned it.

Just then, the clock struck eight and Fr Duddleswell stepped down from his temporary pulpit. The patrons of the pub, having retreated to a safe distance, could all see him as he—rather dramatically for my taste—made a huge, wind-sweeping sign of the cross and hovered over the Chair before dropping down into it.

There were a few loud sighs, a slight shuffling of feet but no other sound until Fr Duddleswell, in his lordliest sanctuary manner, called out:

'A drink, Eileen, if you would be so kind.'

'What'll it be, Father?' Mrs Bowlby's hoarse voice returned.

'What have you got?'

A few sniggers greeted this innocent query but for the most part the customers were aware of being in the presence of greatness.

Mrs Bowlby said, 'Will a pint of dark ale do, Father?'

'Make it a half.' He didn't drink beer normally. 'A *small* half.'

As Mrs Bowlby brought him his drink, a bulb flashed as a local press photographer—forewarned, I had no doubt—took a picture, then five more of Fr Duddleswell enthroned on The Doomsday Chair, serenely partaking of a small half of ale.

He drained his glass in silence. As he rose he must have slipped in a puddle of beer because he landed flat on his back with a thud. Strangely, the crowd in the bar shuffled backwards like startled horses instead of forwards as was natural in view of the plight of a fellow human being. Only Paddy stood his ground, his faith sorely tried. 'Jesus, Mary and Joseph,' he said, 'one half of ale and the holy Father is fallen over drunk. Call a priest to hear his confession.'

With real concern I rushed to Fr Duddleswell's assistance. 'You all right, Father?'

He rose to his feet and adjusted his hat. ' 'Tis only the divil doin' his darndest.' And he handed me the fractured remains of the model chair. Next, he put his hand inside his jacket. When he withdraw it, I saw the palm was bright red.

'You're bleeding badly, Father,' I cried out, much to the consternation of the bystanders.

Fr Duddleswell took my arm and whispered in my ear. 'Get me out of here quick, Father Neil, I have broken something vital to me.'

'What, Father?'

He winked broadly. 'Me red felt pen.'

I supported him as he walked to the door, bidding everyone adieu. 'Until the same time tomorrow,' he said.

'A good dose of absolution, Father,' advised Paddy, 'and sleep it off.'

'Good night to you, gentlemen *and* ladies.'

Outside the pub, his first words to me were, 'I hope to God I have not fatally bruised me spine, like, or spiked me lungs with a couple of broken ribs.'

'You were superb.'

'Wasn't I, just?' After a couple of minutes walking in silence, he slanted his head towards me and said, 'D'you know, that was one of the greatest ordeals of me life. I really *detest* dark ale.'

True to his word, Fr Duddleswell returned Sunday night and Monday. Nothing seemed to disturb his peace of mind. I had never seen such tranquillity in a man who was, in the general estimate, destined to leave us soon. I was more than proud to be under the tutelage of this man of faith who could laugh in the teeth of death.

Walking the streets with him was like striding alongside Elijah who defeated the prophets of Baal, or Christ who drove the money-changers out of the Temple, or St Paul who stopped the trafficking in idols at the temple of Diana or Ephesus, or even dear old St Patrick himself who drove all the snakes out of Ireland into England.

Mrs Pring knew no such serenity. She blamed herself for initiating the whole horrible course of events. 'Father Neil,' she confided, 'only two days and nights of this and I'm a nervous wreck. Even if Fr D survives, I won't. Can't you at least keep him indoors?'

'Not a hope,' I said. Nor was there. I had offered to take Communion to the sick on his beat and to do his hospital rounds for him. All these offers he sweetly refused as if he couldn't see any reason for me to put myself out.

I tried by many ingenious means to keep him in, in case he should be knocked down by an infidel lorry driver or assaulted by some lunatic set on notoriety. But I noticed no change at all in his demeanour or in any of his daily habits.

To console Mrs Pring I told her I was accompanying him everywhere. 'Not,' I insisted, 'that he seems to have a care in the world.'

'His face is buttercupped and daisied all right,' she said, and we both spoke in admiration of 'the faith of the man'.

Mrs Pring held up a large rosary. 'I'm knitting the rosary for his Reverence three times a day.'

Just then Fr Duddleswell came in. He immediately went across to her. 'Me dear old friend,' he murmured. 'What's this?' he said, holding up her hand which was still holding the rosary. 'Saying your beads. Truly wonderful. But promise me one thing, dear Mrs Pring.'

'Anything, Father.'

'Promise you will not pray for me.' He smiled ever so tenderly. 'Things are bad enough already.'

On Wednesday evening at 'The Pig And Whistle', Fr Duddleswell was vested in cassock, cotta and biretta. To a piano accompaniment, he conducted the growing crowd in singing 'Faith Of Our Fathers'.

With the final duplication of 'We will be true to thee till death,' Paddy almost collapsed in tears. 'I never thought,' he moaned, 'to hear such a beautiful tune in a pub.'

Fr Duddleswell, aloft, said:

'I have been holding a holy service here for four evenings already.' He paused to thank Mrs Bowlby for handing him his pint. 'And now,' he went on, ' 'tis about time I introduced you to the most Catholic thing there is.'

Paddy held up his froth-topped glass. 'Guinness, Father.'

'No irreverence from you, Paddy Shea. Not Guinness, neither is it the shamrock, nor the Blessed Virgin, nor even the Pope of Rome himself. While I risk me life once more, me devoted assistant will show you—here he removed the green wrapping—'a Catholic collecting plate.'

He sat down to drink while I was forced to move among the customers like a soldier in the Salvation Army.

Friday was a day of sparkling sunshine. Fr Duddleswell insisted on going for his morning constitutional. He stopped at the end of a line of sycamore trees to watch the sun twinkling through the leaves and stippling the grey pavement with burnished gold.

'Such beauty, Father Neil,' he sighed, 'such intolerable

beauty. There are but two ways to look at the things of this world: as if 'twere the first time and ... as if 'twere the last.' But his face wore no obituary blackness when he said it.

Further on, he stopped in his tracks to ask, 'D'you find me a very attractive person, Father Neil?'

'I do, Father,' I affirmed. 'But what do you mean?'

'You seem to enjoy me company more than most.' He had obviously twigged as to why I never let him out of my sight.

Throughout the walk, as was now customary, people greeted him with, 'Pleased to see you, Father,' and 'Glad to know you're in the pink.' Even from inhabitants not normally concerned for the welfare of the clergy came, 'All the best, mate.'

One dear old lady said, 'Keeping well, Father?' 'Fit as a circus flea.' 'Stay well-wrapped up, Father,' she urged, though the temperature was in the eighties. When we were out of earshot, he said, 'Anyone would think I was a kiddy's Christmas present.'

A most unsavoury character drifted into view: a tramp. ''Ello, mate,' he croaked, grasping Fr Duddleswell's hand. 'May I shake your 'and?'

Since he had no choice, Fr Duddleswell said, 'Yes, mate.'

The encounter lasted but a few seconds, then the tramp broke it off with a fervent, 'Best wishes to you, mate.' He had obviously got wind of the risks my parish priest was running.

'That is the very first time,' Fr Duddleswell whispered, 'that I have ever *touched* a tramp.'

'Unhygienic,' I said. 'I only hope he hasn't given you anything.'

'Ah, but he has.' Fr Duddleswell opened his palm to reveal a half crown.

Then he did the most foolish thing I ever saw. Without looking, he stepped off the kerb in the path of oncoming traffic. The tramp's generosity must have dulled his senses. Three or four vehicles screeched to a violent halt. A small red van in particular stopped within three inches of him. Only the driver's superb reflexes prevented a fatal accident.

The van driver put his head out and yelled, 'You bleedin' fool. What d'ya think ... ?' He had recognized the man who had almost upped his insurance premium for the rest of his life. 'Fr Duddleswell?'

Fr Duddleswell, as unconcerned as if he had just watched a

213

leaf fall from a tree, walked to the side of the cabin. 'Yes, mate? This is a strange place for you to ask me for me autograph, in the middle of a busy thoroughfare.'

The driver, quietly and in a different tone of voice, said 'Bleedin' fool' again, wound up his window and drove off.

I ran to Fr Duddleswell to escort him safely across the road. On the other side, he said:

'When I have bought the Friday fish for Mrs Pring, we shall go to the church, Father Neil, to thank God for that driver's narrow escape.'

'*His* escape?'

'Indeed. He will probably never know how close I came to punching his bloody nose.'

It was then that the awful truth dawned on me. So great was his faith that sitting on The Doomsday Chair, far from making him fear for his life, had made him feel invulnerable. Now I was really worried.

Mrs Pring had reached the limits of anxiety long before. She was testing all the food she laid down before him lest it be poisoned and regularly checking the gas appliances in case death, in its hunger for the parish priest, should devour two more victims.

'I can't go on,' Mrs Pring confessed on Friday evening. 'I can't eat or sleep. I can't even cook.' She promised she would never again accuse Fr D of being superstitious if only I got him to stop.

The consolation I gave was immediately taken away by Fr Duddleswell himself. He came in carrying in his arms and stroking a black cat.

'I just found this little feller wandering around the garden like a lost soul. D'you think, Mrs Pring, you could spare him a saucerful of milk?'

It was a remarkable week and, speaking for myself, a sleepless one. On Tuesday, *The Kenworthy Gazette* brought out a special edition to cover the story. By Wednesday, the telephone was ringing non-stop and, next day, it was national news. Pictures of Fr Duddleswell seated on The Doomsday Chair appeared in the tabloids.

On Saturday morning, Fr Duddleswell's Mass was better attended than if the Sovereign Pontiff had been celebrating it.

Even the Sicilians were there. Spying them from the sacristy, he said to me, as he plunged his head in his chasuble, '*Dio mio*, Almighty God works in mysterious wayses.'

It was probably on the spur of this Sicilian moment that he announced after Mass:

'Tomorrow, holy Mass at nine will be a Requiem for the repose of the souls of three good citizens who died a natural death after parking their backsides on a perfectly harmless Chair.'

Before lunch, I was in his study. There was tremendous bustle and a sense of excitement in the air. I heard him answer the phone.

'*The Express*, you say? Yes, the finale is at "The Pig And Whistle" this evening at eight. Of course you can send a photographer along.' He smartened up his hair and eyebrows as if in readiness. "God bless, now.'

'Another batch of newspaper cuttings and telegrams,' I said, holding them up.

'Not too many with black edges, I'm hoping, Father Neil.'

Mrs Pring came in to announce, 'Three more reporters at the front.'

'Not now, Mrs Pring. Tell 'em I will be holding a Press Conference tomorrow afternoon, even if I have to rise from the dead for it.'

Mrs Pring checked a tear and went out as the phone rang again.

'Fr Duddleswell. And who the divil is it this time? ... Bishop O'Reilly? Yes, me Lord ... No, me Lord. I assure your Lordship there is no need to send an exorcist. 'Tis just a trivial instance of local superstition which I will deal with in the normal course of duty ...'

When his hour of confessions was up that evening, there were still fifty or sixty penitents outside his box waiting to be shrived. I told them to go home because Father had to fortify himself with a meal.

At this point, he emerged from his confessional to say, 'I will be here next week for sure,' and went, head high, via the sacristy into the house.

A quiet meal. Neither of us was keen to speak. At the end, only: 'Pray for me, Father Neil. And tell Mrs Pring to have faith for once in her miserable life and leave the holy oils in their rightful box.'

Near the dining room door, Mrs Pring, already clad in her outdoor clothes, made it plain she wasn't going to wash up the dishes now or maybe *ever*. She was shaking like a leaf but determined to see this thing through.

The streets were lined as for a carnival. There were cheers and jeers and scattered applause which he acknowledged as if he were 'Royalty or higher', as he put it. Tradesmen were selling gigantic balloons with Fr Duddleswell's face on; there were three hot-dog stalls and, in a glance, I took in five ice-cream vans, probably with a new specialty: 'Duddleswell's Delight'. Policemen were controlling the traffic. Fr Duddleswell stopped to sign a dozen autographs.

At the entrance of the pub, the crowd parted respectfully to allow the two priests with Mrs Pring in close attendance to to get through.

The bar was packed with customers, reporters and photographers. The pianist was giving a lively rendering of 'Bless 'em all'. While Fr Duddleswell was putting on his alb, stole and biretta I held Mrs Pring's hand for mutual comfort.

Fr Duddleswell was ready at last. He stood on a specially prepared platform and blew into the mike. A thoughtful patron, anticipating that the crowd would be of soccer proportions, had installed a loudspeaker system so that the overspill in the street could keep in touch with the proceedings.

Tongue-in-cheek, Fr Duddleswell thanked the publican for his generosity and the assembly for their patronage and prayers without which he could not have endured the rigours of the week.

'But, as you perceive, ladies, gentlemen—and all you kiddies outside'—there were cheers—'the superstition has not killed me. And I am about to kill *it*, through me absolute faith in Almighty God.' More cheers. 'First, though, a surprise for you. I have me own challenge to deliver the publican here.'

Fred stepped forward. 'Oh, yeah?'

'You promised, Fred Bowlby, that if I sat on that Chair, you would.'

'Did I? Okay, after you.'

Fr Duddleswell's mocking laughter, echoing like thunder, was much appreciated by the crowd. 'He is still hoping I will die before me week is complete. Perhaps a sudden haemorrh-age.' Laughter. 'Or lightning from heaven.' More laughter. 'Or I will fall from this chair and break'—he staggered. 'Whoops!' —he righted himself. 'Break me neck.' Cheers. 'More likely I will die laughing.' This brought the loudest laugh of all. 'Fred Bowlby, I will give *you* a hundred pounds if you sit on that Chair *before* me week is up.'

Fred squared his jaw. 'Think I'm scared, do you?'

'I do.'

'You're on.' And without a moment's hesitation, Fred sat down on The Doomsday Chair. There was a ripple of applause before a dazed Fr Duddleswell said:

'You are braver, Fred Bowlby, than I gave you credit for.'

'It's easy for me,' replied Fred, ' 'cos I'm not superstitious, see. Now we're evens.'

'And I,' sighed Fr Duddleswell, 'who have borne the burden of the heat and the day do not even get the consolation of a hundred pounds. Only that blessèd Chair.'

The clock struck eight. As he got down: 'Eileen, fetch me me pint of ale.'

Eileen was already on hand.

Fr Duddleswell blew on the froth and scattered it on the bystanders like holy water, so that Paddy and other Catholics present made the sign of the cross. With the microphone in one hand, the pint glass in the other, he sat down for the last time in The Doomsday Chair.

The applause was deafening. When it subsided, Fr Duddles-well drank his brown ale into the mike as noisily as a cow. Then he stood up and shouted so the loudspeaker nearly burst the eardrums:

'Behold me name is Lazarus AND I LIVE!'

Spontaneously the crowd sang, 'For he's a jolly good fellow,' and afterwards there was more applause. When there was a semblance of silence, Fr Duddleswell turned to me and in a whisper magnified by the speaker said, 'Now, 'tis your turn, Father Neil.'

I was shattered by this unexpected turn of events. 'But, Father, I've no stomach for beer.'

'You do not have to drink, lad. Just park your bum there like a good Christian.'

Seeing the strength of my reluctance, he turned disgustedly

to the publican's wife. "Come on, Eileen, if your husband has no objections.

'None at all,' said Fred with a grin. 'Never had any objections.'

With a flourish, Eileen drew herself a short brandy from the bar and went to sit on the Chair which had caused her so many sleepless nights. More cheers.

And then Mrs Pring.

'What's yours?' asked Mrs Bowlby.

'A pink gin.'

'There is no sin hidden,' muttered Fr Duddleswell, 'that will not be revealed.'

Mrs Pring sat down and drained her glass in a gulp.

Shamed by the courage of the weaker sex, I belatedly took my life in my hands and sat down. Diluted applause was all I deserved.

'That's me boy,' Fr Duddleswell said with a trace of irony. 'Eileen, pull me curate a glass of orange juice, if you please. He will need it if he is soon to carry that Chair home for me.'

Everybody seemed happy that evening except me. In the moment of his greatest need, after pledging my support, I had failed a man of God. As we walked home together, Fr Duddleswell, noticing my mood, said, 'Pick your chin up off the ground and show a dimple, Father Neil. Your instincts were absolutely right.'

'But the women,' I began. 'Mrs Pring ...'

'Bone to the tips of their ears. You cannot blame 'em. Ever since Eve ate the apple, they have had no theological appreciation of the mystery of iniquity, if you're still with me.'

'I'm a coward,' I said, grovelling.

'It takes a brave man to admit it, Father Neil. But please take it from me, in my estimation, you are both manly *and* prudent.'

He obviously couldn't see me shaking as I held The Doomsday Chair at arms' length.

I was only too relieved to reach his study and put the Chair down.

''Tis all right, Father Neil,' he said, ' 'tis defused.' We sat opposite each other. 'And now a wee confession.'

I wasn't interested.

''Tis a temptation that comes to us all.'

'What is?'

'First of all, drink. A week past, I loathed the filthy stuff. And now.' He licked his lips.

'What else, Father?'

'Pride without foundation.'

'Father, let's stop sparring, shall we? You're brave and I'm not. You're a man of faith and I'm more of a heathen than Fred Bowlby will ever be.'

Fr Duddleswell coughed in embarrassment. Not at all, at all. I tell you this, now, to show how much more manly you are than I.' I waited with growing curiosity. 'I could not tell anyone before, because, y'see, secrecy was of the essence.'

I wasn't helping him any.

'Me little secret is, I never sat on The Doomsday Chair at all.'

I blinked. Recalling how, in the Junior Seminary, we had coped with masters who used to paste our posterior, I asked, 'Do you mean you put the Holy Bible in the seat of your pants?'

'No, I mean I destroyed The Doomsday Chair before I sat on it.'

This was his story. He had gone down the Portobello Road to look for a copy of The Doomsday Chair. The idea was inspired in him by the realization that if Mother Foundress' picture was not unique, though it had seemed to be, neither was the Chair. Apart from the fact that he was quite an expert on furniture, the Chair was in fact very ordinary.

His task proved even easier than he had expected. He came across one straight away, in Tompkins. Only two pounds. He hid it in his garage till early last Saturday morning—'You will remember, Father Neil, how I was miserable as sin.' He had entered into league with Mrs Bowlby, so on that Saturday morning at three o'clock, according to a pre-arranged plan, she had let him into 'The Pig And Whistle'. She had borrowed the key to the padlock from the belt of her snoring spouse. She and Fr Duddleswell substituted the new chair, screwed the silver plaque on to the back-rest and replaced the gold cushion.

'It was all over in half an hour,' he said.

My admiration for him—undiluted, if a fraction altered—made me enquire further: 'But what did you do with the real Chair?'

He reddened. 'I am not superstitious, mind, but I could not take any chances, like.'

'Go on,' I said, rising from the chair I was sitting in and settling myself comfortably in the replica of The Doomsday Chair.

'I took it to the bomb-site in Ordnance Road.'

'Then?'

He was reluctant to finish his story.

'First of all, I sprinkled it with holy water and spoke over it the exorcism from the Roman Ritual.'

'"To be on the safe side, like," I mimicked. He nodded. 'But what did you *do* with it?'

'Broke it up. I could not burn it, you follow? It might have attracted attention at that hour of the morning.'

'So?'

'I was intending to leave it among the rubble but I thought some kiddies from the district might be using that site as a playground and I did not want to risk them ...' His voice had run into the sand.

Again I urged him to continue.

He coughed. 'In the end, what could I do but take the full responsibility on meself? I brought it back here.' He saw my look of alarm. 'Take it easy, Father Neil. 'Tis quite safe, I tell you. By that time, it was after four, so knowing that you and Mrs Pring could sleep through the Last Trump, I went out into the garden.' I'm sure there was a peculiar kind of terror in each of my bulging eyes. 'And there,' he went on, 'I buried it in the soft earth beyond the distant hedge.'

'I can see Mrs Pring having to do all the gardening in future,' I managed to say.

He nodded. 'Then on that awful, awful, Saturday morning, I really felt more strongly than ever before there was something spooky about that Chair.'

I knew what he was going to say.

'I uncovered Mrs Pring's Hoover.'

My gasp of horror was genuine enough.

'What crank, d'you reckon, Father Neil, would want to bury a brand new Hoover at the bottom of our yard?'

A knock on the door relieved me of the necessity of hazarding a guess. In came Mrs Pring. 'Your humble servant, Fr Duddleswell,' she said, curtseying by the door. Beneath the gentle surface mockery, the admiration showed. 'Shouldn't be surprised if you see the century out, God help us. But you *are* marvellous.'

'Have I ever denied it?' he replied. He indicated the Chair. 'For you, Mrs Pring.'

I vacated it and made a gesture of offering it to her.

'Really, Father? For my kitchen?' He nodded. 'Oh, thank you. By the way, I nearly forgot. A visitor for you. He walked me home.'

From behind her, Fred appeared. His whole demeanour was altered. He looked humble.

'Come to kiss me feet, Fred Bowlby?'

'In a manner of speaking, Fr Duddleswell.'

When Mrs Pring had left to wash up, Fr Duddleswell said curtly, 'No, you cannot have it back. I have just given it to Madame Tussaud for her chamber of horrors.'

Fred said, 'That's not The Doomsday Chair.'

'How did you ...' began Fr Duddleswell. 'I mean, what d'you mean?'

Fred went as red as a poppy. 'Well, Father, as you know I'm not ...'

'Superstitious,' I said in anticipation.

Fred nodded, 'But after Charlie Skinner got drowned three months back I decided to get rid of it. In case somebody else —you, for instance—accidentally died on it and I was had up for manslaughter.'

'So?' encouraged Fr Duddleswell.

'So I found another just like it.'

'In the Portobello Road.' Fr Duddleswell wasn't asking but telling.

'How did you know?'

'The obvious place to look.'

'Only cost me a couple of quid,' said Fred.

'In Tompkins',' I said.

'Yeah.' Fred was more mystified than ever.

'Where else?' I said, pleased to regain a bit of self-respect.

'I put it in place of the real one,' Fred continued. 'Didn't even tell the wife. Too proud to, I suppose.'

Fr Duddleswell's brain was working faster than mine. 'What did you do with the "real" one, Fred?'

'I would have preferred to bury it in the garden but Eileen's a keen gardener.' He blushed again. 'So I took it back.'

'To Tompkins?' I gasped, edging away from the Chair.

'Yeah. Told 'em it didn't suit the decor of my place. Sold it back to 'em for one pound ten.' He shuffled his feet. 'I only came to say, Fr Duddleswell, that though you didn't sit on my Doomsday Chair, you thought you did. That's the main thing, isn't it?'

Fr Duddleswell was muttering, 'I don't know, I don't know.'

'You're the brave one not me, Father. Well, I didn't mean to, but I stole your thunder a bit tonight and I hadn't the heart to steal your hundred quid as well. So *here*.' He handed over a thick wad of notes. 'Now I'll leave you in peace.' He turned to go and since neither of us stirred, he said, 'Don't bother. I'll let myself out.'

Fr Duddleswell collapsed in his armchair, ashen-faced. 'Leave me in peace? he says. I nearly bloody-well massacre meself six or seven times over and that dirty double-crosser says he will leave me in peace.'

'What shall we do with that *thing*, now?' I asked. 'Take it back to Tompkins'?'

'And do the cowardly thing like Fred Bowlby? Never! I will coax herself to let me have it back for fifty pounds. Meanwhile, Father Neil, grab a spade and start digging another bloody great hole in the garden.'

THE END

A SEASON WITH EROS

Ruffo, who had been held at arms' length all through a two-year courtship by his voluptuous girlfriend, marries her in eager anticipation of future nocturnal delights, only to enjoy a brief 'season with Eros' before the realities of a life-long relationship are brought home to him.

This is just one of the tales in a new collection of short stories by Stan Barstow, whose subtle northern sense of humour and observation remains as bitingly accurate and enjoyable as it was in *A KIND OF LOVING*.

'Stan Barstow's books are raw vivid chunks of Yorkshire life. He has honesty, guts and compassion. He has a brilliantly accurate ear for dialogue, a shrewd understanding of human nature and above all, he's a smashing storyteller.'— *Daily Mail*

'Some stories are vicious, others are touching—all hit out with realism and a good deal of wry humour. Stan Barstow has an unerring eye, ear and nose for the north of England.' —*The Times*

0 552 10557 0—65p

A SELECTED LIST OF FINE NOVELS
THAT APPEAR IN CORGI

WHILE EVERY EFFORT IS MADE TO KEEP PRICES LOW, IT IS SOMETIMES NECESSARY TO INCREASE PRICES AT SHORT NOTICE. CORGI BOOKS RESERVE THE RIGHT TO SHOW AND CHARGE NEW RETAIL PRICES ON COVERS WHICH MAY DIFFER FROM THOSE ADVERTISED IN THE TEXT OR ELSEWHERE.

THE PRICES SHEWN BELOW WERE CORRECT AT THE TIME OF GOING TO PRESS (FEB 78)

☐ 09475 7	A RAGING CALM	*Stan Barstow*	60p
☐ 09274 6	A KIND OF LOVING	*Stan Barstow*	75p
☐ 08419 0	THE FIFTEEN STREETS	*Catherine Cookson*	75p
☐ 08444 1	MAGGIE ROWAN	*Catherine Cookson*	85p
☐ 09305 2	THE INVITATION	*Catherine Cookson*	85p
☐ 08821 8	A GRAND MAN	*Catherine Cookson*	50p
☐ 08822 6	THE LORD AND MARY ANN	*Catherine Cookson*	60p
☐ 08823 4	THE DEVIL AND MARY ANN	*Catherine Cookson*	65p
☐ 08538 3	KATIE MULHOLLAND	*Catherine Cookson*	85p
☐ 08849 8	THE GLASS VIRGIN	*Catherine Cookson*	85p
☐ 09217 7	THE DWELLING PLACE	*Catherine Cookson*	85p
☐ 09318 1	FEATHERS IN THE FIRE	*Catherine Cookson*	85p
☐ 09373 4	OUR KATE	*Catherine Cookson*	85p
☐ 09904 X	A VIEW OF THE SEA	*Margaret Maddocks*	40p
☐ 09796 9	HOUSE OF MEN	*Catherine Marchant*	70p
☐ 10074 9	THE FEN TIGER	*Catherine Marchant*	75p
☐ 10271 7	THE MARIGOLD FIELD	*Diane Pearson*	85p
☐ 10312 8	THE RUNNING FOXES	*Joyce Stranger*	50p
☐ 09462 5	LAKELAND VET	*Joyce Stranger*	45p
☐ 09891 8	CHIA THE WILD CAT	*Joyce Stranger*	45p
☐ 09892 2	ZARA	*Joyce Stranger*	60p
☐ 09893 0	BREED OF GIANTS	*Joyce Stranger*	60p
☐ 09431 5	THE BELSTONE FOX	*David Rook*	50p
☐ 10142 7	HEAR NO EVIL	*Jean Ure*	45p
☐ 10230 X	NO PRECIOUS TIME	*Jean Ure*	45p

All these books are available at your bookshop or newsagent, or can be ordered direct from the publisher. Just tick the titles you want and fill in the form below.

CORGI BOOKS, Cash Sales Department, P.O. Box 11, Falmouth, Cornwall.
Please send cheque or postal order, no currency.

U.K. send 22p for first book plus 10p per copy for each additional book ordered to a maximum charge of 82p to cover the cost of postage and packing.

B.F.P.O. and Eire allow 22p for the first book plus 10p per copy for the next 6 books, thereafter 4p per book.

Name (block letters) ....

ADDRESS ....

(FEB 78) ....